WE BELIEVE YOU

ANNIE E. CLARK and ANDREA L. PINO

With

Aditi · Chloe Allred · Anonymous A · Andrew Brown
Stephanie Canales · Julia D. · Fabiana Diaz · Johanna Evans
Sari Rachel Forshner · Elly Fryberger · Abbi Gatewood
Regina Gonzalez-Arroyo · Anonymous H · Princess Harmony
Aysha Ives · Lilly Jay · Anonymous K · Kevin Kantor
Sofie Karasek · Lauren · Ariane Litalien
Katie Rose Guest Pryal · Zoë Rayor · A. Lea Roth
Anonymous S · Nastassja Schmiedt · Elise Siemering
Brenda Tracy · Anonymous V · Liz Weiderhold
Alice Wilder · Kamilah Willingham · Anonymous XY · A. Zhou

WE BELIEVE YOU

Survivors of Campus Sexual Assault Speak Out

A Holt Paperback   Henry Holt and Company   New York

Holt Paperbacks
Henry Holt and Company, LLC
Publishers since 1866
175 Fifth Avenue
New York, New York 10010
www.henryholt.com

Rape and *Winter, Plucked* paintings by Chloe Allred. [Rights reserved.] "The Teal Forks Timeline" written by Fabiana Diaz. [Rights reserved.] "The Elegy of I" and "The After" written by Sari Rachel Forshner. [Rights reserved.] "Disciplinary Education" cartoon by Miranda Friel. [Rights reserved.] "Untouchable: Being a Trans Survivor" adapted from article originally published in *The Feminist Wire* and "The Dangerous Myth of the 'Ideal' Survivor" adapted from article originally published in *Black Girl Dangerous*, written by Princess Harmony. [Rights reserved.] "Again" poem by Regina Gonzalez-Arroyo. [Rights reserved.] "Reclaiming College" speech by Lilly Jay, delivered at the White House on Friday, September 19, 2014. [Rights reserved.] "People You May Know" poem by Kevin Kantor. [Rights reserved.] "An Important Event" speech by Sofie Karasek, delivered at the University of California–Berkeley, February 26, 2014. [Rights reserved.] "College," "Things That Make Me Anxious," "Managing Chronic Anxiety," and "Meditation Vols. 2 & 3" cartoons by Ariane Litalien. [Rights reserved.] "Dear Harvard: This Fight Is Not Over" written by Ariane Litalien. [Rights reserved.] "Accepting Entropy: How My Father Used the Second Law of Thermodynamics to Teach Me How to Survive" written by Liz Weiderhold. [Rights reserved.] "No One Narrative Defines Survivors" written by Alice Wilder, excerpted with permission from the *Daily Tar Heel*. [Rights reserved.]

Library of Congress Cataloging-in-Publication Data

Names: Clark, Annie E., author. | Pino, Andrea L., author.
Title: We believe you : survivors of campus sexual assault speak out / Annie E. Clark
    and Andrea L. Pino.
Description: First edition. | New York : Holt Paperbacks, 2016.
Identifiers: LCCN 2015046702| ISBN 9781627795333 (paperback) |
    ISBN 9781627795340 (electronic book)
Subjects: LCSH: Rape in universities and colleges—United States. | Women college
    students—Crimes against—United States. | Rape victims—United States—Biography. | BISAC: SOCIAL
    SCIENCE / Women's Studies. | BIOGRAPHY & AUTOBIOGRAPHY / Women.
Classification: LCC LB2345.3.R37 C53 2016 | DDC 371.7/82—dc23
LC record available at http://lccn.loc.gov/2015046702

Our books may be purchased in bulk for promotional, educational, or business use. Please contact your local bookseller or the Macmillan Corporate and Premium Sales Department at (800) 221-7945, extension 5442, or by e-mail at MacmillanSpecialMarkets@macmillan.com.

The names of some persons described in this book have been changed.

First Edition 2016

Printed in the United States of America
1   3   5   7   9   10   8   6   4   2

This book is dedicated to

Faith Danielle Hedgepeth,

Tanyesha Stewart,

Elizabeth "Lizzy" Seeberg,

Deah S. Barakat, Yusor Mohammad Abu-Salha, and
Razan Mohammad Abu-Salha,

and to every student survivor of violence, to every victim whose
life was cut short by violence, and to all whose stories have not
been told, or whose voices have not been heard.

We Believe You.

It's true what a mentor once told me:
"Being a survivor is being part of a club
that nobody wants to join.
But once you're in it, you're in it for life.
And it's the strongest group of people
you could ever imagine."

—Julia D.

CONTENTS

V—DECLARATIONS OF INDEPENDENCE

RIGHTS AND RESOURCES

WE BELIEVE YOU

INTRODUCTION

Annie was sitting in front of her computer on her carpeted floor, Skyping me from her tiny living room in Eugene, Oregon. She listened to me, almost guardedly, as she drank her coffee.

Andrea was wide awake—it was four a.m. her time—as she sat alone in her room in Kenan Community (a kind of student housing) at the University of North Carolina at Chapel Hill. She wasn't crying, but I could see her shaking slightly and breathing harder as she finished telling me what had happened to her one night at an off-campus party. "Me, too. It happened to me, too," I said.

"I believe you," Annie said, and with those three simple words, she became the first person to listen to my entire story of surviving sexual assault.

We shared our stories, we believed each other, and we promised to support each other through the entirety of our journeys.

Although we are from very different backgrounds, we had both been drawn to UNC–Chapel Hill by the school's competitive academics and by its strong sense of pride, by the lure of intellectual prospects and by the sense of community and belonging that all students applying to college yearn to feel.

We never expected to be writing a book before turning thirty, much less a book that would detail stories all too similar to events we each once tried to completely suppress.

We never imagined that in our lifetime the president of the United States would say, "Survivors, I got your back," or that revelations about the scope and institutional cover-ups of campus sexual assault would be on the front page of the *New York Times,* or on the cover of *Time* magazine.

But we also never thought that, in our lifetime, we would survive violence.

We've noticed, even with our own stories when we've told them ourselves, that the media often leave out the messy details, as if pining for a "perfect survivor" narrative, something which we have come to learn does not exist. Not everyone was sober when she was assaulted. Not everyone went on to triumph after his experience of sexual violence. With this book, we wanted to delve into the gaps, into the stories the mainstream media often deem not pretty enough to retell; we wanted to share real stories and to make sure to include some of the survivor identities and experiences that are too often dismissed.

The stories of what happened to us, along with thirty-four other individual stories of assault and sexual violence, of betrayal, and of healing, unfold in the pages that follow. We know that there are many who do not want to speak out, or who cannot tell their stories, or who were forever silenced when they tried to speak out. And the thirty-six of us in this book cannot speak for them, but we carry them in our thoughts as we share what happened to us.

PART I

BEFORE

Six years ago, I tore the blue seal of the large envelope that held my acceptance letter to the University of North Carolina at Chapel Hill (UNC). I came from a tight-knit Cuban family that had never had the opportunity to even consider college. I was going to be the first one in my family to make it, and I loved everything about Carolina.

—Andrea Pino, survivor who attended
the University of North Carolina at Chapel Hill

To understand our journeys of healing and survivorhood is also to understand that we live in a culture that warns us to avoid the moment when sexual assault will break us, as if we could avoid that moment—a culture that tells us what clothes to wear, what signs to give, what signs not to give, and what not to drink, as if by making such personal adjustments we might have the power to avoid the violence done onto our bodies against our will.

Even before sexual assaults occur, we live betrayed by a society that blames us for any violence that might happen to us—and blames us for our gender performance or for our lack of femininity or masculinity, and blames us for our willingness to challenge these rigid social expectations, as if these facts about us, as if these qualities inherent in our identities, warrant violence.

Before sexual assault, we were children told of the adventures that awaited us in college—"the best four years of your life!" We were courted by pristine, colorful brochures that invited us, encouraged us, to ask big questions and to contribute to a community that wanted us.

Before sexual assault, there was an element of innocence within us, an innocence that bought into the belonging that the colleges and universities advertised.

We were customers, but we were also dreamers.

Before we were sexually assaulted, the colleges and universities sold us trust, love, and safety; and we bought in with our tuition dollars and our hearts.

Our Stories

ELISE SIEMERING

I grew up in Hickory, North Carolina, below the mountains. Surprisingly, I didn't do mountain things. I ran track all four years of high school, but I was mostly into music growing up. I was involved in all kinds of music—percussion in middle school and high school; the band in high school; and singing. I was in church choirs, and in school choirs in elementary, middle, and high school. I didn't have a favorite musical activity—just anything.

My dad teaches fifth grade, and my mom is a school social worker. Growing up, I also enjoyed spending time with family and friends. I have a younger sister.

I always saw myself attending a small college in North Carolina. Also, I have mild cerebral palsy on my right side, so it was easier to be closer to home for all those doctor appointments. In January of my senior year of high school, my dad came home one day and said one of his coworkers went to High Point University, so we pulled up their website. They had small classes and a small school environment, which was what I wanted, plus, they were about an hour and a half from home. I applied and got accepted and did this thing called Summer Experience, where freshmen can come early and take classes. That's where I met Marie, my best friend. I started there in the summer of 2008. I was eighteen.

I was very involved at High Point. I did campus activities, was pretty much your normal college student. I loved hanging out, was very social, very involved, and had a great group of friends.

My assault happened my sophomore year—the spring of sophomore year—toward the end of finals, when I was nineteen. It was the last week of the semester.

The guy who assaulted me had been an acquaintance. We had the same friends. It made it interesting, after it happened, to see who was really there for me and who wasn't.

LAUREN

I was raised in a very open and nonjudgmental household in Lincoln, Rhode Island. My mom taught me to dream big and to respect others; my dad made sure we had semirealistic goals that would provide for us through life.

Special education was my life dream. I knew that in special education the smallest lessons can help a person communicate with others and become a participating individual in society, and I wanted to be responsible for making sure that happened.

I was a free-spirited teen who wanted independence and the chance to be unapologetically "me." A chance to explore who I really am. College meant growing up and making my own choices. I could choose to stay out all night, hook up with strangers, or drink until I had to be hospitalized and my mom or dad couldn't tell me no. In reality, I didn't do much of anything, because I am not a partyer, although I had fun in my own ways.

Curry College in Milton, Massachusetts, was always the school I knew I'd go to. While researching possible schools, I knew I couldn't get into obvious fantastic schools because of my learning differences and grades. I have ADHD and executive function disorder. Curry has a program for "special needs" individuals in the mild to moderate categories to help them through academics and even the social aspects of school.

ANDREW BROWN

I am the unicorn who is from Washington, D.C., and came back to D.C. after college.

D.C. was actually a really great place to grow up. I went to a great prep school and saw a lot. I carpooled to school and took the Metro back home after school, gradually expanding my reach with my parents' approval. By eighth grade I was able to establish some independence and explore the city a bit. I'm glad my parents gave me free rein. D.C. is a city divided, economically, and I got to see that. The divide was something I became increasingly interested in and studied at Brown. I got a degree in urban studies. My dad works in historic preservation, and my mom is a retired teacher. So conversations about place and why communities matter were conversations shared around our dinner table. It's no coincidence my twin sister and I are going into careers that focus on helping people. She's interested in psychology and social work.

It was incredible having my twin sister go through all the same stages of life with me, always having a friend to play with. When I came out of the closet, we actually got a lot closer. I don't think it really surprised her.

My dad says they knew I was gay. *I quit figure skating because it was getting in the way of my singing.* We still joke about that.

I'm really glad my parents gave me the space to explore who I wanted to be and didn't give me any prescriptive ideas about who I should be.

Why attend Brown? I really wanted to save a lot of money on Sharpies by not having to write my name on a lot of things. Actually, the best joke I heard was my friend who said, "Sounds like it's got your name all over it!" At Brown, whenever I got a letter from home, between my address, which was Brown Street, and my name, and the return address, it would have the word "Brown" on there about four times.

But seriously. I enjoyed getting to know adults who went to Brown; it was clear they had pursued passions they had long held, and Brown gave them the atmosphere in which to pursue those passions. The curriculum has no core requirements, so it encourages you to learn what you want to learn.

I declared a major right away. I had known I wanted to do urban studies when I got there. I almost did a double study and included music. Music continues to be part of my life. I started out as a chorister at the National Cathedral before my voice changed. I sang in college—opera, musicals, revues.

ANONYMOUS S

I grew up in Texas with my sister and both parents at home.

From age four, I was a ballet student with a Russian teacher who was incredibly strict and really focused on discipline. She was relentless, but I progressed quickly and grew to love dance. I learned you have to give your best. Throughout my life, people have always said to me, "Calm down, it's not the end of the world." But I would view any kind of failure as unacceptable. You give it your all, or you shouldn't even try.

I really didn't have any aspirations academically, other than to graduate. My goal was to be an Olympian and that is one of the main reasons I chose Southern Methodist University, in the University Park section of Dallas. I don't really feel comfortable stating which sport, but they had a smaller team that would be able to offer more individual coaching and more opportunities for me to compete at a Division I level.

I was looking forward to going to college and seeing if I could do it academically and athletically. Actually, I knew I could, because I don't give up. Athletes don't give up.

AYSHA IVES

Monroe Township, New Jersey, is suburbia. It's a middle-class town, quiet, small. We had two hundred graduates each year in my high school. The town is predominantly Caucasian. I'm African American.

I lived with my two younger sisters, my mother, and her mother, also two female cousins, one older, one younger. They came when I was eight or nine. Other cousins came and stayed for a bit, too. So we had a full house of mostly women for the majority of my life from the time I was twelve up. After my grandfather passed away when I was sixteen, it was pretty much all women.

My father wasn't really involved in my life. I only recently reconnected with him, in my late twenties, and now we have phone calls. He said he was just a kid himself when I was born, and didn't want the responsibility of rearing a child at the time. He was about twenty.

I have forgiven him, but there are times when I wonder if my life would have been different had he been present. Would I have chosen different relationships? Sometimes I wonder if I would ever have had any contact with the man who raped me if I'd had a father. Those things come up from time to time. When those moments pop up, I reframe them and realize that they're part of my history.

I was raised Baptist. My grandmother was the matriarch. She died three years ago, in November. She coparented me. And she was Baptist, a devout Christian. No makeup, no music, no cards or games with dice. If the game had dice we would hide it or we'd have to wrap them to hide the dots and write the number on the dice. I'm not sure why.

Our church was within walking distance of our house. We were there every Sunday. It wasn't until I was an adult that I was allowed to go to church in pants. You had to wear a dress and patent-leather shoes. I was in the choir until I left for college, and in all the Easter plays.

I stopped going to church when I was in college, but I really rebelled when I was in grad school. I was almost a nonbeliever in grad school. Partly because my mentor at the time wasn't religious. So I lost my faith for a while. It came back around.

> **I stopped going to church when I was in college, but I really rebelled when I was in grad school. I was almost a nonbeliever in grad school.**

As far back as I can remember, it wasn't a question of if I was going to college, it was a question of where. As I approached college age, I could feel it coming, finally, freedom! Dating wasn't an option while I lived at home. Absolutely not. And because I was chubby, academics was my strength.

Cornell was my dream school. I was really heartbroken when I got that rejection letter. Writing was always my thing, but I didn't pursue it because it didn't seem glamorous.

I got accepted into Rutgers and decided to be a biochem major. I started school there in August 1996. I was seventeen. I wanted to find a cure for AIDS. Or be a geneticist, helping to find a cure for genetic disorders.

I thought, "I'm going into a place that celebrates being smart." I was so excited about it. There was also that freedom—my own dorm room. Also, because I didn't consider myself to be very attractive, I guess I was hoping that the experience in college would be different. Younger kids can be so cruel. I was thinking college would be different. I could re-create myself. Finally, I'd be able to date. And find people who would celebrate me no matter my physical appearance.

When I got there, it was good in the beginning. A couple of my good friends were attending also, and I met new people. The first year was good.

One time in my sophomore year I was walking around, still kind of chubby, walking across campus, and someone opened a window and started making mooing sounds at me. It was awful. I was so distressed. I was the only woman walking across the courtyard. That was the only time I felt ridiculed about my appearance.

Mostly, being at college was freeing.

AYSHA IVES

ANONYMOUS V

I came to college because I wanted to learn but also because that is just what girls like me do. I was smart, financially well-off, and from a competitive public school in the Northeast. Back in high school, no one ever questioned that I would go to and graduate from college. I'd heard that people took more than four years to graduate, but girls like me finished in four years. Girls like me went to the most competitive school they could get into and they succeeded. College was the next step on a staircase I'd always been climbing. Each year, I went up; there wasn't an option to go back down or move sideways. There wasn't another staircase. Girls like me graduated from good colleges.

After my senior year of high school, I went south to a competitive, well-known institution. I liked the way people spoke in the South. I thought that saying *y'all* was grammatically efficient. I liked that people nodded as they passed each other on the sidewalk, instead of looking down like they did in the Northeast. I liked that the winter would be mild. I liked that when I graduated, I could tell future employers I went to an impressive institution. Some people are in love with their college; if anything, I was in love with where it could get me.

Going into college, I wasn't sure what my major would be, maybe political science, maybe psychology. Once school started, I moved toward the psych route. The million-dollar question is, what will I do with my degree once I graduate? Originally, before I destroyed my GPA, the plan was to go to grad school and become a clinical psychologist. I wanted to take some time and be involved in research; I fell in love with research. Things haven't exactly gone the way I wanted them to.

Even before I went to college, I had a history of depression. That part of the equation doesn't fit into "girls like me." My high school therapist said I have a "Barbie" version and the "real" version of my personality. When I'm in Barbie mode, I accept endless workloads and push myself to the limit. Barbie me is miserable and stressed, but she pulls it (and my résumé) together. "Real" me used to be very depressed. That version of me failed tests and didn't turn in papers. The dual performances followed me to college. I kept them in balance for the most part until my junior year. Then all bets were off, even for Barbie me.

Barbie me knew how to manage regular depression (wanting to sleep all the time, low mood, forcing myself to get to therapy, etc.); she had no idea what to do about PTSD.

So during junior spring everything got sidetracked, majorly.

FABIANA DIAZ

I was born in Caracas, Venezuela, on March 1, 1994. We left Venezuela in 1999 when I was five—my mom and dad, sister, and me. I speak Spanish fluently, and a lot of my parents' friends speak Spanish. Venezuelans are a very family-oriented culture, not go-go-go like Americans. Caracas is a chaotic city, with a lot of noise and street vendors, but it has a lot of beauty to it, too. Beautiful beaches. Everyone is so welcoming—their house is your house within thirty minutes of meeting you. I hung out with my cousins all the time. I miss the positivity of it.

I'm an American citizen now, and my mom's Italian, so I have a dual citizenship with Italy. But my roots are Venezuelan. And that's how I identify myself. I definitely identify myself as a Latina.

We left because of the political tension, the crime rate. My dad had more opportunities in the United States. He owns his own tool company and makes a lot of tools for auto companies. That's why we moved to Michigan. Lake Orion, Michigan.

It was so different. I knew some English, but there was a still a language barrier. When we got to Michigan, it was snowing. I had never seen snow. I loved it, though. I always wanted to be outside, to make snow angels. My sister and I had seen that in a movie.

My mom was unhappy. She was used to having a lot of friends, and my dad was traveling. School was difficult for me. I was shy and not answering questions correctly. My mom would pack my lunch of black beans and rice and I'd get "Ooh, what is that?" so I told her to not pack me that lunch anymore. After that she packed me peanut butter, and I hated it. But I wanted to be like the other kids.

> **My mom would pack my lunch of black beans and rice and I'd get "Ooh, what is that?" so I told her to not pack me that lunch anymore.**

From middle school to high school I went to the same school, and things got smoother. I became very outgoing. I learned to adapt.

I didn't want to go to the University of Michigan. I wanted to study international relations. My mom speaks five languages, my dad speaks seven, and I speak four: Spanish, English, Italian, and German. I wanted to go to Georgetown, but I didn't get in. I always wanted to be a diplomat, an ambassador.

My parents have instilled in me a respect for service. In high school I did more than a thousand hours of community service—in Mexico, New York City, Chicago, and locally, as well, in Michigan.

When I first started at Michigan, I didn't have a major. Then, in my sophomore year, I ran across international studies and chose that as my major, with a focus on culture and identity.

ANONYMOUS XY

I was raised in New York—downtown Manhattan—in an expensive zip code. I'm from a big family. Both my parents are well educated; between the two of them they have seven degrees, five from Ivy League schools. It was an intellectual household, but not an emotionally nurturing one. I've had people say, "Oh, your parents' style must be an Asian 'tiger mother' thing," but I think the way my parents raised me was more based on who they are as individuals.

It was a strange, very extreme existence. With my dad, one second you're the best, and the next you're dead to him. He was also physically abusive. My mom valued what she thought of as "principles" over empathy.

My parents didn't like me stepping out of the little box they had drawn around me. There was a tacit contractual arrangement: I take care of you, so you owe me. There was a lot of time spent fighting with them as I grew older and looked for independence. The fighting escalated sometimes. There was always a stated or implicit threat of violence in my father's discipline.

My parents were very backward in terms of feminism and sex positivity.

No therapy. My parents were very antitherapy.

So honestly, getting raped was not the first trauma I experienced, but by far it was the worst.

I went to Harvard. Studied economics and math. Undergrads tend to lose perspective. I was so focused on work and studying that if someone had come up to me and said, "A Nobel laureate is coming to campus to speak tomorrow!" I would have said, "Sorry, I have a lot of homework."

I was oblivious to how to really live. All this stuff other people figure out as teenagers, I was shoving into my brain suddenly as an eighteen-year-old, trying to fit into those grown-up clothes.

I was sort of stalked by this guy in college, which annoyed me, but I didn't realize how serious it was. My mother said, "This is your fault this guy is following you. You were encouraging him," even though that wasn't true. I was not good at picking friends. Also I was trying to find myself. I met my Aikido sensei—my teacher, my martial arts instructor, my mentor—while I was at Harvard. Her support became very important to me.

The weird thing is that my assault happened in grad school. It's usually young girls, that's who we think rape happens to. Innocent young girls being jumped in the bushes by evil men. But I was a grown woman and knew how things worked.

It hit home to me afterward how messed up rape culture is.

From "The Elegy of I"

SARI RACHEL FORSHNER

As a child, I was defined by delicious, rollicking peals of silliness.

These were a source of great frustration for my elders:

"Get ahold of yourself!"

"Stop cackling, you're piercing my eardrums!"

"*Enough*."

They thought that unabashed joy would be an obstacle to my success, and that my success was more important, but I knew I could allow myself to revel in my wholehearted amusement in life, and still smile sweetly as I received my As, discreetly stuffing them into a folder in an effort to not hurt anyone's feelings.

How *utterly fun* I was. In constant tintinnabulation, pealing throughout a room. The echo bounced off the walls and back into me. My personality was too big for the everyday, so I brought it to the stage.

My classmates voted for me to play Anne Frank. I was Ebenezer Scrooge, Poe's Red Death, and *The Crucible*'s seductive Abigail Williams.

I could be anyone but I delighted in playing the villain—it was so freeing to express fury without fear of repercussion.

I sought challenge. I sought criticism. "Thank you for the compliment, but tell me what I can do *better*."

I ricocheted between silence and silliness. I was lustful; I was idealistic. I loved fiercely and hated little.

Although my dimpled face sometimes indicated a greater youth than I possessed, I was self-assured beyond my years. Although I wavered in my confidence, just as every adolescent, as every artist does, those waverings were not readily apparent.

I was buying a stack of folders and pencils at Target, and the woman in line in front of me assumed I was a teacher rather than a student. Taken aback, I doubled over in laughter.

By the time I left for college, I had worked at a cell phone store for just shy of two years; at eighteen, I was the employee with the most seniority and the key holder for two locations. No one else wanted to deal with the boss. One by one, they quit or were fired. I insisted he stop calling me babe and kept a private record of my own sales. When he tried to short me on my commissions, I argued on my own behalf.

I devoured books. That was who I was. Laugher, lover, reader, actress, student.

I'm Going to College

ANDREA PINO

Abuela was the first one to leave Cuba. It was over sixty years ago. She and my *abuelo* were in love, but knew that they couldn't come to Miami together. Abuela had four siblings, and though the oldest, she's survived all of them. At eighty-seven, Abuelo's greatest joys are his granddaughters, Christmas cards from the Obamas, and Hillary Clinton. So, Abuela and Abuelo both worked hard and got their families out of Cuba and settled in Miami, but to this day, Abuelo tells me that he wished he could have gone to college.

"Quería ser enfermero," he told me. He wanted to be a nurse, but he never finished middle school, and instead he painted yachts for a living. He told me that I was going to be the first one to make it, that I was going to go to college and run for office. "Vas a ser como Hillary," he still tells me, because he thinks women like me should be in politics. "Nunca, nunca, nunca pares de luchar," he says.

"Nunca, nunca, nunca . . ." Hearing those words still keeps me going some days, and it was fuel that helped me to put so much effort into my education.

～

I went to Miami's Champagnat Catholic School from kindergarten until ninth grade. Many at Champagnat came from lower-income families. It was the only Catholic school that offered reduced tuition, and my parents saw it as a viable alternative to the crumbling public schools in Little Havana. But in ninth grade, I told my mother that I'd had it with parochial school. I'd had it with the overly gendered plaid skirt uniforms, the conservative politics, and the restrictive curriculum. In my head, for a long time, these frustrating experiences had been the price I had to pay to be in school at all. But, by ninth grade, I was ready to move on.

～

In 2008, I began my sophomore year of high school at International Studies Charter High School. ISCHS was located then in the Citibank building in Coral Gables, right on Miracle Mile, overlooking one of the wealthiest neighborhoods in Miami. My favorite part of going to school was getting to venture through the stacks at the nearby Barnes & Noble; if I was lucky, I could read a few chapters of a book I was dying to read but hadn't saved up enough to buy. It was then that my journey to applying to college began. I knew of five colleges, more or less: Florida International University, the University of Florida, Florida State University, Harvard University, and Yale—and the latter, I knew of only because of my obsession with *Gilmore Girls*. Since sixth grade, I had wanted to go to Yale. My first online purchase was, in fact, a Yale sweatshirt.

～

COURTESY OF ANDREA PINO

By the summer after my sophomore year, I was actively preparing for college, and it was a big fucking deal. It was such a big deal that nothing else mattered to me.

That same summer, 2009, while enrolled in an English 101 course at Miami Dade College, through a program that offered college classes to qualified high school students, I was accused of plagiarism. Four times.

"I'm going to submit it to Turnitin.com," my professor said, expecting a panicked confession from the youngest student in her class. "You shouldn't be able to write like this. You cheated."

I didn't know whether to be upset or flattered: it appeared that my first college professor thought I wrote *too* well. She proceeded to accuse me of plagiarism three more times, including on a paper I wrote *during an in-class final*. Despite these interactions with my first college professor, I earned one of the highest grades in the class.

I took nine more college classes before I finished high school in 2010, along with just about every Advanced Placement course ISCHS offered. My school day began at four a.m., when I woke up to study for the SAT, and ended well after ten p.m., when I arrived at home from my evening college classes and sat down to do my high school homework.

~

While reading campus brochures, it's easy to get discouraged if you know that Latino students make up less than 10 percent of many campus populations; it's easy to think that you're not going to be able to compete with applicants who are legacies, or who spent most of their childhoods in prep schools that, by definition, were preparing them for college. Those students started the race before I was reading, probably. I knew that I had to work really hard to make up for where I was in the race. People like me, from families with no previous college graduates, didn't go to Yale. People like me barely graduated from high school. My mom almost got her college degree after starting community college, and as a first-generation American she had opportunities that my grandparents didn't have. But, like my father, who left Cuba at four years old, she wasn't able to get her bachelor's degree. So that—getting my bachelor's degree—was the finish line, and class, race, and money were the obstacles. Proving my worth to people like my English 101 professor—that was always my motivation.

When I asked my parents to give me a college road trip for my seventeenth birthday, the prospect excited me *much* more than my *quinceañera* had, and it was a request that was just about the strangest thing my extended family had ever heard. For many young Latinas, wearing that special white dress and a tiara on the day you turn fifteen is among their most treasured memories; it still is for my mom. But I cared more about wearing a robe that was too big for my body and a cardboard cap that could barely rest on my head. Graduation day would be the day that I would never forget. My mom and dad and sister and grandparents were supportive of this endeavor, but no one else in my community understood it. Why would a girl my age spend so much time talking about school and politics instead of boys and *telenovelas*? My family has always embraced me, but I feel that they have always had to apologize for my actions and attitudes. I'm not sorry, though, for becoming a woman who speaks up and fights for what I believe in, even if it makes people uncomfortable.

The University of North Carolina at Chapel Hill happened to be the first college I visited on my tour.

"What schools are you applying to?" I asked my fellow prospective students as we circuited the campus in the summer of 2009. "Oh, just all the Ivy Leagues, and maybe Amherst College and Notre Dame," said one prep-school-type white boy, with a look that held no doubts about his ability to pick from any one of those schools. "But I'm hoping my recommendations come through, because I want to go here, and it's going to be difficult since I'm out of state. Good thing I have a high SAT score."

I turned away from him. I tried to focus on the beautiful trees surrounding an old stone outdoor theater across the street from the admissions building.

As terrifying as the idea of competing with this boy was, I'd fallen in love with Carolina the moment I saw the Forest Theatre (a stone amphitheater built into a hillside on the edge of the campus), and I felt a connection. "I belong here."

The day I applied to Carolina? I drank *quarto coladas* that morning—four of the strongest espresso shots on the planet. American coffee just wasn't going to be enough. I needed the elixir of my ancestors. "Tonight is the night I'm going to do it. I'm going to apply to the University of North Carolina." And in January 2010, when I was accepted, I proceeded to almost destroy my laptop pounding out messages of joy.

"I did it. I'm going to college."

"Quiero ser abogada," I said on my first visit home, for Thanksgiving.

"Just make sure the boys know you know how to make pie," my late Tia Digna said in Spanish.

"¿Cuantos años te faltan ahora?" Abuela wanted to know. When would I move back home?

"Acabo de empezar, Abuelita." But I'd only just started.

I had only been gone one semester, but for her, my leaving was heart-breaking.

My family didn't understand why I chose to move eight hundred miles away to go to UNC.

~

I love my abuelita, and I often think of what I've never told her. I think of all the conversations we've had and all those we haven't had. I think of all the things I wish she knew about the woman I am today.

NUNCA NUNCA PARES DE LUCHAR.
TU ABUELO ANTONIO

Colleges

High school students and, even more often, their parents ask us, "Which colleges are the really bad ones?" or "Which campuses are rape free?" or "How rapey is this place?," as if there's a way to avoid going to a college where sexual assaults occur. As far as we can tell, people are sexually assaulted on and around every college campus. In recent years, students and other stakeholders have filed complaints with the U.S. government against nearly two hundred colleges and universities for mishandling reports of sexual assaults on campus. Here is the list of colleges and universities that are or have been under federal investigation for possible Title IX violations as of December 31, 2015:

Allegheny College

Alma College

American University

Amherst College

Arizona State University

Barnard College

Bard College

Berklee College of Music

Bethany College (WV)

Binghamton University

BioHealth College

Boston College

Boston University

Brandeis University

Brown University

Butte-Glenn Community College District

California Institute of the Arts

California Polytechnic State University at San Luis Obispo

Canisius College

Carnegie Mellon University

Catholic University of America

Cedarville University

Central Community College

Chapman University

Cisco Junior College

Cleveland State University

College of William and Mary

Colorado State University

Columbia College Chicago

Columbia University

Cornell University

Corning Community College

CUNY Hunter College

Dartmouth College

Davis and Elkins College

Denison University

Drake University

Duke University

Elizabethtown College

Elmira College

Emerson College

Emory University

Florida State University

Franklin and Marshall College

Frostburg State University

Full Sail University

George Washington University

Glenville State College

Grand Valley State University

Grinnell College

Guilford College

Hamilton College (NY)

Hampshire College

Hanover College

Harvard College

Harvard University Law School

Hobart and William Smith Colleges

Idaho State University

Indiana University–Bloomington

Iowa State University

James Madison University

Johns Hopkins University

Judson University

Kansas State University

Kentucky Wesleyan College

Knox College

Langston University

Lincoln University

Louisiana State University–System Office

Marion Military Institute

Marlboro College

Massachusetts Institute of Technology

Medical College of Wisconsin

Michigan State University

Minot State University

Missouri University of Science and Technology

Monmouth College

Morehouse College

Morgan State University

New York University School of Medicine

Northeastern University

Northern New Mexico College

Oberlin College

Occidental College

Oglethorpe University

Ohio State University

Oklahoma State University

Pace University (NY)

Pennsylvania State University

Pitzer College

Point Park University

Pomona College

Polytechnic Institute of New York University

The Pratt Institute

Princeton University

Quincy College

Regis University

Saint Mary's College of Maryland

Saint Thomas Aquinas College

Samuel Merritt University

San Francisco State University

San Jose Evergreen Community College

Santa Clara University

Sarah Lawrence College

Seton Hall University

Southern Illinois University–Carbondale

Southern Methodist University

Southwest Acupuncture College

Spelman College

St. Cloud State University

St. John's University

Stanford University

SUNY at Albany University

SUNY at Binghamton

SUNY at Stony Brook

SUNY Buffalo State College

SUNY College at Brockport

SUNY College at Purchase

Swarthmore College

Temple University

Texas A&M University

Trinity University

Tufts University

Union College (NY)

Universidad de Puerto Rico

The University of Akron

University of Alaska System of Higher Education

University of California–Berkeley

University of California–Davis

University of California–Los Angeles

University of California–San Francisco

University of California–Santa Cruz

University of Chicago

University of Colorado at Boulder

University of Colorado at Denver

University of Connecticut

University of Delaware

University of Denver

University of Hawaii at Manoa

University of Houston

University of Idaho

University of Illinois at Urbana-Champaign

University of Iowa

University of Kansas

University of Kentucky

University of Massachusetts–Amherst

University of Massachusetts–Dartmouth

University of Miami

University of Michigan–Ann Arbor

University of Mississippi

University of Montana at Missoula

University of Nebraska at Kearney

University of Nebraska–Lincoln

University of North Carolina at Chapel Hill

University of Notre Dame

University of Richmond

University of Rochester

University of San Diego

University of South Florida

University of Southern California

University of Tennessee at Chattanooga

University of Tennessee (Knoxville)

The University of Texas–Pan American

University of Virginia

University of Washington

University of Wisconsin–Madison

University of Wisconsin–Whitewater

Valparaiso University

Valley Forge Military College

Vanderbilt University

Vincennes University

Virginia Commonwealth University

Virginia Military Institute

Washburn University

Washington and Lee University

Washington State University

Wesley College

West Virginia School of Osteopathic Medicine

Western New England University

Western Washington University

Westminster College (UT)

Whitman College

William Jewell College

Wittenberg University

Xavier University

Yale University

PART II

HOW IT HAPPENED

Things can change so fast in life. You can plan all you want but life can turn on you really fast.

—Ariane Litalien

From time to time, the flashbacks are so horrible that I can't leave my bed. I feel his hands on me, I smell him on me; I have never had such vivid memories of anything else. Even though this would be hard, even if everything went my way, it was made harder than it needed to be. I implore people to listen to survivors. To know that no matter what gender you are, what sex you were assigned at birth, no matter any other demographic you may fit into, you can still be raped. And that all people, regardless of anything else, deserve to live a life without rape and deserve support if they are raped. Believe survivors. Support survivors. Love survivors.

—Princess Harmony, survivor
who attended Temple University

This section of the book is hard. Really hard. Our hearts are heavy with these stories of pain.

But this section is important, because it's real. These are our real experiences of sexual violence. Some assaults left obvious external injuries, while others of us had no visible scarring. Some of us were fully awake, yet unable to move. Some of us were unconscious, and unaware of the horror to which we would awaken.

Some of us cannot yet quell our rage at our assailant. And some still blame ourselves.

Our stories are as different as we are, but they share the same horrific moment in time. The thread of sexual assault has woven our lives together, and, for too many of us, a collective fabric is dyed with memories of unwanted, unsolicited, intrusive violence.

For some, writing about the experience is cathartic. For others, to purposefully relive that time is yet another violation.

Many still live in fear and cannot identify themselves for safety reasons, which is one reason some contributors are anonymous. There is power in putting our name to an experience, but the ability to be "out" also carries a privilege. Too many individuals, particularly those from marginalized communities, cannot or do not wish to speak out. No one should feel pressured to do so.

There is no one right way to survive. No one should have to tell their full story to a throng of strangers to be believed. But here are the stories of some who have chosen to do so.

This section contains snapshots that help to explain why many of our lives were derailed. We share these images with the hope that our stories will open readers to a variety of true narratives of how sexual assault happens. And we hope readers will understand that there is no hierarchy of pain.

Every kind of survivor story is valid and every survivor deserves the kind of support that they want. We are entrusting you with stories of the moments in time when assailants invaded our bodies without our consent. We still sometimes have flashbacks of these moments, but we are going to be okay, and we know that we are not alone.

Our Stories, continued

ELISE SIEMERING

It was April 30, 2010. That night, we were studying for exams together, me and this one guy, along with another guy. They were in the same fraternity. I was not in a sorority at the time. We all were just studying because we were in a communications class together.

We all three met at the library; then we stopped by the assaulter's place and he dropped his stuff off, and then he offered to take me back to my dorm room, which was not directly on campus. I had a suite, kind of an apartment-style room. We had to take the trolley back as it was kind of late, around eleven or twelve. Me being naïve, I was thinking, "Oh, he's being a gentleman because it's late."

We were hanging out, and all of a sudden, he tries to kiss me. I push him back. The next thing I knew, he pinned me down and assaulted me. He left at about four o'clock in the morning. I had an exam at nine a.m. Growing up with my mom as a social worker, she'd always been open and honest with us about drugs and sex. I have always been close to my mom. Still, I'm lying there thinking, "Holy crap, what am I gonna do? Am I gonna say anything? What would I say?"

Marie was in the room next door, but she wasn't aware of what was happening. The next morning I got up and went and took my exam. I was in extreme shock. I was on autopilot.

He had raped me, and I had bruises on my neck and inner thigh and chest. He had said, "You're gonna keep quiet and not tell anyone, and we're gonna keep this between you and me."

On my way to my exam, I saw one of his friends. And this guy said, "Oh, hi, Elise, how are you?" and I said, "Oh, I'm fine." He said, "Are you sure?" Because I had bruises on my neck. I said, "Oh, sure, I'm fine," trying to brush it off.

I didn't know what to do, who to call. Freshman year, we didn't have any kind of training.

When I got back to my dorm, Marie was there. She was kind of upset because she thought I had been hooking up with someone. I had never had sex before. I was waiting for the special person. She was confused, saying, "Something doesn't make sense." He had texted after my exam, to make sure I wasn't saying anything: "Have you talked? Have you said anything to anybody?" So basically I lost it in her room.

When I came back after the exam, I took a shower. Neither of us knew what to do. I remember having to go to a store to get Plan B. He didn't use a condom. Should we rip the sheets off my bed? Because there's no way I'm going to sleep on these things anymore. After we did all that, his fraternity brother called to check up on me. I told him, and he was in shock. He said, "Elise, you need to report this. You need to go to an RA." I said, "I'm not gonna do that." I was concerned about what our friends would think, what his frat brothers would think, and I was afraid.

Later that night, I went and talked to an RA, who knew the assaulter. I remember him saying, "Elise, it doesn't really surprise me." Which blew my mind. At that point, High Point hadn't trained their RAs in what to do when a sexual assault happens.

The RA, who was a pretty tall dude, said this guy, who had been a high school athlete, was always trying to overpower him in some way. He said, "And you're not the first person to tell me you've had issues with this kid."

I couldn't go back to my apartment. I stayed with some other girls. I didn't sleep that night, didn't eat.

The RA said, "Elise, you need to call your mom." And that was what I was dreading most. Even though we were close, I didn't want to be that disappointment for her.

At six in the morning the next day I called her and said, "Mom, don't freak out, but two nights ago I was sexually assaulted." She dropped everything and came running up there. On the way to High Point she called the rape crisis hotline to see what we needed to do. I completely lost it with her. She told me, "Elise, we need to go to the hospital and get you checked out and have a rape kit done, as they're time-sensitive." We were running out of time.

Mom went with me to the head of Student Life, and that woman said to me, "Do you want me to inform him?" She said they had to get his side of the story also. She said, "Do you want us to wait until you're off campus? Or we can call him right now." I said, "I want to be off campus before you contact him." I was scared of what was gonna happen. In those forty-eight hours, I had had people who knew him telling me I wasn't the only one he'd gotten physical with. I was afraid. So, duh, of course I want them to wait.

After multiple meetings with High Point people, they said, "You need to talk to the head of security and get a rape kit." So Mom and I went to High Point Regional Hospital and got my rape kit done. That's so invasive. I was like, "What the heck?" I was so drained; I had barely slept, barely eaten. Mom was thinking—her social worker side was thinking—"We need to call the police and report this." Her mom side was thinking, "I need to take care of Elise and make sure she's okay." She kept asking me, "Do you want me to call the police?" I said, "No, Mom, the school

> **Mom was thinking—her social worker side was thinking—"We need to call the police and report this." Her mom side was thinking, "I need to take care of Elise and make sure she's okay."**

will handle it." The nurse asked, "Do you want us to call the police?" I said, "No, let's just get this done."

I remember the nurse saying to my mom, "Hey, Pam, can we step out a minute?" Because I had massive bruising on my inner thigh. She told Mom there was no doubt I had been sexually assaulted; she could tell by the bruising and the vaginal trauma. They gave me medicine for different sexually transmitted diseases, just in case. I remember saying, "I don't wanna take this." It made me sick.

I stayed in a hotel with Mom. The next morning we talked to a guy in security, and he's asking me questions, and I'm telling him about the bruising. He looks at me and looks at Mom and says, "Well, it's normal to have bruising when you have sex. It happens."

I remember looking at him and thinking, "What the hell are you saying to me?"

Mom was furious. We went for my meeting with Student Life. They took my statement. Apparently he had already left campus to go home for the summer. High Point promised Mom and me that they would not let him return until he gave a statement, until they had talked to him.

I remember driving away from school for the summer thinking, "It's gonna be okay."

LAUREN

The assault happened three weeks into my freshman year, on September 7, 2011. I was eighteen.

Curry has this Facebook page that lists everyone's contact information, so we could talk before actually getting to school. This kid I had never met asked for my number and I gave it to him. I gave my number to a lot of people in that Facebook group. He texted me that he wanted to hang out. I'll call him A. I said I couldn't, because I had class. And then class was canceled. It was a sociology class. Sometimes I think, if class hadn't been canceled, maybe, just maybe, this wouldn't have happened.

I met A at my dorm room at 11:30 a.m. I knew his name and that was about it. He locked my door, and before he started the assault, he asked if I was single. Maybe he thought that was my way of giving consent. He used force on me. Then he said, "Text me," and left.

My roommate walked in maybe ten minutes later. I was shaken up, and, honestly, had no clue what had just happened. I told her and she told me to tell someone. I went to my next class, a communications class, and then to lunch. I saw him at lunch and ran out and decided then to tell a resident adviser I was very close with (and still am today).

> He used force on me. Then he said, "Text me," and left.

I knew what had happened was wrong, but I didn't know how to put it into words. I wasn't okay. I was shaky. My roommate really helped, and so did my RA friend. She immediately called my community director (CD) and he told her to call a female CD so I could feel more comfortable. From there, they called a female public safety officer. Everyone spoke very calmly to me, as I was crying so hard during the whole investigation. They told me they had called the cops. When I spoke to them, the male officer was very to the point and didn't give me much breathing space. The female officer understood my position and let me take my time. The male officer finally caught on that I needed to breathe, but he wasn't so great at first.

My dad happened to call in the middle of the police interview (he always called me, every night), and I ignored his call.

The female police officer reasoned with me and told me to tell my parents. She also let me take my time. When they left to arrest him, I called my parents. From there, I was brought to a "safe spot," a place no one else would know about. I was with the RA and the female CD until my parents arrived. They spoke to the arresting officers, and then we left for home. It was about nine p.m.

He had been arrested that afternoon and was held in jail for the night.

After interviewing me, the public safety officer wrote my story out. I went over her typed story with the associate dean and okayed it. A few days later, I had to go over A's typed-up story and correct it if he had made errors. He lied on both of his statements, the one to Curry and the one to the police, and I pointed that out. My story matched up everywhere.

My ADHD and executive function disorder can make it tricky to communicate, since I know what I mean to say, but my thoughts don't come out as organized as they would with a typical learner. But in this instance, since I only had to tell my story twice on that one day, I didn't get super overwhelmed. I was very emotional, but I wanted him gone and I wanted to get justice so I wouldn't have minded screaming my story if I'd needed to.

ANDREW BROWN

It was the sixth night of college. It fell within the Red Zone, what a lot of social scientists realize is a critical time frame for college students socially, between arrival and Thanksgiving of freshman year, which is why early education about predators on campus is so important for college students.

I had just met new friends, and we were hanging out, laughing, having a good time until late at night.

It was five a.m. and my friends went home, and I was heading to the bathroom to brush my teeth and get ready for bed.

I was in the hallway and saw someone cross paths with me. I saw his eyes follow me. I unlocked the door to the bathroom—it was a communal bathroom that required a key to get you in—and was at the sink when I heard a knock.

I remember having the fleetest of questions as to why someone would knock, but figured someone else needed the bathroom, so I opened the door. He walked in and said, "You know, you're really hot."

I turned back to the sink as I said, "Thanks, but I'm going to bed. I'm gonna say no, but if I see you at a party I will remember what you said."

He stepped closer and suddenly started feeling me up while he said, "C'mon, nobody has to know."

He then moved me into one of the stalls in the bathroom. He was between me and the stall door the whole time. I just froze. I had no idea what to do, thinking, "Is this how people come on to each other in college?" I was so alarmed that I just completely froze.

Then I was saying no, turning away from him multiple times; then I was dead silent, not moving.

The only sound I distinctly remember hearing is the buzzing of the fluorescent lights the whole time. After assaulting me, he just left.

ANONYMOUS S

I don't believe that anyone goes to college thinking that they will be the victim of a violent crime. Why should they? All I'd ever known was the safety of living at home with parents while going to grade school and high school, and I imagined college would be a four-year extension of that same experience.

When I signed my letter of intent to attend college on a full athletic scholarship, I knew that my future had endless possibilities.

That changed very quickly, however. Only two months into my first semester of college, I was violently raped by another student athlete. The worst part was that I had no idea it was rape. I grew up seeing stories in the media about "date rape," and my parents gave me the lecture: "Always watch your cup" and "Don't accept drinks that you haven't made." I was naïve; I thought that you had to be drugged, abducted, and then dumped somewhere for it to be considered rape. This was not my case. After it happened, I had a sick feeling for a long time. I remember asking myself repeatedly for months, "What the hell happened that night?"

It happened my freshman year. I was eighteen.

He was a fellow athlete, a football player. We were studying together at study hall and then he suggested I should come back to his dorm to study more.

This is when parts of what happened are really hazy. All I know is that he was walking behind me, and I somehow ended up on the ground outside his dorm. I started to panic. I went limp. He told me to get up. Then he grabbed my left arm under the armpit and lifted me back up to a standing position and forcefully escorted me into his dorm. Thinking back, I still get upset with myself that I didn't fight back, but I am glad that I survived the attack; it could have been a lot worse.

Later I kept thinking, "You're a big strong girl, why didn't you fight back?" I'm not a small person. He and I were almost the same height.

I've heard everything in the book, like "Why didn't you scream?" I was just focused on "Stay alive, stay conscious." I was crying the entire time. Tears running down my face.

> Later I kept thinking, "You're a big strong girl, why didn't you fight back?"

When it was over, he reiterated, "If you say a word, I'll find you." It was straight out of a movie. And then he added, "I'm done with you, you can leave now."

I grabbed all my clothes and ran back to my dorm. I had a roommate. She saw how upset I was and asked, "What the hell happened to you?"

I said, "I had sex with somebody and I didn't want to." She jumped out of her bed and said, "Let's get you in the shower. We have practice in the morning." She was an athlete, too.

I stayed on campus and acted like nothing had happened. Everything else is a blur. I don't remember my classes.

But . . . I got hurt three weeks after I was raped. In my mind, it's connected to the rape.

Prior to this, I didn't talk about my problems. As athletes, you don't talk about your emotions, you work through them. I would go to practice and give it my all, and that's what you do. Suck it up. Keep your head down. Do whatever it takes.

My injury was from excessive working out.

I had never been injured before. Then the doctor said, "We need to do surgery." I had four surgeries. I was still thinking of the Olympics after the first two surgeries. But the pain was overwhelming. I couldn't stand it any longer. So I decided to meet with the surgeon again, and that's when he said that working out was making my body worse. That's when I knew, "Oh, my God, my career is over."

When the doctor is telling you that what you love is making you worse, it's hard to swallow. I couldn't use my body to cope with the emotional pain anymore. That was when I hit rock bottom. Being an athlete was my whole life. Being in control of my body was vital to me.

So I had the other two surgeries. I can never run again, and I loved running. I still have trouble walking.

The Attacker

A Chorus

We'd kinda been friends my freshman year.

He was an acquaintance; we had the same friends.

I had met him in passing the year before. Seen him
around campus. He was a visiting student.

He was a fellow athlete and was in one of my classes.

Met him at a frat party. He was not a frat member,
just a guy who was there.

I was raped by a woman, an upperclassman.

This guy had dropped out and was no longer a student,
although he was hanging around.

The cops knew all about this guy. He had already
raped six people and attempted to rape three others.

He was someone I had considered one of my best friends.

AYSHA IVES

I spent a lot of time hanging out with friends at Rutgers. And then, when I was nineteen, I met this older guy; he was thirty-six or thirty-seven. I was still so green. At the time I was a virgin. He put a lot of pressure on me to have sex. Finally I said okay. We were in my dorm room, at the beginning of sophomore year. I was twenty when I finally said, "Fine."

There was not a lot of foreplay. It was sort of like a business transaction. When he actually entered me I started to bleed. It was really painful, so I said, "Stop!" He said, "No." I said, "No, it really hurts, please stop." He said no again.

Then I felt something tear and there was blood everywhere. I bled and bled and bled. He said, "Oh, you must be on your period." It didn't stop.

I went to the college clinic and they sent me to the emergency room. The clinic offered no resources, no literature. So I went to the emergency room and I remember sitting in a wheelchair waiting to be seen. I had put on a pad but it had soaked through. I remember sitting in the chair and my whole pants leg had blood on it. I sat there for at least an hour, and I remember there was a change of shift. I'm still in a wheelchair and when the new shift came on, one of the workers said, "Are there any emergencies?" And the outgoing staff said no, nothing serious. I was soaked in blood, and I remember making eye contact with this nurse and she said, "Oh"—pointing at me—"she's bleeding," and then lowered her voice so I couldn't hear the rest of it.

I asked for a female doctor, because I didn't want another man touching me. I lay back down and closed my eyes, and I heard a man on the hospital staff say, "Well, she wasn't wanting a female a couple of hours ago." I remember opening my eyes; I couldn't believe what I had heard. And he didn't mean for me to hear; it was a joke amongst them. As for all the bleeding, it wasn't from my hymen; it turned out that he had ripped my cervix. The female doctor who stitched me up, the first thing she asked me was "Were you on drugs?" I was indignant: "No!" She was critical, in a "How did you get yourself in this position?" kind of way. I had thought a woman would be kinder, gentler, but a male doctor might have been better.

That hospital was awful. And I don't think the bad way I was treated was because of racism, I think it was because of victim-blaming.

As for the guy who hurt me, I would see him periodically, out and about. Afterward, he called me, and I told him what happened, and he didn't really care.

A couple of years ago he saw me on Facebook, and he messaged me. I brought that up—that what he did was a part of my life from which I'm still trying to heal. And his response was "You need to let it go."

Assault, rape, I didn't say those words to him. I struggled for a long time with what to call it.

I forgive him, but I struggle with the fact he doesn't take any responsibility. He doesn't own up that he hurt me. I've had to struggle with releasing the trauma.

Several months later, I met another man in town. I was twenty-one. He was about twenty-six. He was a socially awkward man. He didn't get along with his family; they weren't allowing him to stay with them anymore. We dated for a little bit and he wanted to have sex, but I made it very clear that because of my first experience I wasn't having sex.

One night we got a room at a hotel near the school. We got alcohol, and we were gonna drink a little bit and watch TV. I didn't drink that much, enough to loosen motor control but my mind was still alert. Things started to get hot and heavy between us and I said, "No, I don't want to have sex." I was very verbal. I said, "Stop, I'm scared. I don't want to." He kept saying, "You're such a tease." I remember getting really frightened because his whole demeanor changed. The look on his face was frightening.

I remember trying to push him off me, but I was having a hard time.

I was fighting him enough that he couldn't do what he wanted, so he started choking me. I had on a nightshirt, and I remember he's choking me and I'm uncoordinated but fully aware and I remember him removing my undergarments and then I remember him entering me and then my whole world just stopped. I stopped fighting, I stopped yelling, stopped struggling. I just went limp and waited him out.

Several minutes later, he stopped. When I stopped struggling, he continued for several minutes more, and then he just stopped. I don't remember him ejaculating.

When he rolled off me, I asked him for my keys. He had hidden the keys to my car, and also my cell phone. So when he stopped I asked him for my keys back and he said no. I ended up staying that night. I was afraid. So I stayed.

The next morning I woke up and he woke up and he asked me if I remembered what had happened last night. I said yes. And he said, "I'm sorry." I didn't say anything. He gave me back my keys and cell phone. There was blood on the sheets and he went outside to throw them in the Dumpster, and while he was outside I collected my things and fled.

ANONYMOUS V

The assault happened my junior year, in the fall. November. I don't like to talk about it a lot, because it feels like I'm trying to convince people that it happened. The first sentence told you I was assaulted; you can either believe me, or you can choose to not believe me. There was a point in time when I was dependent on validation. I needed to hear that my friends believed me and I wanted to hear my school believed me. I don't need that anymore. Now, recounting details makes me feel like my rape is a spectacle or something being consumed. I don't want my trauma treated like a car crash—people say it's awful and sad, but they read all the gory details and thank god it wasn't them.

I will say this: I was twenty when it happened. I had rules that semester about hooking up. I wouldn't go home alone with a guy the first night I met him; I clarified what I wanted to do sexually before we entered the room; I didn't hook up when I was very drunk. Aside from the last rule, I don't have those anymore. Rules might make you feel safe, but they don't keep you safe. The only thing that keeps you safe is someone else respecting you and your wants. That's on them and their rules.

That night, I'd known the person for over a month. As we were walking back, I said, "I don't know what I want to do. I'm not sure if I want to have sex." I didn't think I was in a bad situation.

He raped me.

When it happened, within twenty-four hours I reached out to our health educator, who is also the point person for sexual assault. She let the dean of students know confidentially that something had happened. But I didn't want to file a report then because it was so close to final exams and I didn't think I could handle the pressure. The health educator and the dean told me I had plenty of time to file a report.

FABIANA DIAZ

When I first moved to Ann Arbor in June, I was in a bridge program at the University of Michigan that was mostly for minorities. There were about five hundred students and it really felt like it was just us on campus.

The assault happened on my second night at the university, June 25. It was a Tuesday. It happened at midnight; actually it started at eleven and ended around one a.m. I had moved all my stuff into the dorm room the day before.

I had met him on the day I moved in, Monday. A bunch of us started talking at the cafeteria table, all getting to know each other. That night the guy I was dating at the time drove up to visit me. He was a little older, and was going to Michigan State, so he drove up to see me. We went out and had ice cream. They were very strict about curfew, so I said, "I have to get back." He walked with me and met some of the students, actually met the guy who would be my assailant, before he left.

The next day, all of us students went downtown to get some food. My feet were starting to hurt and I didn't want to be out any longer, so I said, "Let's walk back." So four of us, two girls, two guys, walked back. We went to the dorms, were walking around. We'd had our first day of classes that day. We were all just talking and talking.

Three of us went back to my room, a guy and one of my girlfriends, and my roommate hadn't shown up. Then my girlfriend left and I assumed the guy was leaving, too. I got up to go get my phone in the next room to text my boyfriend, and instead of leaving, the guy walked to the door, stopped, locked the door, and told me to be quiet.

I didn't know what to do. I'd never been in that situation. I had seen it on TV and always thought I would scream and fight. But once it happens to you, you freeze.

I started crying as he pulled my clothes off, and he said, "Shut up." He kept telling me to shut up. I was crying the whole time. He kept repeating, "It's just sex, it doesn't mean anything."

Afterward he got up and left. I found my phone and keys and locked myself in the bathroom. Then I called my boyfriend, and I was crying and crying. He couldn't understand what I was saying. I couldn't talk. It was two in the morning. I was just crying. He thought I was homesick and he said, "Do you want me to come pick you up?" My parents had left for a business trip to Chicago that day and I didn't want to tell them. I didn't know how to talk to them about it. I said, "No, no, no, don't come."

Then this girl walked in and said, "Do you want me to go get somebody?" She got one of my friends and they took me to their room and said, "What's wrong?" I was frozen. I just couldn't talk. I finally told someone, "I think I was hurt." And then two guys came in and I completely stopped talking. It was three in the morning and we had class at eight. The girls made the guys leave.

I told the girls what happened and they said, "We need to go confront him right now, what the hell was he thinking!" I said, "I'm not leaving this room, I'm staying locked in this room." I didn't feel safe.

The next morning, my friends walked with me to class to make sure he wasn't around. They walked me up to within thirty feet of my math class and left. Then I turned around and saw him. I started to panic. I ran and found the girls' bathroom and hid for fifteen minutes.

My boyfriend said he was coming to get me, so I told myself to just get through this class. I was scared the whole time. This girl came up and said, "Are you okay?" I said, "No, can you walk me out?"

I had never met her before. She was the first person I told that I was raped. She and I are still really good friends.

She walked me outside to my boyfriend's car and she told him, "She's not doing too well right now." I was still in shock.

He parked the car and I wouldn't tell him for what felt like hours. I finally told him and he said, "We're going to the police to report rape." I said, "No, that's not me. That's not what happened to me." It's such an awful word.

I went to his house. His stepmom is one of my mom's friends; she's Venezuelan. We had dinner and I was gonna shower and my boyfriend went to get some guest towels and his stepmom followed me to the bathroom and said she wanted to talk.

She said, "Fabiana, did something happen to you?" And I fainted. She threw water in my face and started screaming for my boyfriend.

I woke up on a couch. She said, "I have to call your parents." I said, "I can't call them," and started crying. She dialed my dad at least fifteen times; it was really late, about two in the morning. My dad wouldn't answer and finally he did and I just kept crying. He said, "What's wrong?" and I handed the phone to her and she said, "Fabiana is at my house and she's okay, but something bad happened to her." In the background, my mom started crying.

My dad said, "I want you to go to the police right now. Please do that for me. And we are leaving and will be there as soon as we can."

My dad later said he did one hundred miles an hour on the highway.

At the police station, I was shaking the whole time. I couldn't really talk. My boyfriend would talk and I would nod. I gave my statement and then they drove me to the hospital for the rape kit. I had not showered yet. And then my family showed up. At this point, I'd been up forty-eight hours.

That was the first time I've ever seen my dad cry. It was always a joke in my family he'd never cry. That's probably what hurt most, was seeing him cry.

The officer was fine. The detective came to my dorm and took all my bedding. Everything I had bought for college was gone: a Michigan blanket and stuff from Target; my sheets and all my blankets and pillow and the clothes I was wearing that night. I never saw any of that stuff again.

The hardest thing was when the detective came to take my statement that morning while I was still in the hospital. She later said since I'd had no sleep my statement was invalid and I had to do it again.

The first thing she said to me was "This is gonna be hard because he's attractive, isn't he?" I shut down. She now actually does a lot of Collaborative Reform work with the community. I think she's had a change of heart.

ANONYMOUS XY

My rape happened a week before classes of my second year as a graduate student at the University of Chicago.

I was living in an apartment with three other people: a married couple and this other guy. We were having a housewarming party. It was super safe: my house, my party, not drinking that much. I was very explicit with this guy: we are not gonna have sex.

I had met him in passing the year before. Seen him around campus. He was a visiting student. I didn't invite him to our party, but someone else did—my male roommate did. I was with other people in the apartment. It should have been safe.

But we were in my bedroom, me and this guy, kissing, and all of a sudden he penetrated me, without me saying it was okay. I don't remember how he got my clothes off. I couldn't see anything; it seemed to me as if the lights went off. I felt like I couldn't move. I started screaming, "What are you doing?!" He kept saying, "You're a psychotic bitch!"

I don't know what happened. They said I was screaming a very long time. My roommates busted in. They threw him out. They took care of me. Called a university advocate. Apparently I became catatonic. They had to slap me to get me to wake up.

I remember coming to and a cop saying, "Is she drunk?" The advocate said, "No, she's in shock."

I said, "I know how sex works, and that was not sex, that was rape."

My clothes were mostly on—my roommate had put my underwear back on for me. Somehow I got to the hospital and had a rape kit done. The rape exam was really bad; I remember it hurting a lot. But the staff was great. My roommates stayed with me.

After the exam, the cops said, "We need you to go to the police station right now." At least I managed to say, "I want some food," so we stopped at the apartment first. Hours had gone by at this point; it was the next day.

Then we went to the police station. It was really awful, waiting in that dark place. I don't think I realized before how fucked up the world is for rape survivors. The detective came out and told me the guy had turned himself in. I took that as a good sign. I remember my roommate saying, "No, don't get your hopes up, that doesn't mean he's admitting to it." Then, sure enough, the detective said that him turning himself in was a sign he was not a bad person: *See what a good guy he is, he came in on his own.*

I said, "You've got to be shitting me."

The police had already questioned me at the hospital. And they said my facts matched his, for the most part. Then they had me take out my clothes and show them to them. I had worn a maxi skirt, and they had me put it on and wiggle in it, and they said, "Well, he couldn't have raped you. It had to be consensual if you were wearing that skirt. It's too long for him to be able to rape you unless you helped him."

Wow, usually they say it's a short skirt that asks for rape, now it's a long one!

To this day if I see a cop car and it says, "Protect and serve," I snort, "Yeah, you guys don't do that."

Did their disregard of me have anything to do with me being Asian? People ask me that now. And I don't know. I have a dark sense of humor and am edgy and made jokes, and probably wouldn't have done that had I been more strategic about rape culture. I'm a petite woman and a Ph.D. student and was dressed nicely, so maybe they thought, "Oh, this is a spoiled, privileged brat."

That was my first direct encounter with rape culture. I was never before aware of how much injustice was out there.

Assaulted by Strangers, Twice

ZOË RAYOR

I left home at seventeen to attend New College of Florida, in Sarasota. A young feminist, I wanted to escape the Bible belt of north Florida as soon as I could, and I skipped a year of high school to do just that. When I first arrived at New College, I had no idea what I wanted to study and took multiple classes, including gender studies and Hebrew classes, and became interested in conflict resolution.

After turning eighteen, I traveled to Israel (and ultimately ended up in Palestine as well) as part of a program, geared toward Jewish students, called Birthright. During those few weeks in Israel, I wrote an extended essay for an independent study project about Zionism, the Israeli occupation, and female Palestinian suicide bombers. After this experience I became a conflict studies major and I moved to Israel during my sophomore year to attend Tel Aviv University. While living in Israel, I experienced my very own conflict, one that would rage on for years to come. It was there that I was assaulted for the first time.

One afternoon in the fall of 2009, I took a taxi from my dorm to the beach in Tel Aviv to meet up with some of my family. I sat in the front seat and began to smoke a cigarette. The driver was an Israeli man old enough to be my dad or even grandfather. We were almost to the beach when he pulled into an alley and locked the doors. It took me a second to realize what was happening and then I frantically tried to open the door but couldn't. I froze. The man began groping me and then shoved me into the backseat. I didn't know what to do, I went into shock and completely let go of control. He yanked my dress off, pulled down his pants, and raped me. After he was finished, he crawled back into the front seat, told me to put my dress back on, and then drove me to the beach as if nothing had happened.

I didn't know what to do; I was in a daze. I had no way to identify this person, and my Hebrew was fairly shitty. Confused and numb, I walked out to my family and tried to act normal. One family member asked me what was wrong, and I told her I thought I had been assaulted, but said I didn't want to do anything about it because I didn't think I could and I hadn't fully processed what had happened. It just didn't seem real.

A few months later I spoke to my mom on the phone and she described a date she had gone on during which a man tried to grab her and force her to kiss him. She was very upset and asked if I had ever dealt with anything like that. The question came out of left field and I broke down and told her that I had been raped. She was completely shocked and desperately wanted to be there for me. The reason I had kept it from her was because I didn't want her to know, to feel the distress of having her only child raped at eighteen, in a foreign country, alone. I didn't want her to experience the pain of being unable to do anything. She immediately booked a flight for the next month and helped me move my life back to the United States.

While I was still in Israel, I starting sleeping with a ton of people. I didn't totally understand what I was doing or why, but in hindsight I was desperately trying to regain my power and dignity as a human and a consenting sexual partner. I began to compartmentalize my experience of rape and tried to sweep it under the rug, although my PTSD and the trauma surrounding the experience would continue to dramatically impact my life. I think I was able to psychologically separate myself from what had happened to me because I had escaped from the physical place where I had been assaulted—both the cab and the country. I know this now because when I was later assaulted in my own space I felt very differently about it. After the first assault, I did go to therapy, but I felt that talking about the assault over and over was more hurtful than helpful. For the next few years, I tried my hardest to forget about it.

A difficult part of my recovery was learning to be in a relationship again and to accept love. I had started dating Josh my first year at college and when I came back to the United States I had to explain to him what had happened to me. He was incredibly supportive and loving, but it was horrible to have to talk to him about my assault and infidelities. Having sex with someone whom I loved turned out to be much harder than the random sex I had engaged in overseas.

Fast-forward two years. My thesis research was under way and I had begun my fourth year of college. After I returned from Israel, I had decided to change my major and pursued gender studies and religion. I shared an off-campus three-bedroom house with a friend and Josh. Josh and I usually slept together, but on a night in September 2011 I had come

> **A difficult part of my recovery was learning to be in a relationship again and to accept love.**

home late from a party and Josh had gone to sleep in his own room. I woke up two hours later, around four thirty a.m. I vaguely remember someone embracing me, trying to wake me up; I thought it was Josh. I pushed him off and mumbled, "No," before falling back asleep.

Right after that I suddenly woke up again with someone on top of me, and my body was pinned to the bed. As my eyes adjusted, I could see he was wearing a black hat pulled down to his eyes, and a handkerchief over his face. He said, "Don't say anything or scream or I'll kill you." Time stopped. It seemed like minutes went by, but it really must have been seconds. A million thoughts came into my head. "Is this really happening again? Who the fuck is this? Am I going to be raped again? Am I going to let this happen?" That last thought came up, and I realized that I was *not* going to let this happen. I don't know where my confidence came from, but I decided I wasn't going to freeze this time. I was going to fight.

I couldn't move my arms, but I immediately began screaming and my right leg shot up and kneed that fucker in the balls. He jumped up and ran, and I chased him. I watched as he fled through the backyard, hurdled over a seven-and-a-half-foot fence, and took off. I collapsed on the floor. Josh and my roommate came running into the living room to see what was wrong. I could only keep repeating, "Someone was here! Someone was here!," over and over. They thought I was having a nightmare, but I pointed toward the open back door and they realized that someone had indeed been there.

Someone immediately called the police. They came to inspect and couldn't find anything. They asked what I had been doing, if I had been drinking—they even joked about having a lot of DNA on my bedsheets. I eventually found out that the cops knew about this rapist. He had raped six people and had attempted to assault three others. His MO was that he would stalk his victims and wait until they were either home alone or asleep. The police believe he had been stalking me for months and although I had kept my blinds closed, apparently he could see in through one of the windows at night, a fact that made me feel nauseated.

I later found out that the young woman who lived in my room previously—another New College student—had been assaulted in that very same room eight months earlier by the same rapist. The landlord knew about the previous assault and had never told me and my roommates about this rapist who had not yet been caught. Neither the campus police nor the Sarasota police department had warned the student body about the assailant.

I found out most of my information not through the police but through an advocate at the local rape crisis center who had also happened to previously work as a police advocate (the police casually forgot to grant me a police victim advocate until a few weeks after I was assaulted). My mom had done a lot of research after my initial assault, and I had seen this advocate as a therapist at the rape crisis center (Safe Place and Rape Crisis Center [SPARCC]) in Sarasota. She told me about the other rapes and that the perpetrator had never been caught. He wears gloves, a mask of sorts, and a hat, and he leaves no trace evidence. He basically looks like an average white male, twentysomething, of average height and build. In a college town. After my assault and the publicity surrounding his crimes, he became known as the Bayshore Rapist.

About a month after I was attacked, he attempted to rape a friend of mine who lived down the street (also on Bayshore Road). This time there were four other people at home asleep *and* a dog, and yet he still attacked her. During the next few months, through mutual friends, I ended up meeting other people who were either victims themselves or who knew the women he attacked. He would stalk them for months and then sneak into their houses while the place was empty. He would then sit on their beds and wait for them to come home. He asked them questions about their beliefs and talked to them about religion. Most of these girls were Jewish. He generally sat and talked to them for about an hour before he raped them. They all thought they could talk him out

> **I ended up meeting other people who were either victims themselves or who knew the women he attacked.**

of it. Or that he would not rape them if he got to know them as a person. No one knew if he had weapons on him or not, and I don't think anyone had fought back until I did.

After the Bayshore Rapist attacked me, I was very angry not only about what had happened but also about the fact that he still hadn't been caught and no one was talking about it. I spoke out. I gave interviews to local news agencies and wrote numerous emails to the student body warning them about the situation, the known locations of the attacker, and the fact that the campus police weren't doing a thing about it. I got involved with a group of survivors who met up weekly to discuss our trauma, the patriarchal culture of rape that we live in, healing, and activism. I, along with nine amazing students, interviewed stakeholders, consulted other schools' sexual assault policies, and completely rewrote our college's Title

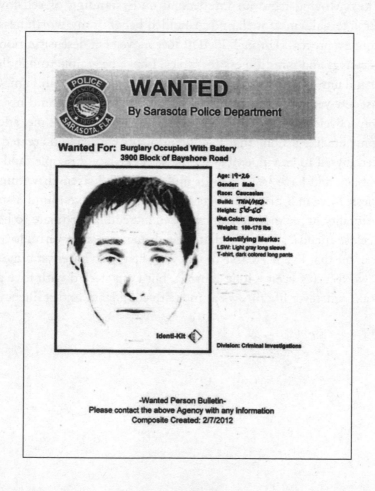

WANTED

By Sarasota Police Department

Wanted For: Burglary Occupied With Battery
3900 Block of Bayshore Road

Age: 19-26
Gender: Male
Race: Caucasian
Build: Thin/Med.
Height: 5'6-6'0"
Hair Color: Brown
Weight: 150-175 lbs

Identifying Marks:
LSW: Light gray long sleeve
T-shirt, dark colored long pants

Identi-Kit

Division: Criminal Investigations

-Wanted Person Bulletin-
Please contact the above Agency with any information
Composite Created: 2/7/2012

IX policy and reporting process. I even spoke publicly to my entire campus about what had happened, about living as a survivor in a society that glosses over the staggering rates of assault, and about what it means to be an activist. To this day, more than four years later, neither my Israeli rapist nor the Bayshore Rapist has been caught.

When I look back, the most important parts of my story are not about what happened to me but rather my strength in healing. For me, self-love—learning to accept, embrace, and respect myself and my story—has been key. Moving from an intellectual understanding of self-love to a truer, internal, emotional, and grounded belief in my worthiness has been quite a process. Through EMDR (eye movement desensitization and reprocessing) and mindfulness therapies, I have been able to handle my PTSD and unravel the stories my past has created about who I am. Over the last few years I've been able to set up boundaries around my relationships, I've cut out the people and jobs that do not serve me, and I'm living my life like it's one that I've intentionally chosen and created. I've allowed myself to be vulnerable with a select group of people (and now the public), and have been able to find power and strength within this openness. I live in a place that lets me exhale, and have found a source of spirituality in the mountains. I've been incredibly fortunate to have a mom, close friends, and a dog that provide me with a powerful love and belief in me that I've been able to rely on when I can barely stand on my own two feet. It's been a long journey, but I am steeled with love and I now take whatever life throws at me with confidence and resiliency.

Dear Abuelita

ANDREA PINO

Dear Abuelita:

I have a big secret.

I was raped.

I'm sorry I've never told you, but I can't find the strength to ever say those words in your language. In our language.

Abuelita, I dropped out of college.

It's a secret that only a few people know, but I carry it like I'm wearing shackles every day.

The truth is that *I feel like a failure, sometimes.*

I feel as if I let them win, and I feel as if I've let generations of Pinos, Silvas, Meriños, Villafruelas, and Cabreras down.

But, Abuelita, I'm afraid to speak with you because I'm afraid you may say, "Me, too."

It's difficult for me to realize that so many that I love have been assaulted. They were scared and embarrassed to tell their story, afraid that their friends would be disappointed. I, too, felt that way. I was raised with high morals like you, with a life enlaced in strong religious duties that always led me to believe that the woman was to be pure till marriage.

I did not have that choice, Abuelita.

It's easy for me to channel this anger into writing, but to explain it is to feel it in a constant cycle: to feel those weeks of denial and of refusal to accept that it was not my fault, and that I am still whole. This is why I can never share this letter with you.

Along the journey, I felt like one of many numbers of Latinas who have been sexually assaulted—and, just like my sisters' families, my family knew nothing of what happened to me. I wore the veil of a victim for weeks before I could remove it and accept that I was a survivor. But I now know that I'm not alone in my silence, nor am I alone in my determination to break it.

I want you to know that nothing you did brought violence

on me, but that I consider you my guide. It was you who worked tirelessly for our family to come to this country, and it's you who has given me the world.

Yo soy una mujer, Abuelita.

And it's thanks to you that I am the woman I am today.

I am smiling today, because I am surviving, and I am healing everyday.

I am a survivor, Abuelita.

I don't know if you will ever read this letter, and I am sorry that I am not ready to put these words down in *español.*

But I want you to know that I am strong, I am fighting, and I hope that you are proud of me.

Te amo, Abuelita.

Tu primer nieta,

Andrea

I Startle Easily

ANONYMOUS A

There is a mark I can't shake, which prevents me from forgetting this experience entirely: my jumpiness. I am unable to suppress the dramatic bodily tensing whenever someone approaches me outside of my peripheral vision or walks up behind me and touches me to gain my attention. Each time, with embarrassment, I deflect—"Sorry, I startle easily"—and pray that they don't press me to explain why.

It was an unusually warm night for the end of January, the spring semester of my first year of college. Some women who lived on the floor above me in the dorm invited me to go to a party with them at a fraternity house. I was pretty studious and didn't go out much back then. I remember feeling anxious because I didn't even really own any good "going-out clothes," and was also worried about going to a party at a fraternity house.

I'm a black woman, who grew up in the South, and was, thus, wary of hanging out with large groups of drunk white men. My friends assured me that this party wouldn't be too raucous, and that since this was the "Jewish frat," there would be lots of other people of color there. My friends were drinking and offered me a tequila shot; I declined, as I didn't drink, but I agreed to go with them.

The first few hours were fine—fun, even. The music was good, and I had fun dancing on the dimly lit living-room-turned-dance-floor. Beer, spiked punch, and liquor were flowing, but I stuck to water and just enjoyed the hip-hop and pop hits booming on the speakers.

Around one a.m., I was standing near the edge of the party, trying to find my friends, when I felt arms reach around my torso from behind. I was quickly and firmly dragged to a dark corner, boxed in, and groped. I squirmed and pushed, trying to get away, but was not strong enough to overcome my attacker's arms. My resistance only caused him to pin me against the wall harder. I remember feeling his hot, alcohol-infused breath on the back of my neck as Ludacris's "What's Your Fantasy" blared in the background. In a panic, I completely froze as this stranger touched and grabbed me in private places, slapped me, bit me. In the longest three minutes of my life, I was molested.

> **I'm a black woman, who grew up in the South, and was, thus, wary of hanging out with large groups of drunk white men.**

Eventually the song ended. He let go, and as he walked away I turned around and recognized him as a guy who was in my drama class—someone I'd never spoken to; I didn't even know his name.

I wandered around in a bit of a daze, holding back tears, trying to find a friend so that I could leave. I found the women I had come to the party with; they were hammered, and didn't understand when I yelled above the music that I needed to go home. Alone, I exited the house and walked into the cool night, waiting for the campus's night shuttle to take me home.

The rest of that semester was a blur. I tired frequently, had trouble concentrating. I felt like I was walking under a dark cloud all the time, and I gained a lot of weight. I remember trying to describe to a few close girlfriends what had happened at the party. It didn't go well. Perhaps they didn't understand or couldn't relate. Perhaps they felt that these experiences were a normal part of college life. Perhaps I didn't know or have command over the right words to fully articulate what had happened to me: "I was sexually assaulted. I was molested. I felt violated. I am afraid." As a result, I didn't disclose to anyone else. I tried to forget about what happened, tried to suppress the experience, and strove to make it through the rest of the semester and move on with my life. One memory, though, is clear: as I packed up my dorm room to move out for the summer, I remember praying, "God, thank you for helping me make it through this semester. Please help me find a purpose. Help me make meaning out of this."

The summer right after that experience, I found myself working with teenagers in a rural town. Many were going through puberty and didn't know how to deal with this life transition, and many of the girls were experiencing sexual harassment from their male peers. I started thinking about how having knowledge of your body relates to the development of self-confidence and self-esteem.

> I remember praying, "God, thank you for helping me make it through this semester. . . . Help me make meaning out of this."

Over the next year, I worked to develop a program to teach youth sex education, and I continued working with this program until I graduated from undergrad. This program was definitely beneficial for the students, but it was also the first step of my own healing and activism. It was a way for me to intellectually process my experience: "Maybe if I'd had more self-confidence, and had the knowledge and language to talk about my experience, people would have believed me," I thought. "I want these girls to be knowledgeable and feel ownership over their bodies, so that something similar never happens to them."

Gradually, the healing continued. Toward the end of my undergraduate career, as I took more women's studies classes and learned more about the reproductive justice movement, I found myself in spaces where I was able to meet other women who'd had experiences that were similar to—and oftentimes much worse than—mine. Hearing these women's stories validated my own experience, and during the summer before my senior year, I finally disclosed my story to someone who, I felt, actually heard me and actually understood.

Despite the healing that took place over time, carrying this secret also left marks on me that would display themselves at various times throughout undergrad. When I look back on my grades from the semester I was assaulted, the mix of As and Bs looks fine on the surface. But that semester I earned the lowest GPA of any semester during my college career.

I had always been attracted to black men, but suddenly I found myself fearful of them. I crossed the street or avoided eye contact when passing a black man who was unfamiliar to me, all the while, my head yelling, "Your avoidance perpetuates the racist idea that black men are predators! Walk down the street like a normal human, because he's probably a normal, nice guy!"

Wearing makeup, doing my hair, and dressing somewhat fashionably no longer interested me, as I didn't want to draw attention to myself. Once, a friend suggested that I try on some wedge heels while we were shoe shopping. My immediate reaction was "No! I can't run from an attacker in those!" She looked at me like I had four heads.

In the few instances when a guy was able to see through the wall I tried to build to keep myself invisible and asked me out on a date, I had small panic attacks—body shaking, breathing heavily—as I worked up the nerve to go. When a friendship with a guy began to look like it was transitioning into a relationship, I found a way to end it. The worst part of it all is that since I never reported my experience, I continued to

"Police won't believe me. They'll think I somehow brought it on myself as a black woman."

see my attacker around campus. By the time I recognized that I should report my experience, other thoughts got in the way: "The black community already has issues with police, don't stir up trouble." "Police won't believe me. They'll think I somehow brought it on myself as a black woman." "Don't start trouble within the black community on campus—people might take sides." "Remaining silent is better." Because my attacker was drunk that night, I don't think he ever recognized who I was. But I never forgot—and will never forget—his face. And every time I saw him, despite trying to hold it together, I eventually panicked and had to leave wherever I was within five minutes of seeing him.

My assault took place seven years ago, and I'm thankful for how far I've come in that time. It took me five years, but eventually I got over my fear of black men and began to feel comfortable dating again. I've dedicated my career to public health, working on issues related to reproductive health, HIV, and interpersonal violence. I've been able to informally offer support to other women who have disclosed similar experiences to me. I feel that by the grace of God, I've been able to find purpose in this nightmare. But there is a mark I can't shake, which prevents me from forgetting this experience entirely: my jumpiness. Despite my furious will, I am unable to suppress the dramatic bodily tensing and the yelp that escapes my mouth whenever someone approaches me outside of my peripheral vision or walks up behind me and touches me to gain my attention. Each time, the person looks at me extremely confused, wondering where this reaction is coming from. Each time, with embarrassment, I deflect: "Sorry, I startle easily—how can I help you?" and pray that they don't press me to explain why.

Star Wars

JOHANNA EVANS

Classes had started that week, the fall of 2006. I was a freshman at Dartmouth, on my own for the first time and struggling to make friends. Not knowing where else to meet people, I followed my floor mates to a fraternity party, but after fifteen minutes of the awkward, vapid frat scene I decided I'd rather be alone.

Some guy offered to walk me home. I said, "No, I think I'm just going to watch *Star Wars* and go to bed."

"I'm going in that direction anyway," he said. "And I've never seen *Star Wars*."

At the time it didn't occur to me I was in danger.

I let him walk with me. He followed me back to my dorm room, where I stood in my doorway and said, "It was nice to meet you." He pointed out my movie posters and pushed his way in. I started getting ready to go to sleep; went to the girls' bathroom down the hall, put on my pajamas, brushed my teeth. I came back and said, "Okay, I'm gonna watch the movie and sleep."

He said, "Well, can I watch it with you?" He was Muslim. This was 2006, and I was very passionately against the Iraq war. I didn't want him to think I was afraid or distrusted him just because he was Muslim, so I let him stay. Then he started kissing me, and I pushed him away and said, "Hey, we're gonna watch this movie." He started kissing me again, started undressing me . . .

There are parts of it I cannot remember, because something in me doesn't want to. But I remember having him on top of me, and feeling his slimy needle dick inside me, and telling him over and over, "No, this isn't a good idea." He didn't listen to me, and I froze in terror and confusion, utterly unprepared for the situation.

Being a survivor is like playing three-card monte for the rest of your life. You think you've figured out how to recover, but you've been following the wrong card. Another piece of the experience resurfaces and unravels your sense of self. There was a time that the worst part was that I was raped watching *Star Wars,* that he took that away from me too.

Don't laugh. *Star Wars* represented my belief that good will triumph over evil. It reminded me of childhood, of family. But I now have my own son, who is helping me reclaim *Star Wars* and rediscover the strength, courage, and hope I had before.

Blackout

ABBI GATEWOOD

How can I forgive myself? I've been led to believe that my poor judgment, my decision to drink like every other college student does, led to the assault. Maybe it did. Maybe my inebriation was an invitation for him to enter me as if I were an ATM.

All you have to do is put in your card to get the goods. All he had to do was put the drinks in to get the goods.

Is a woman's body the equivalent of a car wash? You can put in some money and go in and out whenever you want?

He didn't have the guts to rape me when I was awake. He made it easy for himself.

The saddest part is not that he raped me but that he found it okay to rape me.

Gang Rape at Oregon State

BRENDA TRACY

In October 1997, I met this guy and had an immediate connection. He was a football player. Anthony. Went to Oregon State.

Anthony graduated. Then in June 1998, when I was twenty-four, I accompanied my friend Karmen to her boyfriend's apartment.

We get there and it's the two guys who live there, then two guys from California who were visiting, then a fifth guy who was friends with Anthony—a really nice guy. I remember I had always thought if I wasn't dating Anthony I would have wanted to date him.

They're smoking weed; Karmen and I were not. They were playing video games. Then they wanted to drink, so they sent me and Karmen out for orange juice. When we got back, they suggested to me that I drink and at first I said no, but then I took an orange juice and Tanqueray. I first sipped it, and then gave it back because it was too strong. I started to feel dizzy and warm. I was sitting on a sofa. I remember seeing one of them look at me and he grabbed Karmen's hand and led her to the bedroom. The room was spinning. Then I passed out.

When I awoke I was naked, flat on the living room floor, feeling really heavy. I couldn't move my arms or my legs. There were four men, all wearing white tank tops. I turned my head to the right, and there was a man trying to force his penis into my mouth. So I turned my head to the left, and there was another guy trying to force his penis into my mouth.

A guy was raping me. And a fourth guy was stroking me, and himself, and laughing. They all high-fived each other.

I passed out again. I woke up as they were pouring alcohol down my throat and I was choking.

Another time I woke up and they had propped me up on my hands and knees, and they raped me from behind. One of them was in front of me and I was trying to stay conscious and to say, "You're Anthony's friend. Please make them stop." He had a hard time getting erect and the guys made fun of him.

I was in and out of consciousness. They were tossing me around the apartment like a rag doll. I said I was gonna throw up. One of them picked me up and carried me into the bathroom, and raped me from behind while I was laid over the sink and vomiting.

They used a small flashlight on me. They used an alcohol bottle on me. Toward the end they used ice on me because I was so swollen and dry they couldn't get inside me anymore. So at that point they gave up. That was six or seven hours later.

A Letter to My Daughter

ANONYMOUS K

Me, I worked from home for seven years. I worked fourteen hours a day, and I guess when you work sometimes in your pajamas you lose time.

I lost time after what happened.

I originally wanted to write a letter to my daughter about all this, but then I just couldn't. I get lost in my head, and I'm not a good writer anyway. Besides, I never shared this with anyone. You're the fourth person to ever know.

I was raped my freshman year. It was 1985, so thirty years ago; actually, it was very much around this time of year. Fall. I went to a toga party with my roommates. I had a pink toga on. I was talking to this guy, and he was tall, and I was just really intimidated by the whole college thing, but I was also excited about it.

This guy, he took me into the back room . . . and for the longest time, what felt so long, I was in shock.

I was in shock.

I wasn't fighting back.

He was so strong.

I didn't even have a voice.

I am in shock.

I remember walking back to my dorm.

Being so numb.

Walking through campus alone.

It was just supposed to be a toga party.

After, I had a hard time at school. I really had a hard time at school. There was no one to reach out to. This is 1985. And where it happened— it was a very popular frat. I would never go there again, but I did go out again sometimes.

I ended up dropping out. It was the second semester of freshman year when I left. My parents didn't know. They still don't know. They just know that I went into a really deep depression. I just didn't know how to cope anymore.

So, after that I started going to a local business college. I was so lost.

I didn't know what to do. I was going through motions. I finally told my best friend, who was in nursing school. It was such a different time, back then. I hate to keep saying that, but it seemed like a different time. I was alone and there was no support system. When I told my friend what happened, she just said, "So sorry that happened. . . . So, what are you doing this weekend?" and made it seem like not a big deal. But it was a big deal.

I mean, I don't have some crazy story. I didn't have bruises. I kinda felt like, "Did I let this happen?" But we never talked about rape back then. Rape in 1985 was a stranger pulling you into a stairwell, it wasn't at a toga party with a boy who was in college, at least we didn't think of it that way back then.

It happened, it was horrible.

That's my story, and I'm sorry it's not so eloquent.

~

I wanted this story to be a letter to my daughter. But I have to deal with myself and I still have these ghosts.

I would have shared everything with her before now, but I don't want to burden her with it. I was very strong for her when she was young. I didn't have to rely on a guy for anything. I wanted her to be self-sufficient, too.

I love her. I love her so much, but she can be so self-reliant. I wonder if I did that to her. She's a self-reliant person, you know that.

I never told her.

~

The impact? Oh, I'm not sure where you want me to go.

I went back and finished college. I never got married. I just wanted her to grow and be healthy. I worked odd jobs.

Then when my daughter was almost five, I got a job offer at the university. I was a secretary and then I moved positions. I didn't have day care. She stayed with my parents. I was on the waiting list for day care and every day at lunch hour I would beg and beg to be moved onto the employees' waiting list. It was a beautiful facility and so cheap.

It was like that until she started school. I was always a single mom.

My daughter isn't going to live in a man's world. She's going to live in her world.

She's beautiful and smart and successful and now she can be so self-reliant. But now, I can take a step back, you know. I'm so proud of her.

I don't know. I don't want to think. Because if I wanted to think and if I felt comfortable doing so, then I would tell her something about what happened to me.

I can't write a letter about what happened. If I ever tell her it will be out loud. I'm going to visit her soon, so I might say something then.

But I don't think telling her is going to help her in any way.

I don't ever want her to see her mom as a victim.

Right After

Johanna Evans, photographed one week after the
assault. (Photograph courtesy of Johanna Evans.)

PART III

TRAUMA AND BETRAYAL

Rape by Chloe Allred (acrylic on canvas)

We need to stop assuming that trauma builds character. Sometimes it does. But it also builds fear. It builds pain. It suffocates and it paralyzes. I didn't return from challenges as a stronger person. The bottom line is that it shouldn't have happened. I know it makes other people feel better to imagine that my trauma has made me stronger, but here's the thing: this experience belongs to me, not them.

—Alice Wilder, survivor who attended the University of North Carolina at Chapel Hill

For many survivors, strength comes from moments in time before their assault. When we were girls, our parents told us that we were going to do great things.

I was a competitive soccer player, who dreamed of success after seeing the U.S. Women's National Soccer Team of 1999 win the World Cup. Aside from sports, I was also interested in politics and in following in the footsteps of my grandfather, Charles Whitley, a former U.S. congressman: "I'm going to run for office," eight-year-old Annie said.

```
In sixth grade, I announced that I wanted to go to
college. I, Andrea, would be the first one in
my family to do so. I (literally) dreamed of going
to school, and this goal was fueled by what my
abuelito always told me: "Nunca, nunca, nunca pares
de luchar." Never, never, never give up. I believed
that I could do anything I set my mind to.
```

We were meant to believe that trials were good and that defeat builds character, but those life lessons don't always hold true in cases of assault.

It's comforting to read survivor narratives and think, "What happened was awful, but look how they grew from that experience!" However, the harsh reality is that violence shouldn't be romanticized, and that courage isn't necessarily bestowed by it.

The people in this book are some of the most powerful individuals we have ever met; but they aren't anomalies, and their survivorhood, healing, and activism aren't supernatural. We are all people, just like you. To borrow a phrase from the late academic and disability advocate Stella Young, our stories are not meant to be "inspiration porn." They are merely the truths and daily realities of violence.

Therefore, just as we wanted to actively make space for multiple narratives of assault in this book, we also want to make space for multiple truths in response to trauma. Assault sometimes shatters pieces of ourselves, and the way we put our own mosaics back together—or don't— is an individual process.

Some survivors report their experience immediately, while others wait years, and still others never want to report, or can't report. Some survivors undergo a terrible reporting process that revictimizes them, while others experience a supportive process at their schools. Some people, particularly people of color, queer people, and others in marginalized communities, may not feel safe going to the police.

Survivors who have a negative experience with police, who are not believed by officials at their school, or who are blamed even by their friends often describe the responses of unsupportive individuals as almost a second rape. That betrayal of a trusted institution compounds the already existing trauma. Over 30 percent of survivors develop a psychiatric disability as a result of their assault. Rates of post-traumatic stress disorder (PTSD) are higher among survivors of sexual violence than among combat veterans. Depression, anxiety disorders, and other invisible disabilities are common in survivors, but often, survivors who have these invisible disabilities do not receive the academic accommodations, compassion, understanding, and support that they merit.

Trauma manifests itself in many ways, it can accompany us for years, and it can reappear when we least expect it. Violence, once visited on us, often stays with us after the moment it happens, and its true impact is perpetuated by the society that tolerates it.

Our Stories, continued

ELISE SIEMERING

So the guy who attacked me had already left campus to go home for the summer. High Point had promised Mom and me that they would not let him return until he gave a statement, and I'd driven away for the summer thinking, "It's gonna be okay." But that summer was complete hell. The Student Life people at High Point made me come back to campus three times. Back and forth. After I got home, they called us and said they'd contacted him. He had a "family emergency" and could not travel, so they took his statement over the phone. During our last meeting, they made me come up [to campus], and it bothered me that they were making me, the victim, do more work than the person who did the assault. During the summer, I went for counseling, attempting to make progress toward healing. Each time they called, I felt like I was taking another step back. That summer in June, I interned with my old youth group—we were taking the kids to beach camp—and we got the call that I needed to come to High Point. They then sat down with me and said he denied all accusations. He'd said, "Oh, Elise asked me to have sex."

At that time, they told me that he had done the phone interview and so he would be allowed back on campus. I remember sitting in the parking lot with Mom, and crying, and then something snapped. I said, "We're gonna go to the police."

One of the biggest blessings I had in my whole case were the two detectives assigned to me. A lot of people I've talked to in similar situations didn't have that; I personally couldn't have asked for any better. We went straight to the police station. The detectives were two women, which made them easier to talk to, and they told me I was not the first case at High Point who had been treated that way. They told us they were not surprised.

The police did a whole write-up and they said to me they would contact High Point, and contact him, and that one of the biggest problems was that High Point was legally supposed to contact them as soon as I reported. High Point was not supposed to give me an option of calling the police or not.

The police asked me who I had talked to about the assault. I gave them the names of five of my friends. I still had those text messages.

They had to call my friends, three girls and two guys, as witnesses: Marie, the other guy who had been with me in the library that night, and other friends who were also friends with my attacker.

Later that month, the police called me with an update, and this is when I found out who my friends were. The only one who was willing to speak to the police was Marie. The rest refused. People I had thought would be there for me weren't. They wouldn't talk, so that made the case harder. That whole summer I debated: "Do I go back to High Point?"

I decided, "This is my university just as much as it is his. I'm gonna go back."

That fall I went back a week before classes started. Upperclassmen help freshmen, and I had committed to doing that before the assault.

I was in the student center, and within minutes I saw him, hanging out. Why was he on campus already? He was not helping with freshman orientation, so he was not supposed to be on campus. I called Mom and said, "I've been on campus five minutes and I'm seeing him." My parents were moving my stuff in. At that point, with all the stuff Student Life had put us through, Mom said, "That's it. We are going to talk to the president of the university."

We set up a meeting and met with him. It was the worst meeting I've ever been in. I sat there like a statue. It got heated between my parents and him. My dad was baffled why he wasn't getting this.

I started my fall semester. It was so hard. Rumors started. Some of his fraternity brothers would call me names. They would see me

> I decided, "This is my university just as much as it is his. I'm gonna go back."

in an elevator and call me a bitch, and say, "You're lying!" and yell stuff at me. People on campus were talking about it, and it's a small campus. You see the same people every day. Mom asked if I wanted to get a restraining order. I said I didn't know how much that would help.

We did a verbal agreement with him through the school: You stay away from Elise and she stays away from you. That semester they put me on "Care Watch" and required me to go see a counselor at the school. I had to go through counseling sessions. I was already seeing a therapist. What made me upset was this therapist was working for High Point. It was like she was defending them. It was so hard to open up to her; she was an employee of the school.

That semester, I hated going out. My grades started slipping. Before the assault, I was honors. But I spiraled my junior year. I was still getting calls from High Point wanting to know information. I had the criminal case going on; the police officers told me he had refused to come in and talk with them. They called him multiple times. So they had to get a warrant and come to High Point to find him and talk to him.

My junior year, I went to the head of Student Life because the verbal harassment had gotten too much for me. I said, "He's having people come up to me and say stuff. I'm getting harassed." The head of Student

Life, the woman who had interviewed me, looked at me, and said, "Elise, I don't know why you're still having trouble with this."

Two things I remember most—Student Life and her. She said, "It's been months since this happened. Why aren't you over this?" She told me I could go through student court; it was made up of professors and students.

> She said, "It's been months since this happened. Why aren't you over this?"

I had two professors I absolutely loved. And both of them stood up for me. Both of them went to Student Life for me. One went and basically said, "What the hell?" The other knew about how the judicial board worked, and she said, "Elise, there's no point in putting yourself through that. Rarely do they ever do anything about it." She was so upset. "I want to save you from more heartbreak and struggle. You should just continue with the police." My junior year was very hard. I struggled a lot. My grades went down. My GPA plummeted. I was not social.

LAUREN

We didn't have to come together for a hearing. We had both made statements, and the associate dean and the actual dean of the college sat down with some other people to decide if consent was present, and if what happened was sexual assault. It was determined that it was indeed sexual assault, and about a week later, I received a phone call from the associate dean while in a PAL (Program of Advancement of Learning, my extra-help resource) class, saying it was found obvious there was no consent, so he was dismissed from the school. I was with my PAL advisor and another student, and I cried tears of joy. I was so happy to finally be able to feel safe and free on campus. He had been off campus since the assault, but he did have to be on campus for the meetings. During those times, RAs would escort me to classes by driving me.

A moved out of Curry, since he had been found responsible by the school investigation. The process of meetings with the district attorney's office lasted until the end of January my sophomore year, one and a half years after the assault; at that time, my parents signed on my behalf to put the criminal case on hold. I can resume the case any time in the next five years, which is when the statute of limitations is up. I know I will never be going to court with him since I can't stand to see his face again. I feel that would do more harm than good on my behalf.

ANDREW BROWN

At the time I blocked it out. "One of those crazy college hookups," I told my friends. "You'll never believe what happened last night. Isn't that funny? Ha ha," and it worked, until I would see him around. My blood pressure would rise, my heart would beat faster, my vision would narrow, and I would just try to get out of his sight.

Even though I was experiencing those symptoms, it took me more time to put together that the way seeing him made me respond meant I was trying to protect myself by portraying what happened as something it wasn't.

I was trying to rationalize what happened. But then it all came crashing down.

I suddenly started seeing him every day. I was in an opera and on a different part of campus every day, and there he'd be.

One day I saw him in an eatery, and saw him hug a friend of mine. So I later went up to that friend and said, "Who was that?" It was the first time I heard his name.

I kept seeing him on campus. It led to a complete panic attack in the shower one morning. I just started shaking, couldn't tell where I was. I realized I was not okay, and this had to stop.

So I went to Health Services at Brown. They told me, "Physically you seem okay, but Psych Services might help you better."

Between the questions of "How are you doing?" they asked, "Are there any major stressors in your life?" I mentioned I had been assaulted. That was the first time I said anything to anyone within the Brown administration about what happened. It was to a counselor, a therapist. She responded pretty neutrally, in the sense that she didn't try to put words in my mouth.

I said, "Maybe I was sending mixed signals?" and she said, "Well, you did say no."

She suggested I talk to an advocate, and that's when I met this incredible woman, Bita Shooshani. I started seeing Bita about every week. It was with her that we really started breaking down, "What is it about this experience that is giving you these reactions right now?"

It was seeing him. We came to the conclusion that based on that, the best thing would be to go through the campus adjudication process. So I filed a complaint at the start of May 2012. I submitted an online complaint to the Office of Student Life.

Brown is changing that process, but at the time they didn't have a Title IX complaint form or a Title IX office; I had to file a complaint through the Student Life office as a violation of the student code of conduct.

Typing the complaint brought a bit of panic that something that happened to me that was so personal would be shared with other people.

I got an email about three hours later, saying, "We received your complaint; we have a few more questions for you. Assess which offenses he could be tried under."

It was offense number three, 3a and 3b; 3a is nonconsensual anything and 3b is penetrative nonconsensual contact.

I went to talk to them in the office, and they said, "Well, it's late in the semester for us, so we're going to do this next fall." I just assumed that was the way it was. It was coming from people who did this thing for a living, and I didn't know.

The looming complaint process was hanging over me all that summer. Then the process got rescheduled three times that fall—once due to Hurricane Sandy, but it was rescheduled twice after that.

The Office of Student Life said they couldn't find a panel. So the hearing was set for November. The frustrating thing was that my advisor—a representative provided by the school—had to step out, and then I had a second one. And then she had to step out, so I went back to the first one. On the other hand, my advocate, Bita, was a constant through it all.

No one on campus seemed to know much about the process. No one talked about it much. So I really didn't have a baseline of what to expect going in. I was pretty nervous. Bita tried to help me, but it was still sort of going in blind.

In another step of mismanagement, the attacker never sent in a statement. So we had no idea what he was going to say. It made our job of preparing a lot more difficult.

The panel was made of the head of the Student Conduct Board, a faculty member who was a dean, and an undergraduate student. The dean and the student were both female.

I did get the questions about, "Why, if this was so long ago, is it coming up now?"

Thankfully they refrained from "What were you wearing?"

I dressed nicely but didn't wear a tie. The hearing was held in a room within the Student Life offices. They had already told me he was not on campus that semester. Which was a huge relief for me, because I could stop worrying about whether I was going to see him or not. I could stop looking over my shoulder for that semester. He was a junior, so I assumed he was studying abroad. No one corrected my impression; then, the day before the hearing, someone said, "He's not abroad." They didn't elaborate.

He phoned in to the hearing, which the administrators said would take ninety minutes. There was one piece of evidence, which was a text I had sent to a friend, and one witness, a friend I had told. It took three hours. Everything he said was, "Uh, like . . ."

He would give a small little detail and they would ask him about that and eventually weasel something out of him that would shed light on what happened.

I was pretty lucky he actually said in the hearing that I said, "Not now, maybe later."

He said he heard that as "Maybe now, and yes later." Once he admitted he heard me say no, that was all the evidence they needed.

We had to ask questions through the board, and toward the end he said, "I'm sorry that it happened." It didn't feel like much at the time.

But in terms of the physical details, I was saying one thing, and he was saying another, and the friend I had called was saying a third thing. So 3b was not an option.

The hearing happened, and I got a letter about a week later—an email—from Student Life. He was found responsible for 3a, not 3b, and the sanction was expulsion.

The feeling as I read through it—when I got to the word *expulsion,* my eyes locked on that word and I can really only describe that as total relief. Knowing that I would never have to see him on campus again, so for the next two and a half years I didn't have to worry about seeing him or second-guess where I was going if I was alone. That was very liberating.

There were still physical effects; I remember the stress being there all the time. I behaved more erratically than I normally

> . . . and the sanction was expulsion. The feeling as I read through it—when I got to the word *expulsion,* my eyes locked on that word and I can really only describe that as total relief.

would, doing things and saying things I wouldn't otherwise have said. Being really rude to a friend and feeling really raw much of the time.

And then that was kind of it for a while. I was surprised he had been found responsible for a less serious offense and they had still expelled him. But I didn't want to look a gift horse in the mouth and ask why. I was afraid to know that answer.

Then other stories started coming out. Other people who felt the process had let them down. A friend who had been assaulted, and her perpetrator was suspended for a year and half and his request to reenroll was only denied until after she graduated. Soon it became clear: Brown had a serious issue I needed to address.

ANONYMOUS S

I reported my sexual assault my sophomore year, almost exactly a year after it occurred. We had a guest speaker come talk to all the student athletes and she went into detail, stating, "When you say no, it means no, and anything forward from that is sexual assault."

I couldn't believe what I was hearing. I thought, "Oh. My. God. I was raped that night."

I think the hardest thing for me to accept was that neither one of us was intoxicated. This meant he knew exactly what he was doing every single minute. I now could stop blaming myself because what he did to me was a *crime*.

So the next day I reported it to campus police. To my knowledge they didn't really do anything. I told them I was scared for my life and they said, "All we can do is move you to another dorm."

I said, "You don't understand, he said he would kill me if I told anybody." They said, "You need to have proof, witnesses." I had no proof and no rape kit.

The constant question I kept getting was "Are you sure that really happened?"

I told my parents because the police had said they might question them. To my knowledge, they never did. My mom was in complete shock. My dad was so heartbroken; we're all really close.

So, instead of dropping out of school, I went to counseling. I had to learn how to cope with seeing him around campus and the athletic facilities. If he had been removed from campus, I might have been able to move forward. But I was constantly on high alert in case I encountered him.

I was completely and utterly heartbroken. I had entrusted my life to my university and the athletic department.

What if I lost my scholarship?

Everything I had worked for was truly crashing down. All of those years of putting in extra workouts, all of those parties and sleepovers missed because of early a.m. practice, all to be taken away because my campus police seemed to believe I didn't "make no clear enough for him"? This was my worst nightmare.

I had no idea who I was, but the real upside to being an athlete is that you become very good at putting on a façade. I remember wanting to scream at the top of my lungs just wanting help, but instead I decided to keep my head down, grunt it out, get my degree, and get the hell out.

AYSHA IVES

For years, I didn't tell anybody about being choked and raped. When I was about thirty, I told one of my good friends about it. She said, "Why didn't you tell me sooner?" We had been friends since middle school. She was distressed that she hadn't been able to support me.

And then I told my current boyfriend. And then I wrote and published a book, *Unbroken: How God Made Me Whole Again*, which directly addressed the trauma of sexual violence in my life. It was so hard for me to tell the story, but writing that book was a healing thing for me. It was me reclaiming my voice. Before I wrote that book, I couldn't say the word *rape*. I couldn't even write the word *rape*. It was such a filthy word. That word was such a trigger for me. When someone else said that word, I would flinch.

I never saw that guy again.

In hindsight, I'm sure I wasn't his only victim.

After the rape, I changed my major. I had started out in biochem, and then right after the rape, I changed my major to psychology.

ANONYMOUS V

The last few weeks of fall 2013 were unbearable. I'd followed my own safety rules and I was still assaulted. I didn't want to tell my parents. I kept running into my rapist on campus—in the student center, at the library, and on paths walking into academic buildings. I remember thinking that my lungs didn't know how to breathe the same air around him anymore. Every time he entered a building, I felt hyperaware of his presence and claustrophobic. Switching floors didn't help me escape the feeling. It got to the point that I was so on edge that switching buildings couldn't calm me down. I left school early for the winter break without finishing all of my exams. I still didn't tell my parents: not about the rape or the academic fallout. The wall of things unsaid between us was starting to grow.

Over break, I was diagnosed with post-traumatic stress disorder. I was very resistant to that diagnosis at first. I didn't think it was fair to pathologize my sadness and fear. My experience *was* traumatic. What happened to me *was* awful. I didn't want to hear that I was sick. I thought that what I was feeling was expected and normal.

I understood the diagnosis more when I came back for the spring semester. I was a mess. I still had the same anxiety and trigger response when I saw him. Before the assault, I didn't think about being safe on campus. After, I was hyperaware. I couldn't sit with my back to the door and I had to know who was around. I constantly looked over my shoulder while I walked, or had a friend walk me to class. I felt like our campus wasn't big enough for both him and me to live and study there. I would go to the dining hall, see him, and lose my appetite immediately. I'd see him in the library and lose focus for hours.

So I decided to go through the hearing process. I didn't see how I could stay in college with my attacker on campus. I don't doubt my memory of that night. I didn't file a report lightly. I agonized over it before filing and up until the hearing. I remember calling a friend and telling her that maybe I could call it off if he would just admit it and apologize to me. I thought that maybe I just wanted the truth. I didn't want to ruin someone's life. I spent hours in therapy going over my own behavior that night, checking for things I'd missed that made what he did okay. I couldn't find anything. Every time I searched, I came up with the same conclusion: he knew what he was doing, he knew I didn't want it, and he didn't care. I questioned my own motivations and actions very thoroughly. I didn't report to go on a witch hunt.

During the reporting process, my apartment was my safe space. I would go to meetings about the hearing and then come back and hide. Maybe on weekends I'd go to something social. Mostly, I was drinking too much—self-medicating. The process took months and it took all my energy. I filed in February and the last appeal didn't end until after graduation that May. The night of the first hearing, I thought the process had worked. I had gone through hell by that point. I'd been hospitalized over spring break for PTSD symptoms (without telling my parents why I had been admitted), I'd dropped a class, and my

> **My roommate brought home a huge helping of mac 'n' cheese and ribs, and another friend brought wine, and we were all just really happy. I slept that night.**

friends were shuffling through "check on V" duties to make sure I was still feeding myself and getting out of bed. But that night in April, I thought it was going to be okay. The first panel found him responsible.

While we waited to hear the sanction, my roommates, friends, and I celebrated and breathed deeply for the first time in months. My roommate brought home a huge helping of mac 'n' cheese and ribs, and another friend brought wine, and we were all just really happy. I slept that night.

Then the next morning I got the email: the board assigned him social probation and counseling as a punishment. I didn't understand how they could believe me and give him such a slap-on-the-wrist of a sanction. Drugs and alcohol didn't cause the assault, and we weren't in a relationship. How would counseling change anything? Twice during the [hearing] process he went to drinking events and the school found out about it and did nothing. They said they added it to his file. I had an administrator take me aside and tell me I should file a Title IX complaint. I was too exhausted.

I found out a year later that the campus police didn't know he was on social probation, and my RA didn't know he wasn't supposed to be in my building. The sanction was given in April of my junior year, the spring after the assault, and the final appeal was June. It wasn't until February of the following year that the police were notified. One of my friends had called them in November to say he was violating his sanctions. The police didn't respond to her call because they had no record he was on probation at all. Since all this happened I've heard through the grapevine about other girls my attacker pressured or forced to have sex, people who didn't report.

> **I fell out of love with the school. For three years I had worked as a student caller for the annual fund. . . . I quit that job.**

Throughout all of this, I was angry. I fell out of love with the school. For three years I had worked as a student caller for the annual fund. After this happened I quit that job. Saying "This school's great" would have been disingenuous.

When I tell people about my negative experience with the college reporting process, they ask why I didn't call the police. Part of my assault was anal penetration, which isn't considered rape in the state where I was assaulted. I vaguely knew that before my assault because I had heard about it through activism—that gay men couldn't be raped. A day after my rape, I Googled this to check it out. Today, two years later, I now know that unwanted anal penetration is as serious a crime as vaginal rape in my state, but I didn't understand that from what I found on Google that day. All I understood was that anal penetration was not considered sex under the law. From this correct reading of the law (if incorrect interpretation of how seriously my assault would be taken), I assumed that the police could not help me. If the state did not see my assault as sex, then I didn't believe the state could see it as rape. This made me feel invalidated—like the law deemed me lesser than a victim of forced vaginal penetration—and, above all, incredibly alone.

I trusted the college to help me. They didn't. I took the fall of 2014 off from college to recover from that betrayal and figure out my mental health.

FABIANA DIAZ

I was so ambitious going into college. And I didn't want him to ruin any of that. It didn't hit me until after that summer bridge program at Michigan ended and the fall freshman semester began.

I went through the whole police and university process, which meant being pulled out of class, or not being able to go to class. I missed a lot. I would meet with someone for five hours. It was just over and over and over again, for a month or so. It was so horrible. A nightmare.

For a long time I would say, "I'm fine, I'm fine," even though I knew I was not fine. Life became a competition for me: he wasn't gonna stop me from doing what I wanted to do.

But it's been difficult.

The police didn't want to move forward: "These things never go well for survivors. There's not any hard evidence—the jury will never convict him."

At the school, it was the same thing: I walked in one day and the woman in the Office of Student Conflict Resolution said, "We have a decision, and you won't be happy with the results, but we'll make sure he's not in your classes," and she handed me the letter and a box of tissues and left. I still see her sometimes on campus and I'll look the other way.

Meanwhile, I started getting harassed by the football team because he was friends with them. They were harassing me, and then everyone from that night turned on me. I was really bullied.

That was really shitty. Really hard.

And then lo and behold, in the fall of freshman year, I'm in English 125 and he walks in.

I got up and walked out. I called an administrator and called my dad and it just blew up. But what it came down to was I had to switch classes, of course, not him.

And that's how it was. He'd walk into a room and I'd have to be the one to get up and leave. There was no protective order, nothing.

ANONYMOUS XY

I told my sensei first. I trusted her. She advised me to not keep holding it in, that I should tell my parents because secrets take on a life of their own. "Who knows what their reaction will be?" she said. "Maybe they'll be helpful." She was always hoping for the best in people.

Trauma shakes everything up. Puts things in stark relief. My roommates—we're not friends anymore. They basically abandoned me in two weeks. The married woman and the single guy were about to have an affair, yet they told me my rape was causing tension. I thought, "No, your personal drama is causing the tension."

But my family—I'd been dodging them after the rape. So a few months later, I finally told my mother. I was in Chicago. We were Skyping. I took a deep breath and said, "This thing happened. I was raped. It was pretty bad. I've gotten help, and I'm hoping you can help me, too." She said, "I don't know what to say. I guess I could fly over, but that probably wouldn't help."

Then she just sat there. At that point, I was looking for a lawyer to help me with a civil suit, so I said, "Can you help me with that?" And she said no. She didn't ask if I was well. My father didn't say anything to me. I have three siblings. I didn't tell them. I wanted to, but my mother actively discouraged it.

I went home for Thanksgiving a month after my rape. My mom and I got into an argument (probably about how I didn't obey her enough) and she physically assaulted me. She grabbed me and started shaking me. I don't remember what she said. I had a panic attack.

Long story short, my parents and I went back and forth for three years. There was a lot of victim-blaming, a lot of denial. So I'm not in contact with them anymore.

Why did my rape make them so uncomfortable? My parents had tried to control me, but maybe deep down when they lashed out, they were actually scared. Anger and control really come from fear.

One thing I learned from my sensei: strength and compassion come hand in hand.

For a while it was all very hard. The immediate aftermath was intensely lonely.

Friends

A Chorus

She was the first person I told that I was raped.
She and I are still really good friends.

My roommate really helped, and so did my RA friend.

My assailant and I had the same friends. It made it interesting, after
it happened, to see who was really there for me and who wasn't.

My best friend let me stay with her and sat with me that night when
I couldn't sleep, I couldn't speak, and I couldn't cry.

My sorority—along with my friend Marie—saved me.

His friends cornered one of my friends and screamed at her.

I told a friend of mine what happened and she really
shamed me. I had to go get Plan B with my mom.

Your priorities can shift on an hour-by-hour level. And your
world can feel small compared to what your friends are doing.

At the end of the day, it really mattered who was in my corner.

When I was about thirty, I told one of my good friends about it.
She said, "Why didn't you tell me sooner?"

I called one of my friends and he came over.
If it weren't for him . . .

The Surprising Bravery of Others

ANONYMOUS V

While I was going through the hearings, I had really bad panic attacks—ripping out my hair, sobbing. My friends had to see that, and there was nothing they could do. They couldn't even call my parents. So a lot of my friendships took really big hits. Some of my friends stood by me, but others said, understandably, "This is too difficult and I can't take it." They were powerless watching me self-destruct. And I'm very sorry for that. And there's not a way for me to make amends there. When you're in that moment, you think it's only happening to you, but it's not. It's a whole village going through that.

My roommates were phenomenal; scary stuff happened that spring. When I went back, I didn't want my friends to have to check on me, which they did, though at the time I didn't even realize it.

I did not like myself in the year and a half following my assault (though I'm beginning to now). I was not a good friend or a good daughter, but by and large the people in my life haven't let me give the apology I feel I need to, because my actions were "understandable," "not my fault," or "it was such a hard time." Whenever I speak to a reporter and am characterized as brave or write a piece and receive feedback calling me "strong," I feel like I have fundamentally misled that person in a serious way. I do not see myself as strong or brave. The people in my life who stuck by me are brave and strong and resilient. I don't really have a choice. I'm twenty-one and not particularly ready to hole up in my room for the rest of forever, so I had to find a way to incorporate my assault into my new reality. The people in my life did have a choice daily. And they chose to stay, and they helped me rebuild. Some had to leave along the way for their own mental health, but all of them at least tried to stay and help. That is bravery. I think I've learned gratitude from all of this, but I'm not always able to express it, and people certainly don't let me because they think that I've had a worse lot.

Bravery to me looks like my roommate driving me to a psychiatric hospital my junior year, playing One Direction and talking about who she should ask to a semiformal, as if she were driving me to a mall, trying to make the experience seem normal when it was in no way normal. It was a Sunday night, and when she returned to campus she had deadlines that she wouldn't be excused from. Bravery looks like my friends who answered calls to walk me to class and had to choose whether to say something they thought might be soothing or to try to distract me. Being strong looks like my brother supporting me when I was self-centered, erratic, and a tornado of emotions. That is okay and it is understandable given what I went through. But I think it is also okay to feel remorse for what I put my loved ones through. No matter how justifiable your

> **Bravery to me looks like my roommate driving me to a psychiatric hospital my junior year, playing One Direction and talking about who she should ask to a semiformal, as if she were driving me to a mall.**

behavior is, you don't want to cause your friends and family pain. I hate that in my first attempt at a relationship after the assault (though it never was defined as a "relationship" in formal terms) my assailant was always in bed with us, and that was really hard on the new, caring guy. My mom and dad walked on eggshells around me when they found out about the assault.

Professors wanted to cut me slack, but I let them down time and time again with deadlines. It's hard, because all of my actions are protective and explainable by trauma, but they still impacted other people in real ways. I wasn't pleasant to be around. I feel guilt. I think there's some disconnect between how rape survivors are painted in the media and how we feel. I feel like I was pretty destructive to be around.

Code Switch: 我的家庭

A. ZHOU

When I was two years old, my dad immigrated to the United States on an education visa; I turned four on the plane when my mother and I followed. I am close to my parents. I see them as a gateway to layers of culture, heritage, and ancestry. Even today, trips back to China mean my parents introducing me to relatives I have never met, or explaining various phrases and colloquialisms in Mandarin.

My parents have always made it clear that they love me and hold high expectations for me. I've internalized these expectations and turned them into personal standards. I know what they lost in moving to the United States, and I know that the move was primarily for me and my younger sister. I've never doubted that my mom would sacrifice anything for me. I'm her daughter and her American dream.

It's been three years since my rape and I've never told my mother about it. I'm not sure I will. Every week I call her and every week she reminds me not to stay out too late or walk alone in the dark. She's never said the word *rape*, but we both know that's what she's worried about. I don't want to break her heart by telling her it's already happened. More important, I don't want her to live thinking that it was her fault, which she almost certainly would.

I am also scared, scared that she will reject me, or cope by telling one of her friends, and then the entire insular community I grew up with will know what I've experienced. I don't know if I have enough Chinese to accurately express everything that's hap-

> I'm her daughter and her American dream. It's been three years since my rape and I've never told her about it.

pened, and I don't know if she has enough English to understand. I do know, however, that I don't want to be responsible for the pain I would create by telling my parents.

I've been heavy with hints about survivorship, telling her that I lead the interpersonal violence prevention group on campus and that I sit on committees for sexual assault organizations. Once, I even linked her to a website of survivor stories, knowing full well my story had enough identifying factors and was sitting on page 4.

My mother does not see what she doesn't want to see.

She reads my Tumblr and calls me asking what the word *queer* means, but she does not recognize me as a queer woman. There's a list of things I would tell her if she asks. She never does.

My mother and, I think, many in my Chinese community still live in a 1980s or 1990s mainstream China. They know they are "other" here, but they are not worried because they have ties to a nation where the food is better and the language is musical. Rape is a horrific act only committed by strangers, and good girls are certainly never raped. LGBTQ is a thing that exists, and should be honored and respected, but it doesn't happen in China, nor in Chinese America.

I think I would be perfectly happy hiding my survivorhood from my parents if it weren't for my little sister. Growing up eight and a half years older than her, I started raising her from the time I was ten, making sure she was fed, clean, and not trying to roll down the stairs. I spent summers taking care of her while my parents worked, and I would skip school if she was sick. Many times she's accidentally called me Mom, and in some ways it's true.

I live as a role model for her. I explore Asian America and what it means to be Generation 1.5—someone who immigrated as a child—so that when she asks, I can make sure she doesn't stumble at the same points I did. Much of my activism around feminism and race is to make her world safer.

When I think about my sister going to college as a starry-eyed first-year, my heart seizes. She's becoming a teenager this year, and I have already had many talks with her about consent and valuing her body. I tell her she's beautiful because it's true, but also because white girls can be vicious and sometimes you don't feel pale enough or your nose feels too flat. I tell her she's worth the world and shouldn't have to change for anyone, and I am terrified that my words might not be sinking in.

> When I think about my sister going to college as a starry-eyed first-year— my heart seizes.

I don't know how to talk to my sister about sexual assault, but I have to. I want to be a resource for her if she ever needs it. But I don't know how to do that without telling her that I'm a survivor. If I wasn't willing to tell my mother that I'd been raped because I was scared of causing her pain, there's no way in hell I'll do it to my sister. So I'll insist she keeps me updated on her life, and remind her to call, and get worried when she doesn't check in. Essentially, I'll turn into my mother.

As a part of code-switching between being the perfect, ambitious daughter and whoever else I am, I have created families to fill in for my parents. My parents will never hear me read my survivor stories, but my friend-family will. I won't cry to my parents about the betrayal I felt when I was triggered by the director of a rape crisis center, but tripfam, my closest group of friends, was there.

The first time I caught myself creating family, searching for someone who'd understand when my parents didn't, I found it in my best friend, J. He was the first person I went to about my rape, the person who helped me define my experience. We talked about how isolated we both felt at our universities, and how we couldn't separate our own standards from the ones our parents had for us. We talked about how terrified we were of failing and what it would mean to start a family in the United States. We talked about video games and food, and he tore his hair out trying to teach me how to play League of Legends. It wouldn't be a complete day unless J and I Skyped or exchanged a hundred texts.

Sophomore year, J was hit with a bout of serious depression and it became harder to stay in touch. I'd found my niche community at my university, which meant less time to spend at his. He started cutting me out. I didn't fight as hard as I could have to stay around. Spring of sophomore year, J was diagnosed with cancer. He called me instantly. We talked about treatments. He started chemotherapy the day after. They removed three tumors through surgery. I left the country for the summer, thinking he would enter remission.

Despite all the rounds of chemo or radiation therapy, J died the following April. This was the first serious intersection of my found family and my biological one. I helped J's mom plan his memorial during spring break. My own mother watched and struggled to comfort me that entire week, but I don't think she ever understood how essential J was to me.

My two keys to successful code-switching are: I've never introduced any of my friends to my parents, and I never display extreme emotion around my mother or father. That week I broke both of those rules. During the day, I constantly talked about the logistics of J's memorial, emotionally detached but focusing all my energy on planning the perfect event. I stayed up through the night, struggling to write his eulogy.

Occasionally my mother would knock on the door and try to send me to bed, but it was easy to send her away. We would prepare breakfast the next morning, she would tactfully ignore my swollen eyes, and we'd get my sister ready for school.

That week, my mother spent more time with my father, discussing how best to approach me, than she did in my space. My parents will never bring up difficult topics unless prompted. Silence is viewed as the best comfort. Having been raised to never ask for help, I didn't have the words to demand the emotional support that I needed from them.

My dad drove me the two hours to J's memorial, but he stayed in the car the entire time. My assailant/perpetrator sat in the fifth row as I gave my eulogy. He sat directly in front of me during the reception. I firmly believe that the only reason I didn't break that day was because J was watching over me. He still is. I hope he's haunting the fuck out of my rapist.

I miss J. The weeks after his passing, I was all over the place. I hadn't realized how integral he was to my healing. Losing him sent me back to square one. No one in this world knows my full story anymore. I'm not sure anyone ever will. I won't ever have someone like J to talk me down from panic attacks or understand me at a level where I don't have to say what I'm feeling. It's been half a year and I still don't know how to recover.

> **No one in this world knows my full story anymore. I'm not sure anyone ever will.**

However, I'm lucky to be surrounded by friends who fill in, my chosen family. I draw power and strength from my community, from giving and lending support, and from weathering hard times together. I've found people I can explore survivorship with, to navigate racial identity, queer identity, and immigrant identity together. I feel strong. I am learning that my chosen family does not diminish the importance of my birth family. They augment it, and I no longer have to feel guilt about depending so heavily on them. I know I'm lucky in this regard. One day I'll speak up in my Chinese community, but I feel so much better knowing that I have a second family to fall back on.

Interpersonal violence in Asian communities is underreported. Right now, I am contributing to that underreporting. We need to have serious conversations about why we are so committed to denying realities. We need to learn how to address the silence, stigma, and shame that keep us from supporting each other. One day, I'll begin dismantling the immigrant guilt I've let fuel my ambition and drive, and get rid of the notion that I have failed in some way by being a survivor. Maybe I'll even be able to stop code-switching and come out to my parents.

One of the most valuable things I've learned over the last three years is that this is a process. I don't have to fix all of this now. To my other Asian survivors: I'm here and healing with you. We might not be able to talk about it yet, but that doesn't mean we're alone.

To JS, with all my love

Parents

A Chorus

She said, "I have to call your parents." I said,
"I can't call them," and started crying.

My friend was the first person I called. He told my
parents, because I didn't want to tell them. I don't know
how you tell your parents something like that.

I wanted my parents to trust me. They're so conservative.
I didn't want them to blame me.

That was the first time I'd ever seen my dad cry. It was
always a joke in my family that he'd never cry.
That's probably what hurt most, was seeing him cry.

They try to be supportive but they really don't know
what to do, which I can't blame them for.
They ask me what I need and I say I have no idea.

I drove to my parents' house, and was crying on my hands and knees
in front of my parents, "Please don't make me go back."

It got heated between my parents and [the president of the
university]. My dad was baffled why he wasn't getting this.

It's been three years since my rape, and
I've never told my mother about it.

To question my intentions in coming forward is to violate me once again. Do not ask me why I'm talking about what happened to me.

—Abbi Gatewood

Rape Culture

A Chorus

Campus advocacy is great but . . . a lot of it is victim-centric.
How about telling men not to rape?

If I had only known then that this country is not a perfect system. It does not have my best interests at heart. These representatives don't care about me. The police use guilt and intimidation to bully rape victims away from filing reports.

Rape is the only crime where the victim is guilty until proven raped.

"Oh, he's horny, and we don't wanna ruin his future; maybe he just made a mistake."

It is not just one university that tolerates rape; it is our society, our world. It is a gross injustice to all women and all men. We turn our backs, and tune out calls for change. We don't care to realize the problem until we experience it firsthand. We accept that one in four women will be sexually assaulted while in college, and we watch women's lives be shattered, as if it's okay.

Why is our society creating men who feel like the only way they can have value is by dominating others?

Somebody posted on a girl's door, "It's not rape if it's a freshman." That very much characterizes my experience: "You were young and naïve and you drank too much; how could this poor boy not take advantage of that?"

It's happening all the time, but we're so afraid: "No way this upper-middle-class white boy would do something like this!" But he did do something like this.

From "The Elegy of I"

SARI RACHEL FORSHNER

My sophomore year at USC, I was drugged and raped in the middle of the road.

I thought it was cut-and-dried. I thought I could decide how to handle it, that I could decide not to be a victim. I had always made my own decisions; this would not be different. I would get stitches in my head wound and buy the morning-after pill. I would be grateful that the drugs had taken my memory and I would move on. Something horrible had happened to me, but the people I loved would acknowledge that, and I would not change. The people in charge would acknowledge that; the doctors would be well trained; the law would stand on my side. Something horrible had happened. It was simple. I would remain myself.

But our society doesn't work that way, and if you spend enough time being told that you lost nothing, and that nothing happened to you, even though you know that something did happen, you often lose the agency to simply "decide." You change. I began to doubt myself, to drown in my own shame, even though I had done nothing shameful. My reality shattered and I became someone else. My life experienced a volta.

I had such a clarity once. A deep understanding of my own self. I loved that little girl, bright and strong and complicated as she was. Strange, but sure. So very sure.

She is in a coma, now, and I do not know if she will ever wake up.

I do not say that she is dead—not yet. There is enough of her, still, for me to be ashamed of the fact that she and I are not the same. Some mornings, she smiles in her sleep. Some weeks, I can't find her.

The cocktail of flaws and features that I once possessed was one I was proud to call my own. I was proud to be who I was. Now, even when I demonstrate qualities that I value, I am not proud to see them in me. They are still not enough. There is not a moment of my life that goes by unblemished by shame.

I have become someone who no one knows. I do not even know who it is that I have become; I can only imitate the girl I was. I can only fall short.

Even my body has become alien. My generous breasts became grotesque. Permanently larger as a side effect of postrape prophylaxis, those symbols of my sensuality are now little more than a reminder. My body swelled. Ten pounds. Twenty. Twenty-five. Fifty. Fat and frustrated, fearful of my own naked body and unable to trust, I lost all outlets for my lust.

I exude false exuberance.

My own strength is an insult to me. I have grown strong because I've had to. I demonstrate strength because it is what other people need to see. I do not feel strong.

Tennis Was My Life

ELLY FRYBERGER

When I was little I wanted to be a pro tennis player, but I started too late. Most people start when they're four or five or six years old, go to all the tennis academies, and spend hundreds of thousands of dollars on training. I started when I was ten, and I'm twenty now, so tennis has been part of me for half my life.

I graduated from high school at seventeen and took a year to go to the Weil Tennis Academy. Then I went to the University of Kansas my freshman year; I got recruited there for tennis.

I'd visited Kansas, and I liked it. My major was going to be architecture. Then right before school started the coach who recruited me got fired. And I was still struggling with an injury I got at Weil, so Kansas tennis didn't work out. I started looking at other schools and ended up visiting Arkansas, where I could still study architecture and play tennis.

The Arkansas coach was super nice, said, "We'll take it slow, get you healthy." Talked to my parents for two hours. The facilities were really nice. I expected to play tennis there and get my degree. That was that. That was the fall after my freshman year.

Then some stuff happened. I was supposed to travel to regionals over fall break, in October. Everybody does. I texted my counselor to make sure all my tutors were canceled. She said to check with the coach to make sure I was traveling. And he said, "No, you're not." I said, "Why? Because of my ranking?" Which was low, because I hadn't played any matches. And he said yeah. I found out later it wasn't because of my ranking; it was because of my grades. So the coach lied to me. And that was weird.

That weekend I didn't play, and the following Monday I was raped.

I had hooked up with him one time in August, and he hit me up again. He kept wanting to hang out late at night. I would say no. Finally, over fall break, he wanted to hang out, and I felt bad I had kept blowing him off, so I said, "We're not going to hook up, but we can be friends." He said, "Okay, I can do that." I was in my dorm room getting ready to settle in for the night as I had early practice the next day. He came over and I was in my pajamas with wet hair. He was super drunk. But I've hung out with drunk people before and it had been fine.

I was watching TV and he locked the door. I didn't know he had locked the door until afterward; that's when I realized it was premeditated. He pulled me to him and tried to kiss me and I said, "No, we talked about this, it's not gonna happen." He said, "Oh, but I really like you," and I said, "If you really like me then eventually it could happen but not tonight."

He got more forceful. He pulled my wrists, put me on the ground. I tried so hard to hold on to my pajama pants. He got those off. Then he said, "If you do this, and this, then I will leave." So I did, and he didn't leave. I kept saying no, over and over. I've never said no more in my life. For some people, I feel like you're lucky if you were drugged or drunk or don't remember it. But I was upright sober, and I feel like that was the worst. I can't get what happened out of my head. He was really drunk, so he had trouble getting hard. About thirty minutes later he finally quit.

> I feel like you're lucky if you were drugged or drunk or don't remember it. But I was upright sober, and I feel like that was the worst. I can't get what happened out of my head.

After he left I called a guy friend in D.C. (he also knew the perpetrator), and he said, "You need to report this." I said, "I don't want to go through all that stuff."

The morning after, I texted my trainer and said I can't practice. I told her what had happened and said I didn't know how to tell Coach. She said, "Don't tell Coach, come to the facility and I will take care of it."

She said, "Hey, just meet with the Title IX people." They suggested I go to the hospital and get a rape kit done, so I did. It took four hours. I hadn't taken a shower but I had changed clothes. I gave them my clothes. I had some bruises on my inner thigh.

My friend from D.C. ended up flying out to Arkansas. He told my parents because I didn't want to. I don't know how you tell your parents something like that.

They flew out the following weekend. Eight weeks later, my dad helped me move out of the dorm. I couldn't stand to be there.

The whole time I was in the hospital, I was on the phone talking to my friend in D.C., who said, "He's gonna do this again if you don't report him." (Later we found out the perpetrator should have been off campus a long time ago.) So I went to the campus police, and from then on all my time was spent dealing with Title IX and all the paperwork I had to do to make sure I got a hearing at school and to make sure the hearing happened before the end of the semester. The police gave my case to the district attorney and I had to keep up with responding to all the things the police and the district attorney were asking me for, but, in the end, the district attorney said there wasn't enough evidence to go to court.

Dealing with Title IX was hard; I had to hire an advocate. The Title IX people made me email my teachers, find accommodations for my work. I also had an advocate through the school and she was nice, but she also worked for the school, which was dragging its feet about literally everything. So I was concerned.

If I hadn't had Laura, the advocate I hired, and who helped me get the accommodations I was entitled to under Title IX, I don't think I would have gotten anything taken care of. She helped me prepare for the Title IX hearing. She was in there with me.

The hearing went really well. There was a panel of three judges, faculty and staff, two women and a man. They interviewed him first, for over two hours. They had to push my meeting back so I wouldn't run into him.

HBO recorded my whole part of the hearing. Someone had told HBO about my case and they asked me if I would wear a wire to my hearing, for the *Vice* episode "Campus Cover-up," which was about how colleges handle sexual assault cases, and I said yes, I would. I knew it was going to be fine: I usually don't get too nervous. Tennis matches, I don't get nervous.

I was in there for forty-five minutes. Laura helped me form a statement, which included where I'm from, why I came to Arkansas, what happened, and what I thought the ideal punishment would be. The worst the school could do was expel him.

The panel asked me some offensive questions, like "Why didn't you have more bruising?" and "Did you feel pressured by him?" *Really?*

Within twenty-four hours, they found him responsible and expelled him. When I first got the letter, I was crying because I was so happy. It was a huge relief.

He appealed the decision before winter break, apologizing for his actions and saying he just wanted to get his degree. He was supposed to graduate in December. And the hearing was in December.

The school had thirty days to respond to the appeal. They said they had to wait until winter break was over. On January 30, 2015, they responded to his appeal and I got a link to an email from student affairs. It said he had to do x amount of community service and x amount of work with a therapist, and then he could get his degree and then be expelled, on May 10, which was after graduation.

I was like, "What?" I honestly didn't understand it. It was all legal language. I sent it to Laura, my advocate, and she sent a book-length letter to the school that asked, basically, "What are you doing?" They responded twice, defending their decision. An Arkansas news reporter heard about what happened and did a story on it. My assailant was named in the reporter's news coverage.

> He had to do x hours of community service and x amount of work with a therapist, and then he could get his degree.

The day after the story ran, I got a third email saying, "Oh, disregard the previous email. He was expelled December twelfth." The journalist did some research and called the chancellor's office, and the chancellor said that the first email to me from student affairs had been a mistake.

The *Vice* segment aired in June. Obviously I can't tell the story without tearing up, but the HBO people were really nice. They made me feel comfortable.

One of the main reasons I hadn't wanted to go through with reporting the rape at school was because he was an athlete. He was in the Olympics, all-American for track, a star athlete, and an asset. Just like

Jameis Winston. You get special treatment on all levels when you're an athlete. Everybody knows they get let off the hook for stuff that if normal people did, they'd get in trouble. The University of Arkansas is known for track. They've won over forty championships. It doesn't look good for the school to have an athlete known for this kind of thing.

So that fall I received incompletes in two of my classes, and I had to drop my economics class because the professor wouldn't work with me on my attendance and grade. One professor was nice and let me take a test at home and send it to her. I'd had Bs and I started getting Fs.

I went back in the spring. I thought I was gonna be okay; I had gotten an emotional support dog and an apartment off campus. But I ended up dropping all my classes except for one, history. I got an A in that. But I needed to be around family more. So once the semester was over, I moved back to Denver. Got a place here. I'm not going back to Arkansas.

I lost twenty-five pounds in three months. I was able to sleep, but I wouldn't go to bed until almost morning. Then I would sleep during the day and still be exhausted. I still have nightmares. I'm still depressed.

I initially got a full-time job teaching tennis, but I took on way too much. I wasn't ready. Shit got really bad. I almost committed suicide. It was everything; all of it. I called one of my friends and he came over. If it wasn't for him . . .

After that I started seeing a therapist. My dog helps. I'm not ever alone-alone. Denver helps. Denver has such a good vibe to it. Being around my family and friends helps. I've started eating again.

How do I spend my time now? I try to sleep. I work behind the front desk at a public tennis club. It's nice that I've had time to relax. I haven't had to be busy all the time, getting a workout in or whatever. But tennis was my life. I feel like I'm missing out. What am I supposed to do?

People You May Know

KEVIN KANTOR

When my rapist showed up under the
People You May Know tab on Facebook,
it felt like the closest
to investigating a crime scene
I've ever been.
That is, if I don't count
the clockwork murder that I make
of my own memory every time
I drive down Colfax Avenue.

Still, I sit in my living room
& sift for clues:

Click
He is smiling
& I see myself caught
in his teeth. He is dancing
with his shirt off in a city
I've never been to //

Click
He is eating
sushi over a few beers with friends
& I am under his fingernails //

Click
I know that alley //

Click
I killed the memory
of that T-shirt //

Click
This is an old photograph.
It's a baby picture.
There is also an older man,
presumably his father.
They are both round & bright,
& still
smiling //

Click
He is shirtless again
& I catch my reflection
in the weight room mirror.
Hashtag #BeastModeSelfie //

I call him The Wolf
when I write about him,
so as to make him as storybook as possible.
The Wolf,
when I write about him,
which is to say, when my memory
escapes the murder,
or when the Internet suggests it.

Facebook informs me that we have *3 mutual friends //*

which is to say, he is
People You May Know
& I am
People You May Know.

& there are people that know
& people that don't know
& people that don't know
that I want to know,
but I am afraid to let know,

& probably people that know
him that know
of me that know //

    the word *No*.
        No.
        No.

No was a flock of sleeping sheep
sitting in my mouth.
& now I know
The Wolf's middle name
& what he listens to on Spotify
& the all too familiar company he keeps
& he can no longer be a wolf,
or the nameless grave
I dig for myself on bad days.
We have 3 mutual friends on Facebook
& now it feels as if they are holding the shovel.

64 people *liked* the shirtless gym pic,
4 people told me they'd rather I said nothing,
2 police officers told me that I must
give his act a name,
or it did not happen; that, obviously,
I could have fought back //

    which is to say, no one comes
    running for young boys who cry rape.

When I told my brother,
he also asked me why
I did not fight back.

Adam,
I am.
Right now
& always.

Every day I write a poem titled
Tomorrow.
It is a handwritten list
of the people I know
who love me
& I make sure to put
my own name at the top.

The Punishments

A Chorus

They gave him social probation and counseling: He was
not allowed at events where there was alcohol. He had to have
drug and alcohol counseling and relationship counseling.

They suspended him for a year.

My senior year, I was still running into him.

The school wouldn't tell me his sanction due to
privacy laws, but "Wink-wink, nudge-nudge, he's not here"
led me to believe he'd been expelled.
I wish he had plagiarized, because then they'd have
kicked him out for sure.

They said he had to do *x* amount of community service,
x amount of work with a therapist; then he could get his
degree and then be expelled.

We graduated the same year. He got one of the
highest honors the school gives.

He graduated early.

The last time I spoke with the university's police, they told me they'd reached a conclusion, even though they never did an investigation. My rapist went unpunished.

The subcommittee recommended probation. But the board decided to just admonish him, which is doing nothing.

DISCIPLINARY EDUCATION AT ITS FINEST...

Betrayals

ANDREA PINO

My first semester in college was a culture shock. After finding out I was from Miami, one of my classmates asked me if I "came to America on a boat." I was completely taken aback by this question, since I expected that everyone at the University of North Carolina at Chapel Hill must have worked as hard as I had to get into college and had at least learned something about Latino culture. I had never seen myself as an "outsider." It was then that I realized the Miami Latino community was a bubble. I grew up in a low-performing school district, most of my family doesn't speak English, and my grandparents were Cuban immigrants, blue-collar workers who came to America in search of a better life. I had never experienced the life I saw in movies, that lovely suburban life with large backyards, white fences, and a sense of safety. My house was first broken into when I was ten years old. I thought my parents were joking at first; it wasn't until I saw glass on the floor and our belongings flung everywhere that it hit me. I ran to my bedroom, worried that they had stolen my Game Boy, wanting this nightmare to end.

At the time, I expected the police to do something. After all, if there were police costumes next to superhero costumes, police must be superheroes, too. But at seven years old, I experienced betrayal for the first time. The police didn't help us—not then, and not the three more times our home was broken into. They didn't do anything even when we had photos, witnesses, and fingerprints. When I was seven, the police didn't protect me in Little Havana, and I knew that at twenty years old, the police wouldn't protect me after my assault. After I publicly came forward as a survivor, I learned that the biggest triggers aren't actually the nightmares of my assault but the nightmares of the betrayals that I've had to survive.

When the media tells your story, it feels like open season on your truth. It's exposed to commentary, and a part of you loses control over it and the vulnerabilities that you intended to share. When you tell your story to the media, you're at the mercy of their portrayal and the portrayal of others.

I've been betrayed by friends who struggled to understand what happened to me and to accept that the same person who put forth strength and composure could fall apart. I wish I could have said the right things to get them to understand that I was broken, and that my confidence was a lie to both of us.

I've been betrayed by my culture, by the toxic masculinity of machismo that historically keeps Latinas quiet after our bodies are violated, and that prevents us from healing as a community. *Nuestro dolor y nuestras historias siguen en profundo silencio.*

> **I've been betrayed by friends who struggled to understand what happened to me and to accept that the same person who put forth strength and composure could fall apart.**

I've been betrayed by the white society that polices my gender, my sexuality, and my race; that tells me I speak too loudly, and too fast, and that I don't "pronounce things right"; a society that tells me I should make sure to have makeup on at all times "to bring out those green eyes" so that I attract "the right husband," and that encouraged me to stay silent in the face of racism because wasn't I "lucky enough to pass."

I've been betrayed by the university that I love so dearly, whose seal I wear around my neck, and whose quads and bricks hold pieces of me—pieces of who I was before and of who I am today.

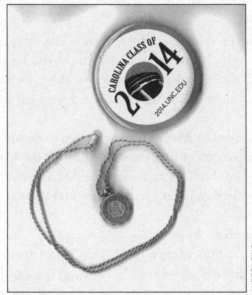

ANDREA PINO

Untouchable: Being a Trans Survivor

PRINCESS HARMONY

FIRST SEMESTER, FRESHMAN YEAR: RAPE AND ITS AFTERMATH

It was the end of my first semester at Temple University, and as the first student known to have been raped in the 2013–2014 school year, I was to be the school's warning to the student body. After my assault, the school newspaper published an antidrinking article that mentioned my case.

I was their warning because I was intoxicated when I was raped. I was at a bar on campus, hanging out, trying to get a feel for college life. He bought me a beer. And I'd had a few drinks before then. I don't know if something was done to the beer, but that particular night, I got drunk faster than I usually did. We headed back to my dorm, where we were able to enter unhindered because the security, which normally sends intoxicated students to the hospital, didn't notice that I was drunk. In my room, he told me to take off my shirt and I did it, without thinking. He asked for oral sex and I said no. I attempted to resist but it wasn't enough and he ended up raping me. I blacked out while it was happening. When I woke up, he was masturbating over me.

When I went to check him out of the residence hall, the security guards noticed that I was drunk. I didn't want them to know. I really didn't want to go to the hospital or deal with any of them at all. But, as protocol dictates, they called the police, more guards, and the EMTs. The responders were three EMTs and two cops, and they all looked at me and could tell I was drunk, but didn't care that I had my rapist's semen all over me. In hindsight, it seems really wrong to me that they were nonchalant with my rapist, could tell I was drunk, and could tell "something" had gone on between me and him but either didn't put it together or didn't care to. They were too busy chatting and laughing it up with my rapist to notice. They let him go, and he ran out of the building like it was on fire.

Deep down, I knew reporting my rape could backfire, but I didn't have a choice. As part of an administrator's inquiry about my drinking that night, I was asked what had gone on with my "guest." I was already facing sanctions for drinking; I was explicitly told that not reporting what happened would earn more disciplinary action. So I was forced into it.

The school's administration told me that they felt uncomfortable dealing with a transgender survivor, particularly a trans woman survivor. The administration's behavior didn't make sense. They helped both men and women who were survivors, but not me? But now I understand that they'd bought into the idea that trans women are unrapeable. In their eyes, the lack of consent didn't matter.

From the start, the investigation was mishandled. University police, working with Housing and Residential Life, destroyed evidence that they possessed—my rapist's name, and the time I checked him in and the time I checked him out—and dismissed evidence I presented. They ignored the semen-stained carpeting, and even though anyone could see that I was covered in my rapist's bodily fluids, I was never asked if I wanted a rape kit. So, because there was no biological evidence, the rape investigation was damned from the start. I was forced to report, retell, and relive my rape over and over again to different administrative officials, including several housing administrators, but there was no Student Conduct Code hearing, and no closure whatsoever. The last time I spoke to the university police, they told me they'd reached a conclusion. My rapist went unpunished.

I would tell other trans survivors at Temple to not report. There's no point. The administrators who worked in Temple's Wellness Resource Center would see me come to their offices and resource centers day after day and ignore me. They sent their student workers to ask me what happened and lead me on as if I would get help. Then I'd be told that they wouldn't or couldn't help.

Misogyny keeps women from speaking up because society is not inclined to believe them. I met misogyny and transphobia. To me, it seemed that the administrators exhibited a kind of doublethink. On the one hand, they believed that on August 24, 2013, I had been raped in my dorm; on the other hand, they didn't seem to believe a trans woman could be raped, as they never offered me any postassault medical services. Even though it was rape, as a trans woman the message I got from the school was that I deserved it and that this particular rape didn't matter, because he'd targeted a transgender woman.

> Even though it was a rape, as a trans woman the message I got from the school was that I deserved it and that this particular rape didn't matter, because he'd targeted a transgender woman.

The only support I had was the woman who would eventually be as close to me as a sister. Had it not been for her presence in my life, I would have killed myself. And that's not hyperbole. I owe her a debt that is unpayable.

Sometimes the flashbacks are so horrible that I can't leave my bed. I feel his hands on me, I smell him on me. And this experience was made even harder than it needed to be because healing and recovery were impeded by a school that refused to believe that I was the victim of violent sexual assault. I implore people to listen to survivors. To know that no matter what gender you are, what sex you were assigned at birth, what demographic you may fit into now, you can be raped. All people deserve a life without rape and, if they are raped, they deserve support.

Believe survivors. Support them. Love them.

FIRST SEMESTER, JUNIOR YEAR: HEALING AND SURVIVAL

If you're a survivor, there are spaces for you—support groups, therapists, even online groups where people can share their feelings. But when you're a transgender woman, you're not welcomed by these services that anybody else—even cis men—can access. So how do you heal?

The short answer is that you really can't. Without access to even the most basic service, such as a trans-competent sexual assault nurse examiner, you won't get even an investigation into your rape.

The long answer is that, even though it's hard, you can heal on your own. I originally thought of fighting through the pain, continuing to go to school, and never mentioning the things that happened to me. But then I made the jump and chose to become an activist because, through helping others and working to change policy for the better, I could heal my own pain.

I spoke to whoever would listen; I filed my complaints and made them as detailed as possible. In the beginning it was painful, but over time, after telling my story over and over, I became numb. I no longer cried, no longer hurt. I just stopped feeling it. While numbness may not be the ideal form of healing, it was the best I could hope for.

My best piece of advice to trans survivors, honestly, is to not risk your mental health for activism. I did what I had to do to survive, but although I found healing in it, there has to be a better way.

Despite all the advances I made and the changes in policy I helped make happen, and even though I was able to numb my pain, participating in the movement made me bitter. Trans-misogyny and other forms of bigotry and bias exist in the movement, as they do anywhere else. I try to engage, to fix them, and people acknowledge what I say and sometimes fervently agree, but then they'll go back to doing what they always do. It's heartbreaking.

My healing happened in three phases: coming out with my story; working with trans survivors individually; and then disassociating from a movement that hurt me just as much as the rape had. Those phases were messy, and probably lack the finesse of a proper healing via therapy, but I gained experience and knowledge. The campus antirape movement hurt me. I was shouting into the wind at people who were supposed to have been supportive and who claimed to want to help my activism, but I don't regret that pain because it made me realize that the antirape movement, much like everything else, can be and is deeply flawed. And I don't regret my time with that movement.

The Dangerous Myth of
the "Ideal" Survivor

Institutions of higher education often retraumatize students who survive gender-based violence by invalidating our stories and denying our experiences.

While survivors on campuses all over the country are rising to claim justice, in this sea of people clamoring for change there's a media focus on a particular, "ideal" type of survivor: a cis, white (or white-passing), heterosexual woman. The patriarchy also delivers the message that "innocent" people who get raped are worthy of dignity, but "other" people are deserving of rape or cannot be raped. Many people believe these lies; many more continue to believe that the only legitimate form of rape is that perpetrated by a stranger.

However, survivors are not all "ideal." Typically, people who were date-raped, trans women, and women of color fall into the category of "other." And many of us don't get our stories heard, because we don't get the space or attention to tell those stories. Not every survivor in the campus antiviolence movement was raped. Some were stalked, or were physically, verbally, or emotionally abused in relationships, or were sexually harassed at school, at work, or on the street, or had other horrifying experiences. Our movement is diverse because the people in it are diverse and their experiences of abuse are diverse.

While the movement has been led by enterprising and intelligent people across the spectrum of race, sexuality, and gender, classic activism, in the form of rallies and teach-ins, isn't enough to make universities change. The media is the most useful weapon, with its power to share our stories with the world and threaten the university's brand. Unfortunately, the media also helps shape the problematic image of the "ideal" survivor.

Sometimes when reporters ask for survivor stories, they reject stories from us in the QTPOC (queer and trans person of color) community upon hearing who and what we are. And sometimes, queer and financially suffering survivors within the movement have felt betrayed by other survivors, when the other survivors focused their organizations to cater to those with privilege.

If the movement to fight gender-based violence on college campuses is to succeed, it requires the voices of all survivors. So when members of the media or members of the movement ignore survivors of color and queer survivors, call them out on it. Someone who perpetuates myths and erasure isn't an ally.

Many of us joined the campus antiviolence movement because we experienced the pain of institutional betrayal. When our university ignores or punishes us after we report gender-based violence or harassment, our movement and community should not betray us as well.

—Princess Harmony

THINGS THAT MAKE ME FEEL (OVERLY) ANXIOUS

COFFEE

ALCOHOL

BEING LATE

BEING EARLY

HEALTH ISSUES

ELEVATORS

FOOD

EMAILS

Sexual assault in the News

MONEY & BILLS

THE THOUGHT OF PEOPLE NOT LIKING ME

MY STRUGGLE WITH ANXIETY

Ariane Litalien

Anger

A Chorus

For months, I focused on a quote that I put on my mirror:
"Holding on to anger is like swallowing poison and expecting
the other person to die."

I resent the anger.

I was very angry for a long time after my assault.

I threw my anger from my assault at anyone I felt threatened by.

It took one of my very close friends my senior year saying to me,
"You're kind of a bitch, and mean to people for no reason."

I wanted to feel less angry every day. My anger was exhausting.

I still get angry sometimes, but now I recognize that anger and
channel it: "What's a better use of this energy?"

I ran into him in the lobby. I couldn't believe I didn't
kill him. I was consumed by rage and a desire to
enact violence on him, very depressed, suicidal.

Why didn't I murder him? Because I wasn't the strong,
badass woman I think I am.

Unaccepted Students Day

A. LEA ROTH AND NASTASSJA SCHMIEDT

Lea: We met at an off-campus national gay and lesbian "Creating Change" conference. We were randomly assigned roommates at the conference and hit it off immediately.

Nastassja: I was a freshman and Lea was a junior. I'd started Dartmouth in 2011, and was thinking about African and African American studies, and women's and gender studies.

Lea: I started in 2009, studying sociology and public health, focusing on global health and social inequalities. I was premed and was an activist around global AIDS policies.

Nastassja: I was born in Italy—my father is Italian—and my mom is African American. I had gone to an all-girls Catholic prep school since fourth grade in Miami. It was a very small, pretty feminist school. I was one of the few black students on campus.

My parents are free spirits—they've always supported racial justice and LGBT issues. My mom was a model and actor, and I started modeling when I was six months old, and acting soon after. Because I was a young, black female model, some people assumed I was just a pretty face, but education and the pursuit of knowledge were so important to me.

Lea: I had a difficult time, growing up in Minnesota, because my parents were very unsupportive of me being gay. My high school was maybe at the point where they could have accepted it, but it was 2008 and everyone was saying "That's so gay!" and "Fag" all the time. So in my senior year I moved out of my parents' house and enrolled in a state program about an hour away that allowed me to attend classes at a state university for my senior year of high school. I went to Winona State University, in Minnesota, and it was beautiful, freeing. The atmosphere was very supportive. I was able to be myself.

Dartmouth was a very different culture. Small, elite, tight-knit; really a culture shock. It has intense traditions; being a member of that community means participating in those traditions, including using the lingo and jargon. It's very competitive.

Nastassja: At Dartmouth, the Clery numbers, which are a school's accounting of violence and hate crimes on campus, were all zero when I applied to the school—I'm a black city kid from a feminist school, so I asked. Plus, my mom was very active in making sure I would be safe.

Lea: One month before I went to Dartmouth, I was assaulted by a woman, a fellow student at Winona. She was an upperclassman and we were in a relationship over the summer. She was struggling with depression and an eating disorder, and she sort of snapped. She had restrained me—tied me up. I told her she was raping me, and to stop; she said, "This isn't rape"; then she became more forceful and she said, "This is rape." I started fighting back more and she finally stopped.

As a queer person, I didn't know who to tell. It felt like something I needed to deal with on my own. I started having PTSD symptoms. Meanwhile, I was going to Dartmouth as a freshman rejected by my family. The drive out there started with my mom asking me to take off my rainbow-beaded bracelet; it turned into a nightmare three-day road trip.

> As a queer person, I didn't know who to tell. It felt like something I needed to deal with on my own.

But I was excited to be around so many passionate and brilliant people, and excited about the opportunities and resources there. So at first that excitement overshadowed the traumatic things I had experienced. I created a new self. My second year, I took over the mentoring program for LGBT students, because I kept hearing from so many LGBT students how isolated they felt, or that they had experienced hate crimes, or had been raped, and how isolating and depressing being on campus was for them. I took it upon myself to try to create that safe space that I was looking for.

My junior fall, there was a high-profile hate crime on the gender-neutral floor in a housing unit: someone wrote graffiti that said, "Kill all the fags," and the floor was vandalized.

Nastassja: That was my freshman fall. It created terror, honestly. Hate-speech graffiti was relatively common on campus. The N-word on Obama posters. People would tear down things about black students or LGBT students.

Lea: A new dean had arrived, and she held this meeting with a room full of LGBT people and we went around the circle and shared different "bias incidents"—

Nastassja: —which is a softer way of saying "hate crime."

Lea: The dean was taking notes on her iPad. We were all very open about what the campus climate was like, and that we had an active sense of fear. But not only did they do nothing, we found out later that none of those incidents had ever been reported. The Clery reports continued to be zero.

Natassja: Lea was exactly the type of person I was looking for. I was hanging out with one of their friends in the LGBT resource room, and Lea came in and my friend was like, "Yeah, they're practically married, don't even think about it." ("They" is Lea's and my preferred singular third-person pronoun.) I said, "Are you sure?"

Lea: Months later, when my relationship had ended and we were at the conference together, we went to dinner together. We were flirting a lot. Nastassja had a lot of energy.

Nastassja: We were making eyes at each other. The next day we went to the same workshop, and then went to Subway for lunch. We went back to the room to talk over eating, and I had hoped to kiss, but we got caught up in conversation. Then we were packing up the food and started walking out and they just grabbed my hand and turned me around and kissed me, and it was like, "*Yeah!!!*"

Lea: I had just ended a relationship, so I was not looking for one, but I really liked Nastassja.

Nastassja: I had never been in a relationship, and I wanted to prove that love did exist. We spent time talking and holding hands. I had never held hands with a woman before, or been kissed in public before, and they

> We spent time talking and holding hands. I had never held hands with a woman before, or been kissed in public before, and they just kissed me while we were standing on the corner there.

just kissed me while we were standing on the corner there. And it really meant something to me, that they weren't ashamed to be out with me. [Nastassja cries as they say this.]

Lea: We ended up together.

Nastassja: It was meant to be. And being out and open with Lea was very different from what I had known in high school. Then, I didn't feel comfortable coming out or presenting as genderqueer. There was this fear in my school, or in general I guess, that men and queer women of color were more aggressive sexually, so I was worried that the girls would be afraid of me if I came out as lesbian. I would wear some masculine things, a bow tie with my uniform, or pants instead of a skirt, but I'd always pair it with something pink or feminize it in some way.

In senior year of high school, I went to this Halloween costume party and I kissed a girl. I hadn't really accepted myself, and so even though I liked it, I was trying to numb myself, I guess, so I started drinking a lot. I thought some of my classmates might have seen it happen and I felt like I had to counter it somehow by kissing a guy. The bartender seemed to like me and gave me free drinks. We kissed, but then he took me into the bathroom. It was okay until he wanted me to give him a blowjob. I said I really didn't want to but he tried to force me and I shoved him away and walked out. I was really drunk and pretty upset about everything that had happened at this point, and I guess this other guy thought he could take advantage of that, because he dragged me outside to the alleyway and raped me. I was a virgin. He threw my Spandex shorts away, and dragged me back inside as my dad drove up. It was really, really terrible. Before I went out to my dad, someone gave me a pair of worn-out pants to wear. My dad was really concerned about how much I had been drinking, but at the time I didn't tell him I was raped, I sort of blamed myself, but everyone was drinking and I thought I would be safe around my friends. I told a friend of mine what happened and she really shamed me, she told me I didn't have any respect for my body. I had to go get Plan B with my mom. The rapist told everyone that he didn't use protection and that I wanted it outside like a black animal, and people at school were all talking about it. It was the worst thing that could have happened for my first time.

At Dartmouth, the first Monday of classes, there's a party at this fraternity, and some of my friends and I decided to go, and someone there kept handing me drinks. I was trying to pace myself, but I didn't know that the drink was a hundred percent alcohol, with powdered Kool-Aid added. It was in a trash can. It was red. It tasted like fruit punch.

Long story short, things took a bad turn, and something I didn't want to have happen happened that night. It happened in my room. It was the first time I had ever experienced sex with a woman, and it was really violating. Later she told me she knew I would not have been into it if I had not been drinking, that she had planned it to get close to me. Afterward, I really started having issues connecting with my body. And then I met Lea.

Lea: By spring 2013, we'd been dating about a year. Both of us were processing our sexual traumas. Both of us were really active in LGBT organizing. And we were balancing how our experiences affected our relationship.

Nastassja: I had experienced a lot of violence. I really opened up about everything. Lea was really closed off and didn't know how to trust. So here was this beautiful soul who had been through so much, and I wanted to create this intimacy and trust between us. But it was hard.

Lea: We both had a lot of trauma, and people don't know how to respond to that. So we found ourselves pretty isolated sometimes. We had to depend on each other for support and it brought us close together. Our lives are intertwined now. But at the time, both of us felt powerless and limited in the ways we could be there for each other.

In the spring of 2013, we decided to engage in a form of protest with this poetry event, #realtalkdartmouth, that Nastassja organized with a collection of other students for the week when admitted students come to campus.

Nastassja: We wanted to show them, if you come to this campus as queer or a person of color, you need to be aware of what the climate is like.

Lea: You're more likely to experience violence your freshman fall if you're not aware.

Nastassja: We made posters and did chalking to advertise the event the night before students arrived. But by eight a.m., the safety and security officials had erased all of our chalk. Someone had called it in as hate speech because it was mentioning rape and homophobia. It made people uncomfortable but was definitely not against the rules.

> You're more likely to experience violence your freshman fall if you're not aware.

We had put up posters of facts about violence at Dartmouth around campus, and we saw students and administrators taking them down. There were stacks of them in the garbage. We posted a video to the admitted students' Facebook group and that video was taken down.

So our poetry event started with only three admitted students, and mostly current students. I read bits from op-eds from the school paper written by students of color and queer students, and then students with masks that said "Anonymous" over their faces read the actual horrible responses that people had made in the comments section.

But we still hadn't reached the newly admitted students. So we decided to do a protest at this big show that's like the Super Bowl halftime show of the admitted students' weekend. Freshmen pretend to be admitted students and mingle with them, and then reveal their true identities in this show, get onstage, and dance and sing about how much they love the admitted students and the school.

We had wanted to add the poetry program as a skit, but the organizers told us no. And they had been tipped off that we were planning a protest, so they had security in the form of frat guys and administrators.

The program took place in the cafeteria, and they would not let us in. We were so fed up; we were going to get inside the cafeteria to do our poem. We resolved to not touch anyone. Some people got scared, but a few people at the core said, "We'll do this, and we know what the rules are!" Everyone had experienced activism, but it was still terrifying.

So we walked up to the doors and said, "This is a public place, and the fire code limit for the room has not been reached. We have something to say; let us in."

Lea: A frat guy tried to bar us by slamming the door on our bodies. An administrator said, "You can't do that to a student." Another administrator tackled a very small transgender student who had been smashed in the door. It was shocking. We just kept repeating, "Dartmouth has a problem!"

Nastassja: There were about fifteen of us. We came in chanting, and the students in the show, who were wearing rainbow tutus and other outrageous clothing, started standing in front of us, trying to block us.

Lea: Hundreds of high-schoolers were watching.

Nastassja: The freshman students started crying, "You're ruining my life! How dare you!" They decided to get back onstage and tried to sing over us.

We got in front of them, chanting, and we were louder. We were some pretty hard-core activists, and we were not going to be silenced.

The high school kids' eyes were big with shock. Freshmen started chanting, "We love Dartmouth!," and soon the admitted students started saying, "We love Dartmouth!," like robots. This whole time I'm holding a poster in front of my face that says, "I was called a fag on my freshman floor."

Lea: Then we left. No one tried to obstruct us. And it was raining. So dramatic.

A few people went back to their rooms. Others stayed and talked to groups of admitted students about why they did it. Most of us went to a house off campus and sat in the basement in a state of shock. But someone had filmed the protest on their phone, so we decided we'd have the impact we were looking for if we posted it online.

Nine thousand people saw it that night. It went viral. A conservative paper called us "ungrateful minorities."

Nastassja: Since we weren't an organized student group, no one knew who to blame. So hatred grew toward any people who had those identities—interracial couples, lesbians, queers, Latin@s, Native American students. We didn't anticipate how disgusting and extreme the reaction would become. "Freedom from slavery is a privilege and it can be taken away." "There's gonna be a lynching of the realtalkers at noon tomorrow." There were also tons of rape threats.

It was shocking to see such explicit hatred coming from the mouths of thousands of our peers. Most of the threats and hate speech were posted on an anonymous forum for Dartmouth students (you need a school email to access). The comments on the school newspaper site were also really bad.

Lea: We knew the rules, and we hadn't violated them.

Nastassja: There was a lynch mob mentality. The school paper said we had attacked people and been violent. They published a poll: "What do you think should be the punishment of the real talkers?" The chair of the board of trustees sent a letter to the campus and alumni about a "decline in civility."

> **The atmosphere got so bad that neither of us could leave our room to get food.**

The atmosphere got so bad that neither of us could leave our room to get food. I had this idea we should print out posters of threats and the hate speech and hold it while walking around campus.

Thirty of us went to a meeting of administrators, carrying the posters. They were thinking of canceling classes. We said, "Before you begin, we want you to read these posters out loud, and say the words out loud, because this is what it feels like for us to walk around here every day."

The administrators read the words out loud, and they all started crying. The dean of the school was crying. We said, "We're not going to leave this meeting until you cancel classes tomorrow," so we could all process what had happened. They finally agreed. And in the morning they did an event for all the tenured professors to explain what had happened.

The day after the protest, we met with our deans and asked them to send emails to our professors explaining that we were in the protest and were being harassed and might be behind on assignments or miss class. The deans said they would, but they didn't. Luckily, I personally contacted my professors anyway, and they all said I didn't have to come to classes that week.

The next week, I had to attend a class that would discuss the topic of online activism. It was a large lecture class and lots of students were always posting on the anonymous campus forum where we were being threatened. Especially with the topic of the class, I knew our group would be called out, and I said to the professor, "I don't feel comfortable coming to class. I'm scared." He was an adjunct, so he hadn't been at that faculty meeting and didn't know about the degree of the harassment. He said, "Not only do you have to come to class, but you need to take your midterm later today." I said, "I have been having panic attacks, and there are people threatening my life and threatening to rape me."

He said, "Did you talk to the administration in advance about your protest?" I said no, we didn't have to, that was the point of a protest.

He said, "If you weren't ready for the backlash, you shouldn't have participated in the protest."

I said, "I'm sorry, I didn't expect people to threaten to rape me or kill me."

I felt he was assuming I was just trying to dodge work in his class. I had a 98 percent average.

So I went to class. Everyone was staring. As I sat in the back of the room, I saw the faces turn and I started hallucinating that they were the faces of rapists. I had to be hospitalized for a week for PTSD.

Lea: I couldn't go to classes, or do even the simplest assignments, even though I was an honor student. I couldn't focus. I was so overwhelmed by the situation; it totally derailed me, even though I was only weeks from graduating. I was falling apart.

I was still living just off campus, with threats coming in all the time and Nastassja in the hospital. People were threatening to come into our house and attack and rape us. Meanwhile, we had reported all the hate speech and hate crimes but nothing had been logged or investigated. None of the administrators seemed to be willing to address the situation, they all wanted it to blow over but it kept getting worse. Dartmouth didn't have a Title IX office. So we started organizing alumni and others on

> We had thirty-seven testimonials of rape, hate crimes, and religious discrimination. We hoped our complaint would be a positive catalyst for change.

campus to do a Clery complaint. We had thirty-seven testimonials of rape, hate crimes, and religious discrimination. We hoped our complaint would be a positive catalyst for change. We knew if we filed the complaint we'd be protected from retaliation. So we were in a rush to get it filed. We were very afraid for our lives.

Nastassja: The school did file disciplinary charges against us and a handful of other #realtalk protesters the week after we filed the complaint for "not following directions."

Nicola Schmiedt

Lea: Ultimately the two of us had to leave campus that spring, due to the backlash. We both ended up withdrawing from school, but we couldn't just stop the work we were doing. We needed to focus on healing, but we also traveled around the United States presenting workshops on intersectional coalitional organizing and campus violence at conferences and universities, and participating in the national movement against sexual assault.

Note: On May 30, 2013, Dartmouth students and alumni filed a complaint with the U.S. Department of Education against the college for violating the Clery Act. In July 2013, the U.S. Department of Education opened its own investigation into Dartmouth for possible violations of Title IX.

In December 2013, Nastassja and Lea founded Spring Up, a partnership offering workshops to student organizations and supported by sales of handmade bow ties. Lea graduated from Dartmouth College in June 2014. Nastassja has not yet been able to return to school. Spring Up (timetospringup.org) has since evolved into a multimedia activist collective creating a space for learning and healing, and a style representation project about the healing power of self-love called *Imagine a World: Everyday Heroes*. The two self-published a coauthored collection of educational short stories about the sexual culture, titled *Millennial Sex Education*. As of November 2015, they are engaged to be married.

PART IV

HEALING AND EVERYDAY ACTIVISM

Everyday activism: the radical notion that everyone can play a part in ending violence and oppression by resisting rape culture, supporting survivors, and challenging our institutions.

Believing survivors is a type of radical everyday activism, since we live in a society that suggests that you do completely the opposite.

So, to every survivor reading this book: We Believe You.

There are hazards to openness, but they seem minor compared with the possibility that some readers may find comfort, perhaps even inspiration, from the close examination of how an ordinary person, with strengths and weaknesses like anyone else, has managed an extraordinary journey.

—Sonia Sotomayor, *My Beloved World*

Vulnerability is terrifying. Being vulnerable about your life's hardest moments? That's a nightmare. But we have come to realize that sharing our experiences, even just pieces of our struggles and triumphs, can help us feel that we are not alone. While it was heartbreaking to recognize that there are so many of us, there is immense strength—and a great diversity of activism—in our numbers.

Survivors of violence heal in different ways and there is no one right way to react after experiencing trauma. We cycle through many emotions, and sometimes those emotions are conflicting.

There are days when we feel as if our assaults happened decades ago, but there are other days when our hearts are beating so quickly that we clench our chests as hard as we did on those nights from years past.

Some students might lose interest in school or lack the ability to concentrate, while others might regain control by hyperfocusing on grades.

Less than a week after her assault, Andrea ran a half-marathon; in the days after the marathon, she couldn't get out of bed to go to class. She had graduated as valedictorian from her high school, yet she dropped numerous classes and struggled to focus on classwork in college after developing PTSD.

Annie, meanwhile, obsessed over her schoolwork, using academics as one way of regaining control, and graduated Phi Beta Kappa.

Some survivors use having immediate consensual sex as a way to gain control, while others do not want to be touched at all. Others might develop or revisit an eating disorder, while still others might immediately want to process their assault in therapy. Some may want to confide in a close friend and not in their family, and others may tell no one at all. Substance abuse, cutting, and other behaviors that do harm to oneself are also common among survivors.

Trauma isn't something you "get over," but you can get through it.

If someone comes to you and tells you they have been assaulted, it is of utmost importance that you say that you believe them, and that whatever happened, it's never their fault. You, as a friend, have neither an obligation nor the right to ask *what* happened. Some survivors find power in sharing details, in naming their experience, while others might not be ready yet, or may never choose to name what happened. It's critical that you offer a survivor options and let that person remain in control. They might make a different decision than you would make, but it is their choice all the same.

> Trauma isn't something you "get over," but you can get through it.

There is no timeline by which people heal from violence, even though the media have taught us otherwise.

There is no blueprint to "moving on" from trauma, and there definitely isn't a wrong way to heal.

Even if the narratives in this book are the only survivor stories you've heard, we guarantee that we aren't the only survivors you have met.

When we chose to share our stories, we didn't anticipate that we would become activists. Annie was fresh out of undergrad, working with students at the University of Oregon, while Andrea was still studying at UNC.

However, what we didn't understand at first is that thanks to the everyday conversations we were having, we were already activists. And since this realization, our lives have been changed.

Challenging our culture is not what we were taught to do, but every person has a role to play in changing our culture of violence. This is what we call everyday activism.

Our Stories, continued

ELISE SIEMERING

My sorority, Alpha Chi Omega—along with my friend Marie—saved me. I joined in my junior year—went through the interview process, got accepted, and it was amazing. Every sorority on our campus chooses a different philanthropy to support. Our philanthropy was domestic violence. I felt like the work was my way of giving back and helping people who had been through situations similar to mine.

In the summer of my junior year, the rape kit results came back, and there was not enough evidence. There were photos of the bruises, along with other medical evidence, but there was not enough evidence overall so the rape kit was deemed inconclusive. As a result, the DA would not be pursuing rape changes. There was not much the police could do.

I had to take an extra year to finish school. I had always been a good student and it was hard to accept that I would have to take a fifth year of college—hard financially, and also at school. That's when I decided that I wanted to do something, to have a voice. Alpha Chi Omega gave me that voice. I was on the philanthropy committee, and I got my rhythm back.

My senior year, I was still running into the assailant. We both worked at the athletic department. I had to tell my boss about the situation and he went to Student Life and the head of the athletic department and said, "I don't want him there." And basically Student Life said they couldn't let him go.

At one alumni event I had to work in the same room with him. I was so uncomfortable. Even after that, Student Life just said, "Oh, well, stay away from him."

So my senior year, I focused on the sorority.

In my women and gender studies classes, we had to do an activism project. I was put in a group with the other guy who had been at the library with me the night the assault happened. I said, "The Clothesline Project would be really cool, and Alpha Chi could sponsor it." He agreed, and we got it approved. One day after class, this other guy said, "Elise, can I talk to you? I want to apologize." He said, "I should have been more supportive of you. I shouldn't have taken his side. I should have talked to the police, but my dad didn't want me to. The Clothesline Project is what I can do to make it up to you."

All these guys—even the guy who took me to see the RA and then wouldn't speak to the police—it seemed to me they all felt "Brotherhood

is more important." The assailant had made them think it was my fault.

I had girls come up to me and say he had physically harmed them. I would say, "You should report it," but they all said, "What's the point?"

A Clothesline Project is for women and men who were affected by violence or knew someone who was. They decorate a shirt to express themselves, and the shirts are hung on a clothesline in a public place so that everyone can see them. It helps bring awareness to the issue of violence against women and men.

High Point wasn't supportive of the project. The adult we went to for permission gave us the back of the student section of the Student Life building. Inside, not outside. The adult said it was because they didn't want us to put stakes in the lawn and make holes.

We actually had a lot of people show up for the exhibit. It made me feel like I'm not alone, and I gave someone else a way to speak out. I still have all the shirts. I'm thinking of making them into a quilt.

I then completed my fifth year. We actually ended up graduating the same year, me and the guy. Senior year, he got one of the highest honors that High Point gives. I was in the auditorium when he got it. How the hell can you honor somebody like that?

Courtesy of Elise Siemering

The professor who had helped us put together the Clothesline Project had brought me into her office and said a guy in that same frat had sexually assaulted a girl, and the school had swept that case under the rug, too. Apparently we all graduated together.

I've had thoughts of "Should I have transferred?"—but then again, I would never have found Alpha Chi, never done the project.

After two years, I talked to one of the detectives. She said she was there the day I graduated, that she had to hold herself back from running up to me and hugging me. She told me, "I was so proud of you for sticking to your guns and graduating." Which made a huge impact on me.

And then I got involved with Annie and Andrea. I read an article about their work and I thought, "This is really cool. Once again, I'm not alone." I had Alpha Chi, but those girls didn't really get what it was like. I remember reading what Annie and Andrea had written and thinking, "Wow, it's not just High Point University." I emailed Andrea and talked to her and Annie and honestly, it was one of the best conversations I had had with somebody. Finally, someone who got me. I had therapy, and support from my wonderful family, but it was wonderful to have someone understand what I was feeling. I've been involved with Annie and Andrea on different projects for about two years, and I got to meet them in Boston a couple of months ago. They are two amazing women who I am eternally grateful to because they helped me so much.

I am starting out in communications and sports marketing, but I would love to do what Annie and Andrea are doing: help men and women get the help they need. I have thought about going back to school and getting a degree in counseling. No matter what, I will do social justice work. I have a sister who's in college now. And I want to give that guy or girl who reads this that same feeling, of "Oh,

> **And I want to give that guy or girl who reads this that same feeling, of "Oh, my gosh, there's some girl who knows what I'm feeling."**

my gosh, there's some girl who knows what I'm feeling." I want to be that person in someone's life. I want to do something to give back.

LAUREN

After my assault, I wanted to make a difference. For the first year and a half, I would go to therapy, then call my mom and tell her how it was. I would be open with friends as well, since talking helps me get through just about anything. When I was a sophomore, I became very involved in an event called "Consent Day." We would teach students about consent—what it is and how to obtain it. Of course, the event had free condoms, so that was the incentive for pretty much everyone (especially the guys) to show up.

Regarding consent, it is very important to know yourself before starting a conversation with anyone else about what you want. If you like to be kissed, but maybe not touched certain places, that is more than okay! It is *always okay* to stop. You are 100 percent allowed to stop or take a break at any point in any physical interaction with a partner. When I said that to the students I was working with, they really opened their eyes, like, "Wow, yeah, you're right!" It may sound simple, but it's true. You only have to do what you want to do—nothing more.

As I was approaching my junior year, I stopped therapy and began to self-soothe when I faced flashbacks caused by post-traumatic stress disorder. I learned how to handle every flashback, even the moments of remembering. When I realized that I could control how the flashback makes me feel and how I choose to feel afterward, it completely changed my outlook.

In the summer, I had gotten into a new relationship with a guy I had known for five years. I was very open with him about what I had gone through, but he asked me not to tell him the specifics. He helped me through my flashbacks; he knew how to squeeze my hand and say my name to bring me back. At first, when I came out of the flashbacks, I would bawl my eyes out. When I saw how much that affected him negatively, that was my "aha" moment, that I could change how I feel and how he feels. Rather than be sad that the flashback happened, I could be happy that I got out of it and that I'm not actually there.

My senior year, I really thrived as a survivor. I was involved in a "Blue Lights" walk on campus to see the glowing telephones that call Public Safety at any time, day or night, and to identify places on campus where new phones should go. During this event we showed a public service announcement from "It's On Us," the White House's initiative to raise awareness about sexual assault on campus. After seeing it, I told my friend Caroline, and one of the therapists I was working with for the event, that we should make a Curry "It's On Us" video. I talked to the associate dean of Curry and she loved the idea. So Caroline and I produced this video with the help of only students, no faculty involved. After seeing our video, the dean of the college decided that the college should make its own video, so I also helped make that happen.

My moment of healing started when I could understand the point of view of my assailant. I know this sounds crazy, but that's what it was. Since I didn't know my assailant—only his name—I thought this was a supermalicious act (which sexual assault is). I thought I was targeted and that he was a monster. When I talked to my mom more in depth, she said the arresting officer told her that when A was arrested, he honestly had no idea he had done anything wrong, let alone sexually assault a female. He was a stupid kid starting college with no idea of the concept of consent. He had no clue that continuing to pursue me the way he did was wrong.

> He was a stupid kid starting college with no idea of the concept of consent.

When I processed that information, it helped me heal a lot faster. I am not yet completely done, but I am so much closer to that point than I was two or three years ago.

I graduated from Curry in May 2015 with a liberal arts degree and an education minor (I was originally a special education major). I work at a school in Providence, Rhode Island, for children and adults up to twenty-one with severe and profound disabilities. I was in therapy for two years and then thought I didn't need to continue, so I haven't been back.

My parents and I moved to our new house in North Attleboro, Massachusetts, two years ago. I wanted more decorations, since my old room didn't have much, and my mom said it would have to match my color scheme (purple and turquoise) or just be a very special message. On Etsy, I saw decals that read, "Stay Strong," but they were tiny! My mom messaged one woman selling them and she said she could blow it up big enough to go on my wall!

Demi Lovato has "Stay Strong" tattooed on her wrists, since she used to deal with depression and bipolar disorder. I love this message. It's

universal; it could mean anything for anyone. I made rubber bracelets that say, "Stay Strong," as a reminder of how far I've come, and I gave them to all my friends, since they all had something they needed to stay strong for.

I strongly believe everything happens for a reason, the good and the bad. I did go through something terrible, but I came out a better person than before. If I hadn't learned that horrible lesson, or gone through something so hard, I wouldn't be as strong as I am now.

ANDREW BROWN

I've taken my experience and passed it down so that others may begin in a place of learning, even though we weren't able to. The protests, the talks, the conversations in hallways, it was all part of leaving a legacy. And this was something a speaker mentioned at our commencement— that our 2015 class was defined by a lot of resistance and a lot of protests. The university wasn't listening to us and was mistreating us. The protests happened because our class wanted to make our community better. We were willing to put ourselves on the line to do it. And as lonely and isolated as we felt in the moment, we were never alone, because we were continuing the long line of people at Brown who have cared enough to fix things.

The speaker's words were really cathartic to hear. So that's what our class's legacy will be: that we fought to make Brown a better place. And as for what I did—through being open about my story, the sexual assault peer education, the work with my fraternity—hopefully, my legacy will be that I helped enact real change.

Now I'm moving forward. Being a peer educator taught me how people heal. For me, that's come to be about forgiveness.

I wrote a piece—a letter—for myself and ended up sharing it at an event. The reaction was overwhelmingly positive, which I'm thankful for. In that first version of the letter, the feelings I expressed were pain and anger. I was writing in an attempt to feel I could let go of that anger. Since then, I've kept coming back to the letter and rewriting as my feelings change.

Two weeks ago I reread the letter. It asked a lot of questions, because I wanted to know why he did all these things. But this time around, I changed it to read, "I *used to* ask a lot of questions." Writing that helped me let go of the way my attacker was continuing to control me.

In that first letter, I'd managed to write, "I forgive you." I don't know if I meant it then. I mean it more now. Writing about forgiveness helped me reframe my thinking and get around to forgiving.

A Letter to My Rapist

I used to ask a lot of questions: Why did you do it? Were you even listening to me when I said no? Why did you keep going as I turned away and as you tried to take something away from me I could never get back? It's only now, three years later, that I understand the irrelevance of those questions. I'm not going to waste any more energy trying to imagine a different world for myself.

In your effort to use your power to oppress me, to humiliate me, to destroy me, you've created a monster. Do you know what this monster does? This monster loves. This monster has more power than you ever will. This monster has compassion and caring and sensitivity he never thought he could have.

I forgive you. It's taken me a long time to be able to say those words, and I've thought and dreamed and prayed to get there. But I forgive you. You helped me see who I really am. I'm not broken. I'm not dirty. I have more love and beauty than I ever thought myself capable of. And all because you seemed to think you could take those things away from me. So I hope you see what you did was wrong, and I pray to God that no one else has to go through what I did, especially at your hands. But that's not my battle right now. My battle is in my heart. And you can't fill my life with hate, no matter how hard you try. So think about what you did, but know that you can't take my heart away.

> *Signed,*
> *Andrew Bearden Brown*

MARGARET HOUSE

ANONYMOUS S

For three long years, I kept my head down and my mouth shut. I told as few people as possible because I didn't want to draw attention to myself. I didn't want to be punished any more than I already had been. Yes, I would see my attacker more than I ever thought possible, but I just had to get my degree. I wouldn't let him ruin my ability to get an education.

Every single day I walked onto that campus, I had to give myself a pep talk: *It's gonna be okay. I'm one day closer to getting my diploma, and after that I don't ever have to return.*

I would get so anxious before I went onto campus, and I would spray my wrist with a perfume from Paris, France, that my grandmother wore. It smelled just like her. It was something sensory to remind me that I was safe and okay.

ANONYMOUS S

I graduated in May 2015. When I walked across the stage to receive my diploma, I realized I would never have to set foot on campus again. It was the most exhilarating feeling. I have learned that a lot of people don't graduate after being raped in college. Somehow I did.

I had been surviving. Now I could begin to thrive.

It was the first step in feeling safe again.

The second step was when I packed up my moving truck and my dad and I drove away from school. I didn't realize how toxic the situation had been until I left that campus. I was smiling as I left the city limits, and I realized I could put this whole thing behind me. There was no greater feeling. I wouldn't have to be scared for my life anymore. I could move forward and rip down the façade I had made to stay alive.

I can now say that I survived. I have moved to a state far away. I'm learning that I don't have to look over my shoulder anymore, that I can finally have peace. I am trying to learn not to live in fear. I have a wonderful man in my life who can protect me and be there for me. I am now learning that it is safe to allow my heart rate to slow just a little bit more each day. Having my family's support when I decided to move made the decision that much easier. We still talk every day.

The small town I'm in is wonderful. There are tons of kids here, and I love hearing their laughter. There are older people happy to see a friendly face in the grocery store. It's nice, because nobody knows about SMU.

And I feel really safe. We know most of our neighbors.

It is a 100 percent fresh start. Nobody has to know what happened to me. This is a safe place to learn who I truly am.

AYSHA IVES

I graduated from Rutgers in 2000 with a degree in psychology. Then I took a year off, because there was so much going on with me that I needed time to just be. Then I went back to graduate school at Virginia State and got my master's in psychology in 2003. I had my son in 2005. He's ten now. I'm not in a relationship with his father. We dated for about four years. I was in my early twenties when I met him and he was almost fifty. Then my son was born. As I got older, I got more assertive, and my son's father got less tolerant. So it ended. He's part of our son's life sometimes.

I now live in a suburb of Richmond, Virginia, and I'm in a relationship with a wonderful man. We've been together eight years. Hopefully we'll be married soon. I started writing my book about three years ago. I knew I was still healing, and I didn't know what else to do. I had tried therapy and the therapist wasn't a good fit. She opened a big can of worms near the end of a session one day and then tried to rush me through it, looking at her watch. I said, "It was safe in my unconscious, and now you've opened it up and left it here!" I felt really unsafe. On the drive home I decided I would not go back to therapy.

Instead, I went back to writing, which has always helped me heal. I wrote every day and finished the book very quickly, within a couple of weeks. I remember crying as I was processing it. I remember at some points not wanting to write any more. But I also remember that when I finished, I could say the word *rape*, which I had not been able to say before. I had finally reclaimed power over what had happened.

> I remember at some points not wanting to write any more. But I also remember that when I finished, I could say the word *rape*, which I had not been able to say before.

Then, when my writing was published, I was able to complete the healing process. I had been afraid of what people would think of me. One person actually said, "In order for him to rape you, he had to get your underwear down, so you must have helped him." That person had been a friend.

My other two books were celebrated. This one, it was almost too painful for my family and friends. "Keep quiet about that. Why are you telling your business?" Well, it's my story, and now I was no longer afraid of the stigma. When the book came out, I could say, "This happened, and I don't have to carry the shame of it. It doesn't matter what the circumstances were. It was my body and someone wanting to take control of my body is not okay. It wasn't my fault. And this is not going to victimize me anymore."

I attribute my healing to the love of God, my boyfriend, writing, and my son. I would say God helped me the most. Now, as my thirty-seven-year-old self, I look at twenty-year-olds and they seem so much younger to me. Twenty is so tender. They're so young. I want to protect them and help them.

I've been a therapist for about twelve years. I work for the Department of Juvenile Justice with incarcerated kids, high school kids. In juvenile detention centers. It's interesting. They wanted me to get certified to do evaluations on sex offenders. I declined. But as I got more training and realized that sexual violence is a cycle, that helped me to forgive my attackers. I try to look past what they did to me and see them in that dynamic—as an abused child. It's such a vicious cycle. Some of the young girls I see tell horrific stories.

My goal is to write more books and do speaking engagements on the topics of healing, infiltrating rape culture, blaming the victim. I want to help demolish rape culture and help the victims heal.

As for my own healing, I can't pinpoint a specific moment. I just evolved. I went from living in shame to trying to suppress the experience to depression and then to triggers and still trying to bury it. When I was not whole, I didn't sleep a night through. Every night, I would wake up between twelve and two. It took me so long to tell my story, because I was fearful people would point fingers. But then I started writing and I felt better, freer. It was the removal of the shame, which had been such a heavy burden. All that victim-blaming—"Well, if you hadn't been drinking," or "You brought him to your dorm room. You opened the door." When I stopped buying their story and made the decision to heal, I was able to start thinking about all the other hurting people out there.

> But then I started writing and I felt better, freer. It was the removal of the shame, which had been such a heavy burden.

ANONYMOUS V

Looking back, the first real step to healing was taking a semester off and giving myself permission to not graduate in four years. I am a rape survivor and I am strong, but I am not the girl I was when I started college and I might not be on the same staircase. Accepting that as my reality doesn't mean I like it, but it's made me more grateful for what I do have and less spiteful of those who are more fortunate.

When I stopped tracing every present problem back to that night someone violated me, the images stop coming up as easily. As time goes on, I've stopped having the dreams so much. I went to a women's group for PTSD, and I'm glad I did that. It helped a lot.

After reading about Emma Sulkowicz at Columbia, I made a conscious choice to try and let go. I wanted to feel less angry every day. My anger was exhausting. To me, Emma's mattress project is the physical manifestation of my ruminations. I thought about her mattress project and how terrible it must be to carry it around every day. It forces her to think about her assault for twelve hours a day. I didn't understand how you could carry such a burden and move forward, find new things, and do something good.

I didn't want to carry the weight of my rape anymore, so for a while, I purposefully disengaged from the national conversation about assault. This was when the *Rolling Stone* story about "Jackie" and the University of Virginia was blowing up. I thought, "I don't have to read this today. Or tomorrow." I realized I didn't have an obligation to be on top of the "assault on campus" news. I gave myself a little bit of permission.

There can be a lot of pressure in the community to go forward and *do* something. But you don't have an obligation to anyone besides being in this moment, or any other moment. Don't let even well-intentioned people pressure you. Allow yourself to take a break. Sexual assault has been affecting everyone for generations. You can take a month off or a year off, and come back to it. Sometimes, for me, an accomplishment is not doing something; turning down an event or an invitation and just focusing on myself is an accomplishment. Knowing when it is not healthy for me to listen to conversations about assault or see a screening of *The Hunting Ground*, setting healthy limits—these are the victories that we don't take enough time to praise.

There are no awards at graduation ceremonies that say "This person got out of bed and went to class every day, followed up with therapy, and took her medication." Success in life after assault can be measured with long-term goals, but my days were broken up into so many short-term goals that seemed like mountains. Your goals can be on an hour-by-hour level. Those goals are just as important as the big goals, because there will be days when getting out of bed and making yourself walk by a building that is triggering will be a huge victory. There are anniversaries of assaults and hearings that will make putting on shoes seem too exhausting to even consider. You could read a news story that shakes you. The world is unpredictable, and it takes a lot of time to feel like you have control again. You won't get enough recognition from other people for how much work it takes to keep moving through the world, so try to give yourself praise.

> There are no awards at graduation ceremonies that say "This person got out of bed and went to class every day, followed up with therapy, and took her medication."

It is hard to find pride in cleaning your room, doing laundry, and cooking a meal. Your world can feel small compared to what your friends are doing. I've had those days. When I need to, I look back on where I was four months ago, six months ago, a year ago, two years ago—and it's okay. I'm okay (so much better than okay now, actually), and it feels remarkable. Most survivors I know feel this way; life was a black hole and then you look around one day and it's not. You didn't think you could get from point A to point B and suddenly you're at point C. I'm not complaining.

I don't believe in that saying "time heals all wounds." Time passes. I found peace and meaning in my life again when I went looking for it. A big part of mindfulness is being aware of yourself and your emotions. I had to take stock, look outward. When I was in the PTSD women's group, I realized how my trauma had hurt everyone in my life, not just me. It got me out of self-pity mode.

Then, I focused on behaviors. I started exercising again. I read a lot of Mary Oliver's poetry. I found a goal: to go back to college in the spring of 2015. It gave me a purpose. I tried for acceptance. For months, I focused on a quote that I put on my mirror: "Holding on to anger is like swallowing poison and expecting the other person to die."

Overall, thinking about this time last year and my life today, I'm so much happier now, and I realize that you can't rush the process of healing. It sounds trite, but I don't think that putting on a brave face is helpful. You couldn't be more of a mess than I was, but I wasn't crippled by this experience. There's something called "post-traumatic growth." I think we all get there; we find meaning out of our experiences and we find more value in the positives we do have. It's very hard to see when you're at the beginning, very hard to see, but at some point, you'll be okay. I remember I wanted an exact timeline for how long it would take (six months? a year?), and I can't offer that. But it does come.

I will graduate this spring with my rapist. I know a lot of people transfer. I didn't because of the way my brain works: I felt that my leaving would be because of him, and that any new environment would be tainted because of that outlook. Staying was also because of him, so both ways were problematic. I wanted to show I have some sort of resilience. If the rape hadn't happened, I would have stayed, and I wanted to stay on course.

I have two thoughts frequently:

1. This is my life. This is it. This is where it's going.

2. It's amazing how you can adjust to anything, and anything can become your new normal.

Those ideas can be baffling and scary, but also comforting. Although it takes a while to put change into practice, as time goes by I identify myself less and less as a "survivor." That idea used to be in the forefront of my mind, but now it's in the background. The overall issue of sexual violence can be disheartening when you read about colleges failing to provide justice, the staggering rates of attacks, or prevalence in the military. It can make you feel sick, like it's everywhere and insurmountable. But the huge challenge of dealing with it creates such a wonderful community. You can find support in places you wouldn't even know to look.

I got an email a week ago from a father in France who read one of my articles and responded across oceans. When I read it, I was in my room, and it was a moment for reflection. He said, "It seems like you found some peace," and I thought, he thinks I sounded peaceful when I wrote that article in November; now this is July, and I am so much more peaceful than I was then. I felt proud of myself for the distance I'd come since November and gratitude toward him that he'd bothered to write me, a stranger from a foreign country.

I messaged him back, which was actually pretty embarrassing. His was a French name and at first I thought it was a woman but it was a man. I just said thank you. It shocks me that what I say gets so far.

An International Facebook Exchange

Dear V, I came across your story. . . . While looking for legal terms for a translation!! Strangely, I read it all, and I wanted to praise your courage and maturity when you are only 21 or 22. With two girls (I'm 33) you can imagine how such a story moved me. . . . All the best, Jean

June 26th, 10:55pm. Dear Jean, Thank you for taking the time to write to me and I really appreciate your kind words. I never thought that I would correspond with so many women after writing the article. It goes to show, unfortunately, that stories like mine are not particularly unique. There are a lot of people who feel like the violence I experienced is familiar to them. They see it in their personal lives, the communities they live in, or in their countries. It's overwhelming how common sexual violence against women is. I hope that the increasing awareness campaigns can help reduce it. Anyway, I have done a lot of work to "move on," and I am in a much happier place now. There is pain after violence, of course, but there is so much good left in the world. There is a life of happiness. Thank you so much for your congratulations! I don't take enough time to stop and think about how far I've come from my low point. This message made my night. Be well. Sincerely, V

FABIANA DIAZ

The summer is the worst ever, because of the reminders. It's been almost impossible; all that pressure of reminders that come just from living a normal life. No one talks about that part of it. And it's almost worse because it's reliving it. It doesn't end. I will have my really bad days and good days. The rape changed me, for sure. My sister calls me this boring grandma. I don't schedule things for after sunset. I don't go out. If I do, I have to make sure I have really good friends with me.

In my junior year I said, "This university needs more activism." There was something missing. I started working with the Dean of Students office. I felt like she believed me. She's been an ally for me; actually, the whole office has. I knew them from my process.

I decided to apply for a residential staff position, like being an RA. My RA had helped me. The dean gave me an assistant's job, in charge of her advisory board, and I got involved with the Sexual Assault Prevention and Awareness Center. I had started doing peer counseling for other survivors and I began to take part in "Carry That Weight," where you carry your mattress with you across campus as a form of protest against sexual assault.

One day I was getting ready to walk out with my mattress by myself, and I was in the community center and all of a sudden I saw a friend and she said, "I wanna come with you," and suddenly I wasn't carrying it by myself. Walking with that mattress showed me I have the ability to make an impact on somebody else. I got affirmation from people I didn't even know—people would come by and help me carry it, even for ten seconds. Survivors do that for each other. We're struggling, but we're here and still standing.

That showed me that I'm not alone. And that I can be that support for others. People care. And people want to help. And that's really cool.

With that motivation, I decided to start a movement called Culture Shift. There was a white football player who had raped a girl his freshman year, and he played all the way through his senior year before he was finally dismissed from the school. I told the vice president if that person had been a different race, his punishment would have happened more quickly. There's privilege in sexual assault. And people get more upset about a [football] losing streak than a sexual assault.

> **People get more upset about a [football] losing streak than a sexual assault.**

We wanted to name the movement Culture Shift because that's what we need.

We had a retreat for student leaders, a two-day thing with a ton of material, to start a dialogue about what we can do as students. We've just started, but we have a lot of goals.

Sometimes we forget how powerful activism can be. In the Diag, the large open space in the middle of Michigan's central campus, we created a giant "M" out of forks. They were all teal, because the National Sexual Violence Resource Center polled groups that fight sexual assault and the groups voted the teal ribbon as a symbol of sexual violence prevention. We calculated the number of students on our campus who had been assaulted, using 27,999 as the total number of undergraduate students and using the statistics of one in four women and one in six men. We wanted to use 5,806 forks, a fork for each survivor; but we were only able to get our hands on about 1,200 forks, so we decided one fork would equal five survivors. People would come up to the display, read the signs, and walk around and really look. It was very powerful, one of the most powerful things I've done.

It's cool because you see the power of the survivors' voices; they're actually being heard on our campus. We're not afraid anymore. Before, it was a stigma, but it's my identity now. There's an empowerment that comes

KENDAL ROSALIK

The display of forks on the Diag created by Fabiana and other students at the University of Michigan. (Fabiana is pictured with Jeremiah Whittington, who is now her fiancé.)

with it. But it's hard to do this. It's exhausting. You get burned out so easily.

I'm trying to read Harry Potter. My fiancé got me a bunch of paints and a stand and I've been painting. It's peaceful and quiet and that's what I've started to do as self-care.

The picture of the first painting I did is one of my favorites. It's peaceful, not too dark. It's spring coming to life, new life, joyous. It's also

JEREMIAH WHITTINGTON

Fabiana's first painting

serene: you're at peace, relaxed, no worries, nothing dark, nothing wrong, you're just there, breathing.

When I'm in places like the one in my painting, I can use all five senses. I can breathe the fresh air and smell it and I'm lying on the grass, looking at the sky, smelling the pine trees and the fresh air, and I see the beauty.

My job and the work I do are always fast-paced, but painting calms me down and brings me back. My dad says, "When you're about to have a panic attack just remember your five senses and that will bring you back to the present moment."

Painting got me all excited about creating something, seeing how I can adapt it. It's like creating a culture shift—you can change a painting whenever you want. If you don't like it the next day, change it, add more detail. It's not set in stone.

That's how I see my life. It stopped for a moment, but it's not over. When I'm reading a book and I see a semicolon, that's what I identify with: "You're a sentence, but it's not done." There's still so much I want to do. So, to others, I say, "Take time for yourself and for self-care. Learn to love yourself again, and remember, your life may have come to a semicolon, but not a period."

To my parents, sister, friends, and fiancé, who have been through this difficult journey with me—thank you.

ANONYMOUS XY

If I had to pick a favorite quote, it would be this one, by Albert Camus: "In the depths of winter, I finally learned that within me there lay an invincible summer."

For a while, the family trauma was almost as bad as the rape trauma. It would hit me and I would cry—this full-body, convulsing thing. But now it's better. I can talk about [my situation] pretty calmly.

Things would have been a lot worse if it weren't for my sensei. Also, I had this friend back east—we're identical twins, except he's black and I'm Asian—who was great. Very nonjudgmental, supportive. And there was a guy who lived downstairs in our apartment building. One day I just confided in him. We're getting married in a year. My parents are not invited to the wedding.

So on the one hand, I felt this intense loss and loneliness, like something was wrong with me. If I went out, I felt like people were staring at me. On the other hand, I began to find a mother figure in my sensei. And my friend out east started being my brother figure. And this neighbor downstairs—well, he became everything to me. On one hand I was feeling very loved and taken care of and, on the other hand, betrayed and hurt.

My case never went anywhere with the police. They said the prosecutor declined it. I tried to go the civil route, and the attorney I talked to told me no on that, too. But I did the campus adjudication, and I won: he was found guilty of sexual assault. Take *that*, rape culture!

Rape is the only crime where the victim is guilty until proven raped.

The school wouldn't tell me my assailant's sanction due to privacy laws, but "Wink-wink, nudge-nudge, he's not here" led me to believe he'd been expelled. I wish he had plagiarized, because then they'd have kicked him out for sure. Turns out he hadn't gotten expelled, because we got invited to the same party. I saw his name in the email. I thought, "What the hell?" I went to the Title IX coordinator and said, "You said he'd been expelled!" She said, "Oh, no, we didn't

> **If I had to pick a favorite quote, it would be this one, by Albert Camus: "In the depths of winter, I finally learned that within me there lay an invincible summer."**

say that, but after this month he'll be gone." Way after that, he was still here. The Title IX coordinator said, "Oh, we thought he'd be out of the country by now."

I got involved with advocacy work. Campus advocacy is great, but a lot of campus services are geared toward college-aged, hetero women, and it's very victim-centric, as if the victims are the ones who need to be changed. There's still a lot of rape culture: how about telling men to not rape?

Rape, family trauma—they will always follow me, but I don't have to react to trauma. It doesn't get in my way anymore. I'll always be sensitive to it, but I'm not full-body sobbing anymore.

I don't know that I will finish the Ph.D. program, and it doesn't matter as much. The few administrators who knew what happened tried to give me allowances, but working on a Ph.D. requires you to be 100 percent focused, and I've stopped feeling that. And I don't know if my brain is 100 percent there.

Being raped has shifted my priorities, made me reassess everything that was important to me. I'm now more focused on friends and people who matter. Because, at the end of the day, it really mattered who was in my corner. My rape separated the wheat from the chaff and helped me start nurturing the wheat.

Before my rape, I don't know if I was that happy with myself. Now I've become very happy with the person I am. Trauma shifts you down to the bare essentials. You find that part of yourself you didn't know existed, and discover you can really like and respect yourself. Even in my extremely triggered stage, I still liked who I was. And I like who I am now. I strive for compassion.

Being a rape survivor reminds me of the Japanese word *kintsukuroi*. It's where pottery pieces are repaired with gold or silver and so they are better for having been broken. I like to think we rape survivors are *kintsukuroi*. Through all our hard work, we filled ourselves back up with gold, and we're beautiful.

MANAGING CHRONIC ANXIETY

Expectation

Reality

1. HOW AM I FEELING?
2. WHY AM I FEELING THAT WAY?
3. IS MY REACTION REASONABLE GIVEN THE SITUATION?
4. *BREATHING EXERCISES*

1. HOWAMIFWORUFN HBGOEJR?FNVOEJFN VORWFNOWHRJBFHWB PERIJGQPRIFEPIJFG ...?!?!

Ariane Litalien

My Dog, My Best Friend

ZOË RAYOR

The last few years have been a tough emotional roller coaster. I've been dealing with the trauma, so much shame, and PTSD. Through therapy and a lot of introspection, I've begun to engage in the art of self-love—and I've found the perfect partner in crime: my amazing Australian shepherd support dog, Poppy. My friend Emily worked at a humane society and found Poppy in the drop-off when she came in to work one morning last year. Emily starting sending me photos of Poppy even though I didn't think getting a dog was the best idea. Then she sent me videos. Then I went and met Poppy . . . and totally fell in love!

Poppy is an awesome fuzzy dog with crazy bright blue eyes that are slightly crossed. We love to go on hikes together, exploring the beautiful mountains of Colorado, the state we call home, and we love to cuddle. Poppy likes to sit on my feet under my desk when I'm working. We live in a tiny six-foot-by-ten-foot camper, and Pops keeps me warm during the cold Colorado winters by sleeping on top of me.

Initially, I didn't expect Poppy to become my support dog. But many times when I was triggered and had a panic attack or completely dissociated, Poppy immediately sensed my fear and came over to lick me or even to jump on top of me and try to bring me back to the present. After she did this a few times, I realized that she was an awesome support canine. We are so emotionally connected and are together almost all the time; I call her my Velcro dog. She's helped so much during my healing process and transition, even though she's deaf. She checks in with me constantly; she is incredibly attentive and in tune with my emotional state.

Having Poppy has allowed me to regain my power as an individual. I love living off grid and exploring in the mountains by myself. Having Poppy around lets me feel safe while engaging in some of my favorite activities, without having to have a partner or friend with me. She's a very human-friendly dog and loves attention, but ultimately I'm her mom and I know she's loyal to me and would attack in my defense if need be.

Having Poppy in my life is one of the best things that has ever happened to me. I think we rescued each other.

GARY RAYOR

Our First Conversation

ANNIE CLARK AND ANDREA PINO

[8/24/2012 5:11:38 AM] Annie Clark: sometimes it hurts

[8/24/2012 5:11:40 AM] Andrea Lynn Pino: every time you talk about it?

[8/24/2012 5:11:47 AM] Annie Clark: like a harry potter scar

[8/24/2012 5:11:51 AM] Andrea Lynn Pino: even though you feel powerful . . .

[8/24/2012 5:11:52 AM] Annie Clark: ha. but for real

[8/24/2012 5:11:56 AM] Andrea Lynn Pino: but really

[8/24/2012 5:11:58 AM] Annie Clark: yep

[8/24/2012 5:12:04 AM] Annie Clark: and it gets better

[8/24/2012 5:12:09 AM] Annie Clark: but never 100%

[8/24/2012 5:12:26 AM] Annie Clark: b/c you're always striving to make it a better world than the one you experienced

[8/24/2012 5:12:27 AM] Andrea Lynn Pino: because you can be bruised . . . but not broken

[8/24/2012 5:12:40 AM] Annie Clark: exactly

[8/24/2012 5:12:40 AM] Andrea Lynn Pino: and it hurts you again when you see that others don't understand

[8/24/2012 5:13:06 AM] Andrea Lynn Pino: and that's what makes it fresh . . . when people talk about it like a #hashtag

[8/24/2012 5:13:07 AM] Annie Clark: and that's why it's sometimes easier to type than speak

[8/24/2012 5:13:25 AM] Andrea Lynn Pino: and it's okay to just let the words sink in

[8/24/2012 5:13:30 AM] Andrea Lynn Pino: in whatever voice

[8/24/2012 5:13:33 AM] Andrea Lynn Pino: in whatever speed

[8/24/2012 5:13:40 AM] Andrea Lynn Pino: in whatever power

[8/24/2012 5:13:46 AM] Annie Clark: however long the process

[8/24/2012 5:13:54 AM] Annie Clark: it takes time.

[8/24/2012 5:14:06 AM] Annie Clark: but within all your time you have power to change things

[The conversation paused for a few minutes.]

[8/24/2012 5:23:24 AM] Andrea Lynn Pino: But . . . despite the years . . . apart . . . the places apart . . . know that your story . . . your tears . . . your work . . . your project . . . brought me comfort . . . I put something on paper . . . even if it broke my heart to check the boxes [on the form, answering yes to so many questions that verified my assault]

[8/24/2012 5:23:43 AM] Andrea Lynn Pino: you . . . you gave me an avenue . . . even though you never would have met me

[8/24/2012 5:23:48 AM] Andrea Lynn Pino: or known my story

[8/24/2012 5:24:10 AM] Annie Clark: thank you

[8/24/2012 5:24:17 AM] Annie Clark: not necessary to be known but thank you

[8/24/2012 5:24:33 AM] Andrea Lynn Pino: it's important to me

[8/24/2012 5:24:49 AM] Andrea Lynn Pino: because . . . I want to do something that will help strangers I'll never know

[8/24/2012 5:25:12 AM] Andrea Lynn Pino: because . . . for me . . . comfort . . . it comes with peace . . .

[8/24/2012 5:25:34 AM] Andrea Lynn Pino: with knowing . . . that I can do something . . . something that will not let another fall through the cracks . . .

[8/24/2012 5:25:46 AM] Andrea Lynn Pino: because . . . I almost did

Speak Out

JULIA D.

I was raped in February of my sophomore year. I was nineteen. Met him at a frat party. He was not a frat member, just a guy who was there. We had both been drinking. I told him at the party I wasn't interested in anything but dancing and kissing.

He kept asking me if I wanted to go back to his place. I said, "No, I don't wanna have sex with you." I knew what I wanted and had no trouble saying it. So as the night went on and I was more and more intoxicated I gave in about going to his place, but I was still adamant that we were not having sex. "We can kiss and then sleep," I said to him. I was very clear.

We got to his room. He wanted me to take off all my clothes. He pushed me on the bed and lay on top of me. I kept saying, "I don't wanna have sex with you!" He just kept going.

I felt like I couldn't move under his weight. I said, "No!" and he still did it. He was very aggressive in all the things he wanted. I let it happen but hated it and was upset. I waited until he passed out, and then I ran home.

Looking back, I was really drunk. But that shouldn't have mattered. I told him no many times.

He texted me the next day: "Hey what's up." I didn't know what to say.

I was a virgin. It took me a while to come to terms with what had happened, including what to call it. I settled on *assaulted*. *Rape* is such an intense word.

> **I was a virgin. It took me a while to come to terms with what had happened.**

A few days afterward I went to see *The Vagina Monologues* with friends, one of whom was cochair of a safety and empowerment group on campus. We were walking and talking afterward and she asked me what I did over the weekend, so I told the story.

I passed it off as the guy wanted to have sex and I didn't want to. Told it very casually: "I didn't want to, but he did it anyway." My friend just looked at me. She was really great in that moment. She said, "Well, that sounds like an uncomfortable experience for you, and not how things should be." And she did a very good job of following up afterward. In my own time, I began to realize what this was.

March was spring break, and my friends and I were driving to Florida. My family had a vacation house along the way. I left early to stay a night with my parents before we drove south.

I had told my mom about the assault over the phone. She was about to walk into a grocery store and had just pulled into the parking lot. She was really angry with me: "How could you do this? How could you let this happen?" She blamed me for drinking.

It was not the reaction I'd expected. My mom was my best friend. I got scared, and told her not to tell my dad. But I didn't realize how awful that was, for her to keep such a horrifying secret from her partner about their baby girl.

For that couple of weeks before I came home, she was very distressed and anxious. She ended up telling my dad. She kept calling me, telling me they wanted to pull me out of school so I could take a semester off. I said, "If you want me to be more depressed, that's the way to do it." I needed support. So I went to see the dean of students to see what my options were about becoming financially independent, so I could stay in school.

When I drove to see my parents, my dad and mom opened the door and gave me the biggest hug in the world and told me how much they loved me and how glad they were I was there.

We sat in the living room and talked a long time, and they were extremely supportive.

My mom apologized for what she had said. I said I understood why. Because she had done so much to protect my sisters and me when we were young kids, she was thinking, "I sent you to college and you were supposed to keep protecting yourself." I think she felt as if everything she had worked so hard to protect was for nothing.

April is Sexual Assault Awareness Month, and we had an event on campus called "Speak Out." We kept a blog, and over the year anybody could post an anonymous testimonial. Then we would collect the testimonials, and members of our safety and empowerment group would read them out loud on campus where people walk by. It was an organized event, with food, music, and advocates—in case someone got triggered—and an open mic at the end so people could share.

It was the hardest night, but a healing night. You knew that everyone there had a story, knew someone, was a survivor, or was blown away by what was happening.

I read my testimonial; nobody knew it was mine, because we do it anonymously. We print the testimonials and members pick the ones they want to read.

It was so scary. My hands were shaking, my voice shook. I felt like my heart was beating a thousand miles a minute. I didn't cry. I looked down while reading it—afraid to look up. I was sharing my story and I didn't want to care about what anyone else thought or felt. This was my moment. I didn't want to ruin it by seeing a look of disbelief. That never happened. Everyone was supportive. I've been to every Speak Out since.

I did do an anonymous report to the school.

I didn't want to go through a trial. I just wanted to be over it.

I threw myself into activist work. That summer I worked at the local rape crisis center, and in my junior year I threw myself into on-campus activism.

I also started thinking differently about sex. Part of me wanted to be promiscuous: "Yeah, I'm having sex, but I'm doing it on my terms." I didn't trust men. I wanted to be in control of my body.

I became very angry and got involved with guys I wish I hadn't gotten involved with. Not because they were abusive, but because they didn't treat me the way I really wanted to be treated. I was sex to them and nothing more. For a long time I'd felt as if I was broken and didn't deserve anything better than those types of relationships.

One of my close friends my senior year said, "You're kind of a bitch, and mean to people for no reason." And I had to think about it and admit it. I threw my anger from my assault at anyone I felt remotely threatened by.

He said, "Thank you so much for sharing with me; that was very brave of you. And none of this is your fault."

Then I met my partner. It was at a party overseas, when I got a job there teaching English after graduation.

We opened up to each other soon after that night. He told me a lot of things from his past, and I told him about my assault. He's a very good listener. Very quiet.

In the end, I felt like he was grieving. He said, "Thank you so much for sharing with me; that was very brave of you. And none of this is your fault."

I was blown away: "How do you know all the right things to say?"

It was very rare to have that reaction, except from my female friends.

Guys were on the bottom of the list of people who know the right things to say.

He always tells me that was the night he fell in love with me. I feel the same. I tell him, "It's because of how safe and supported you made me feel when I was most vulnerable."

I still get angry sometimes, but now I recognize that anger and channel it: "What's a better use of this energy?"

I've gone back to school. I've started my master's in social work and public administration. I want to be a director of a nonprofit or rape crisis center. Anything's possible. I think, "Look at what you've created from that experience."

I consider myself lucky to have met such supportive people in my life—my family, my loving partner, and my college friends—the friend who came up to me while I was reading my testimonial and crying. She held my hand so I could finish.

This is part of what I read:

Knowing

These are things some people know about me:
I like pretty dresses and wearing makeup.
My favorite pastimes are eating, talking, and dancing.
I like having a plan, but I need spontaneity.
I can be really loud and share more information than most people want
     to know.
I trust too many people.

I trusted him that night. I trusted that he knew that no meant no. After *one* time. After *two* times Even after *one hundred* times.

I told people, but I treated it like just another funny story from a night out. I didn't realize it was a problem until the definitions of rape and consent were on a giant screen in one of the bystander intervention trainings I was leading. I never thought that I would have to use the resources we provided to survivors. They weren't for me. They were for those "one in four women." Not me.

Some people know that I can't refer to him, or what he did, by name. But people don't know that's because I still believe it's my fault. I shouldn't have drunk so much. I shouldn't have left with him. I shouldn't have taken off my dress.

People don't know about my constant battle within myself to practice what I encourage others to believe. They don't know that I'm still unsure of how to define what happened, or if I even want to. I mean, I should know, right?

I'm afraid to scream about my pain because I'll have to explain it. I am afraid that people will think I deserved it.

These are things no one knows:
I scrubbed my skin raw and cried on the shower floor the morning after it happened.
I haven't been able to wear that dress since that night.
I take a detour to my first class to avoid passing him.
I had sex with a "friend" because I wanted to prove that I could be in control of my body.

I'm tired of feeling dirty, angry, scared, and ashamed. I don't want to feel guilty and undeserving. I want to love myself again.

I'm learning to trust myself again.

If It Happens to You*

A Chorus

Remember, you don't have to go through this alone. Some people
may point fingers, but many more want to support and embrace.
There are people who will support you. It's not your fault.
And it's going to be okay.

It's not too late to heal. It doesn't matter if
the assault happened five years ago or ten.

Speaking out, even if it's to a friend, reclaims your power.

Confide in a friend or someone you trust. Release that poison.
Release it in some kind of outlet. Because time does not heal these
wounds. You have to deal with the trauma.

Do whatever you're comfortable with. Don't be embarrassed or
ashamed. There's so much scrutiny that comes with
talking about sexual assault. Some people understand and
some people are assholes about it.

If you can, report the incident. Tell someone, anyone,
because it's not right and the perpetrator probably
should be punished for what they did.

You're not alone. It takes guts to not feel that way. Open up to at
least one person, like a therapist or family member. 'Cause there are
times you will still feel alone and you just have to work with that.

Get an animal; get a dog. That helps a lot.

Surround yourself with people who care about you. Take time
to take care of yourself. If you don't take care of yourself,
the trauma's going to be a lot harder to get through.

If you're reading this and you're a survivor, I would like to say,
"Just trust how you feel." And know that you are right.
That's the only thing that matters.

It can be really hard. Sometimes people won't listen, or won't
acknowledge how you feel. At the end of the day, whenever I have
doubts I always go back to how I felt that night and how I still feel
about it, and all the anxiety and the trauma that I have now because
of that night, and that's how I know I'm right.

It's okay to report, or not report, to write about it, or not.
There are all these expectations. I always thought if I were assaulted
I'd be one of those who'd report immediately. And I couldn't.

You do you.

Do what you think is best for you.

---

*Every survivor experiences the aftermath of sexual assault in their own way and
finds healing and support in a unique combination of strategies and resources. Here,
survivors offer heartfelt, individual, various, and sometimes differing bits of advice
based on what worked for them. But there's no one right way to heal. And nothing on
these pages should be taken as professional advice.

Accepting Entropy

HOW MY DAD USED THE SECOND LAW OF THERMODYNAMICS TO TEACH ME HOW TO SURVIVE

LIZ WEIDERHOLD

When I was in sixth grade, my dad retired from the army after spending twenty years thriving as a faithful disciple of aerospace engineering. His passion for this field was as limitless as space itself. At bedtimes during my childhood, I would ask him which star he liked best, and he would regale me with facts about Betelgeuse, the red supergiant, the Goliath of the night sky, whose surface is shrouded by a complex, dissymmetrical, cancerous cloak, an outgrowth of incalculable mass loss. He emphasized how this crimson runaway's stellar evolution will end in a triumphant death as a supernova within the next million years, and how this twinkling Leviathan's winds are piercing the circumambient interstellar medium.

My enigmatic dad almost continuously groomed my affection for science with his romantic insight into current research, but this behemoth of a bard did not know that, although I loved his intergalactic vignettes, I rarely—if ever—fully understood him. My dad's emotional latitude coupled with his boundless wonder made him a difficult person to know. He rarely talked about himself and rarely asked me about myself, choosing instead to swaddle me safely in a blanket of concepts—protected there from our infallibilities, fears, and failures.

But by my freshman year of college, I was entrenched in suicidal melancholy, unable to stop reliving the details of a rape. This rape had too recently launched me from a sprightly, naive undergraduate ready to find my place in this world to a mere nebula of that glowing girl, now cool, dying, and swollen, culled into a vortex of antipathy for myself and for men. I was scared. I was angry. I was reduced to a fractured skeleton of my former self. And, worst of all, I was alone. The educational ecosystem in which I had flourished and into which I had been ushered by my dad's careful, intellectual company was now polluted with deathless shame, a certainty of self-defeat, and a simmering resentment of authority. A barrage of questions, which I never voiced, orbited within me as the magnitude of my pain reached its apogee. Could I have done anything to prevent this? Did I do something to provoke this? How could I fix this?

But sound doesn't travel through space.

I felt I had lost so much. I had lost opportunities to relish the last days of my childhood. I had lost friends, and I had lost fights. Worst of all, I had lost my vision of my future, and I had lost my once-close companionship with my dad, who seemed as distant, as impossible, and as unattainable as outer space. Once my dad had proffered biographies of the visible heavens that lifted me into an untroubled sleep; now I was too choked by my misery to ask my dad about my own biography. Why had a man raped me? My dad sang his lullabies no more.

After my rape, it took nearly ten years for me to realize that my dad could not teach me how to heal. No finite string of warm words could ever articulate the amalgam of inexorable distresses, relief, bewilderment, burdens, and fury that, for years, governed my pursuit of self-actualization. I am certain now that my dad knew that, and that his own questions haunted him and his own grief stayed unacknowledged in the ether of our cragged relationship.

After my rape, it took nearly ten years for me to realize that my dad could not teach me how to heal.

Although my dad knows about my rape, he and I have still not had a conversation about it. And we likely never will. But he is not the enemy. He is my buried hero. He was the first good man I ever knew, the antithesis of my rapist, and the one who gave me eighteen years of unencumbered and unconditional love before the perversion of my virtue and virginity. His love winnowed the mass of truths I couldn't face yet. It distanced me from the depravity of the act, and it is the nuclear fuel for my endurance through life still. Only now, as a teacher myself, do I recognize that my dad translated the data he aggregated from his vast knowledge of space into a narrative that reflected themes of life and death, love and loss, sickness and health, injury, persecution, injustice, and faith. Though he spoke of the stars, he had all along been answering those questions I once thought he had ignored. No matter how corrosive and insidious some truths, the narrative of the night sky can be my compass after all.

My dad helped me grow up. Grow past. Move forward. Heal. Survive.

Again

I am a time traveler. I first discovered my superpower lying on the edge of the sidewalk with a sweet boy. Our romantic friendship left me lonely and confused. I thought the first time we touched, it would feel perfect and satisfying. See, I needed to prove to myself that I could still live the dreamed teenage life of lust and recklessness, but the boy would not touch me. He knew about my history; he knew a wrong turn might offend me, and so we lay still. Overcome with inadequacy, I put my hand on his face and he finally pulled me closer. The familiar tug and pull began, reassuring me again of the surviving potential in my existence. Somewhere in the middle of an embrace or a word, I realized the world around me had flared in and out of focus. I wish I could remember exactly what he did that initiated the process, but from one moment to the next, I went from the sidewalk, to the floor of a dark, cold room. I recalled this room from a month earlier. Immediately, I sensed danger and then fully recognized that I had somehow traveled back a month to a horrible night. I didn't want to accept the reality of reliving what I knew would happen next, so I punched and kicked indiscriminately around me. I screamed at the monster on top of me. I beat him and myself in the hopes

I would wake from this nightmare. The monster rolled over and left me alone on the floor. I cried and closed my eyes until I knew I had transported myself back to the present. When I opened my eyes, the sweet boy stood above me, transfixed in suspicion. I told him I had Band-Aids in my room, but he hurried home.

—Regina Gonzalez-Arroyo

Relationships After

A Chorus

I met another guy, who was also in a frat, although he
was very different. I told him what had happened and
he was supportive and careful and cautious.

We started a relationship, and it was definitely difficult. One night
we were hanging out and we were horsing around and he grabbed my
shirt. I started screaming and crying and collapsed on the floor. That
happened multiple times. It was bad.

I found myself in a manipulative relationship. Just got out of that.

Someday I will date again and have a sexual relationship.
I've been with someone since. It was really rough, but it helped me to
detach myself from labeling my sexual experiences. It helped me put
my bad experience into a separate category.

I had never been in a relationship, and I wanted to prove that
love did exist. We spent time talking and holding hands. I had
never held hands with a woman before, or been kissed in
public before, and they just kissed me while we were standing on
the corner there. And it really meant something to me, that
they weren't ashamed to be out with me.

In the summer, I had gotten into a new relationship with a guy I had
known for five years. I was very open with him about what I had
gone through, but he asked me not to tell him the specifics of that

day. He helped me through my flashbacks, and he was and still is always there to listen when I want to talk about it. I am not saying that you cannot help yourself, but it is nice to have unconditional support from everyone in your life, which is what I have.

I did talk to my partner at the time and told him what happened. It was really hard for me to talk about it. After I was raped, I had cheated on him, having sex with random people. I felt really guilty about that and tried to explain why, but I was having a really hard time having sex with him again. He was sad. He was really sad for me. He felt horrible. He felt like shit. I felt like shit.

For a long time as a survivor, I felt as if I was broken and didn't deserve anything better than those types of relationships. Then I met my fiancé. I had never believed that what I have with him could be possible.

I was always a romantic growing up. I always wanted to be in love forever, like in a fairy tale. But then I was assaulted and I thought, "That's stupid and it doesn't exist, it's not real."

You don't know who will support you. Someone had said, "Have you told Bobby?" And I had said, "Oh, no, because he will come to school and beat the shit out of this guy." But, no. Bobby never even asked if I was okay.

I had a five-year affair with a sixty-year-old married man. He was safe, effeminate. He wouldn't rape me.

My partner is supportive and kind and generous, really wonderful. I'm very huggy. He's very much a feeler, like me.

Olivia Benson Believes Me

ANONYMOUS H

I had never heard of *Law & Order: Special Victims Unit* until freshman year of college, at the University of Maryland. My roommate loved the show, so one night I decided to join her. The first episode we watched focused on college sexual assault, portraying victims who, like us, were students who had just arrived on campus. The story line didn't just unsettle me—it struck a nerve. I felt intensely connected to the characters, especially Mariska Hargitay's Detective Olivia Benson. I ended up watching every episode, even though I couldn't explain why *SVU* impacted me so profoundly. There was something deep at play. And as I watched, I slowly began to realize the connection.

It had started when I was fifteen, in high school. I had a crush on a boy who presented me with this concept of "friends with benefits." I took that to mean he liked me, but all he wanted was the benefits. Soon, I started having problems with anxiety.

Then, two weeks before my sixteenth birthday, a guy named David gave me a ride home from a party where my crush had just ditched me for some random girl. I had known David for years, and he and my crush were friends. My crowd didn't drink or smoke, so I was sober. I was under the impression that my "friends with benefits" thing was secret. But David knew and, looking back, it's easy to tell he knew I was vulnerable because I was upset. He ended up forcing me to do what he wanted, which was to pleasure him.

I don't even remember exactly how it ended. I remember him laughing. I was in shock. Something felt wrong, but I assumed I was overreacting, and I believed that because we didn't have intercourse, I wasn't entitled to my feelings. I told three people what had happened, and one of them—my best guy friend at the time—responded that he had expected more from me. He said he held me to a higher standard and I had disappointed him. I convinced myself that David's actions were okay and I needed to get over it.

> I don't even remember exactly how it ended. I remember him laughing. I was in shock. . . . but I assumed I was overreacting, and I believed that . . . I wasn't entitled to my feelings.

After the thing happened with David, I turned to boys, telling myself, "I'm gonna use them. I can't be used because I'm the one calling all the shots."

I was hooking up with a lot of guys—not intercourse, but everything else. I was convinced that I wasn't the girl that people wanted to date.

Once I began college, I told myself I wanted a fresh start. But during my second semester, I regressed. I was having a bad week, anxiety-wise, and I turned to what I knew: coping via boys.

I texted this kid Ben who was in my class and invited myself over to his apartment. I remember asking him how drunk he was and he said, "Four out of ten." I was maybe tipsy, but I was in control.

All of a sudden he started taking my clothes off—we hadn't even kissed. He pulled me on top of him and started pushing me down. He kept pushing. I resisted. He's a big guy, muscular. I'm five foot one, 115 pounds.

He forced me to perform oral sex and other acts. I dissociated, leaving my body behind while my mind went elsewhere. I knew what had happened was wrong. I left his room crying, and I hardly ever cry. But, like before, I didn't deem it an assault. I believed it was my fault: I knew my state of mind that night, but I went to his room anyway.

I told my mom. Her response? "You should never go to a guy's room alone." I kept watching *SVU*, and the characters' struggles reminded me of my experiences. I deeply sympathized with them, yet I felt conflicted. I still didn't feel entitled to my emotions. However, as I made my way through the series, it became clear that what I had gone through wasn't okay . . . and that terrified me. I had never considered that I was assaulted, but everything made sense. I began to understand how my high school experience had affected me, tainting my understandings and expectations of relationships.

Finally I told my psychiatrist, and she called it rape. When I admitted that to myself, I flipped out. I was a mess.

And then I had another incident, and this was the worst of all. Afterward I thought, "What is it with me? This doesn't happen three times. This is absurd."

I had flashbacks and anxiety and I went from never drinking to drinking a lot. It was really rough and that forced me to have compassion for myself: "I can't keep doing this."

A month later, there was publicity about a sexual assault case involving some football players. I followed it intensely. Watching that trial, I started to feel. I felt passionate about making a difference. And one day I just decided to call the district attorney's office and see if they had any internship opportunities. Now I'm a victim witness intern. It's really cool. I'm trying to raise awareness and to advocate. I can make a difference in people's lives. My goal is to work on criminal sexual assault cases. I'm still very hard on myself, but definitely on the upswing.

I've come so far since my freshman year, when I started binge-watching

Law & Order: SVU. It was one specific episode, "True Believers," that really flipped a switch for me.

> "Healing begins when someone bears witness. I saw you. I believe you."

After a grueling trial and subsequent "not guilty" verdict, a young survivor lashes out at Olivia Benson. As the girl turns to leave, Benson grabs her shoulders, looks her in the eye, and exclaims, "Sending him to prison

ANONYMOUS H

isn't gonna heal you. Healing begins when someone bears witness. I saw you. I believe you."

When I watched this scene I broke down. In one line, Olivia Benson shattered the self-blame and uncertainty I had endured for years. In that moment, I could finally show myself compassion. It was like Olivia Benson was speaking directly to me, and for the first time I didn't feel alone.

Olivia Benson is much more than a TV character—she's a support system and role model. I can count on her.

The After

SARI RACHEL FORSHNER

It used to feel like there was horror
in my DNA.
I tried changing the color of my hair;
I dyed it repeatedly, almost to the point
of destruction. I became a redhead,
but the roots still grew in *raped*.

Never again will I be that bright little person from the before, poised
on the brink of my life, poised
without the knowledge
of how horrible the world can truly be;
I am so sorry, darling, but we cannot
unknow what we know.

Recovery is not
waking up in the morning
and everything is back to normal,
but recovery exists.

It is waking up one morning,
and your roots are just roots, so you go to CVS
to pick out a completely different color, just because.
It is waking up one morning and your body is not
a reminder, is not
repulsive, is not
broken—
it's just sleepy. It just wants you
to press "Snooze" one more time before class.

Recovery is having rape remain
only at the back of your mind, instead
of in all of it.

I cannot promise you
that it all goes away,
that you will never
be afraid to go to Trader Joe's alone
ever again. I won't lie to you.

I cannot promise you that the sex you have will only be easy
and fun, that you will never need
to stop in the middle because
you can't breathe, because you need to go
cry in the bathroom, again, because you
are supposed to be young
and adventurous, but everything
still scares you, sometimes.

I can promise you only this: change.
I can promise you progress.
I can promise you that

it is possible to look in the mirror
and really stop blaming yourself, someday.
It is possible to stop
thinking that you are shattered beyond repair,
or not worth loving, anymore.

It is possible to begin to smile
in such a way that it reaches your eyes again,
in such a way that you are not always lying
when someone asks how you are (curse that question!)
and you say, "Good, and you?"

It is possible to find someone who
does not mind any of it, who knows that none of that
is who you are, it is only
what happened to you.

One day, someone will ask, first,
if they can put their arms around you when you're sobbing.
They will look you in the eye, with understanding, and say
"How can I help?"
To them, you are a whole person who happens to be
in pain, who is not pain itself, who is not contagious,
and you will shake your head and answer "Oh, oh, sweetheart—
you already have."

I must begin in the darkness
so as to show how light
the light is, to understand how far
from the beginning the now is.
I must pause in the middle of the race—
not to reflect on the fact

that the finish line is still too far away
for comfort, but to turn back and realize
that I also have to squint
to see where I began.

I must start with loss; I must mourn the girl-child
whose ignorance really was bliss, then the woman
with head trauma, heart trauma, trauma of the soul,
so that I can show you that no matter how obscure the night is—
no matter the depths of depression or the heights of panic—
it is still possible for there to be a morning, someday,

when you celebrate the person you have become.
When you stop trying so damn hard to imitate who you used to be,
because you're starting, ever so slowly,

to prefer who you are.

Slowly, You Start Forgetting

ANONYMOUS V

Slowly, you start forgetting. Then one day you realize you haven't been thinking about the assault all day. Then one week you can't remember the exact date of your hearing or an appeal or the way a letter from a dean was worded. You start to forget, and you feel a bit guilty. If you're forgetting, maybe it wasn't as traumatic as you said it was. Shouldn't this be burned into your memory? Then you start to feel lighter. It is nice to not have these images readily available 24/7. It is nice to go back to day-dreaming or to more recent memories. Then you feel a bit hopeful, like here is a new beginning.

Then you feel unsure. What *is* the new beginning? That's where I am now. I had my life before this assault. I had my life after the assault. Now I think I'm in my life "after the after." I'm again in a new territory where I'm no longer measuring things in firsts (first time I've had sex since the rape; first time I've gone back to school since the rape) or thinking in terms of "before that night" and "after that night." So I'm trying to navigate this new territory now and figure out who I am, as someone who has integrated "rape survivor" into her person but is no longer consumed by it. It's a little bit frightening, honestly, after this singular event having defined so much of my values, thoughts, and even activism and aspirations over the past almost two years. But it is also freeing.

f(Survival)

A FUNCTION OF SURVIVAL

ADITI

When I was thirteen, I strove for invisibility. I struggled with my weight, my hair, and my lack of belonging. I had few friends in a school where I was the one angry brown girl. The popular (read: white) girls never missed a chance to tell me I wasn't worthy of sharing this world with them. I reached out to my family and was met with silence. I learned to keep my pain, ideations, and everything else hidden, and to assimilate. I planned my life to protect myself.

I was assaulted during my first year at college. My best friend, S, was at the party and gently comforted me while I blankly sat in the backseat of the car afterward, speaking only to mumble an apology to the driver, whose room had been the setting for my assault. S let me stay with her and sat with me that night when I couldn't sleep, I couldn't speak, and I couldn't cry.

- I didn't black out. Will they think I consented if I wasn't wasted?
- He cornered me in the bathroom. Will they say I could have gotten away?

- It wasn't that violent. Will people think it's assault if I'm not physically scarred?
- I tried to joke and stop it, but he didn't care. Will they think I tried hard enough?
- I got away the second he was distracted. Will they still blame me?

My healing was analytical; I proceeded in the most efficient manner, as I had with the other pain in my life. Going home for the summer, I pretended everything was okay so as not to alarm my progressive, but still very Indian, parents.

Life in an immigrant family is complicated. You learn to celebrate the highs and lows as more than your own individual achievements and failures. You become the culmination of everything your family sacrificed in order to provide you with this life. Email chains about your successes are sent to family members far and wide, so that everyone knows you (and by extension they) are one step closer to the ever elusive American dream. My mother constantly tells people that when she grows up, she wants to be just like me. It is utterly sweet, stressful, and heartbreaking all at once.

> **Life in an immigrant family is complicated. . . . You become the culmination of everything your family sacrificed.**

While home, I became reclusive. I dissociated when I was alone, told my family that first year was okay but "I wish I could have changed some things," and counted down the days until school started.

During second year, my assailant lived one floor above us in the dorm. He was in clear sight. He would lean over the railing outside his suite and taunt me with a wave, as if to remind me I was still within reach. S and I made up names like "Sharkboy" so that I wouldn't have to say his name and so she would know he was near. We would laugh about it, and through that laughter and quiet normalization I began to heal.

But soon after school started, I entered into an abusive relationship. It was as if the world were playing a cruel joke. I so deeply craved a safe male relationship that I ignored the little ways he was trying to control me by denigrating my analytical tendencies. He made me feel I was so undeserving that I wasn't even worth breaking up with; he just disappeared. Everything I had ever relied on to persevere was destroyed in the span of a few months. To this day what he did still affects my psychological and physical behavior with partners.

Fearing his retaliation, I spoke only to S and one other close confidant, M, while we were together. After the relationship, I involved myself in every kind of activism that wouldn't compel me to personally share. I managed to hide from my emotions because there was always an exam, a rally, an experiment . . . anything could distract me from myself. Everything was okay; I was *fine*.

Despite everything, I still couldn't reach out at home. It's not that my parents aren't people you can talk to; my mother is incredible. She has lived through every individual, career, and familial trauma I can imagine, yet she is still warm, self-sacrificial, and an absolute badass. She is one of the strongest people I know, and I've always tried to emulate her. She carries our jumbled mess of a family on her back and keeps moving forward.

But my mother also hides. She speaks about her experiences as if she's recounting a particularly compelling memoir; as if these aren't pains she's struggled through, as if they don't still affect her. We are more alike than I am willing to admit. Almost every one of my friends has a close relationship with my mother. They go to her for advice, and they openly talk to her about their lives. Almost everyone has a close relationship with my mother, except for me. Maybe I'm still holding on to my teenage grudge of not being heard. Maybe she's reaching out, and I'm too blind to see.

I still relied on M and S for my peace of mind, but at the end of fall semester, in less than twenty-four hours, M died of a bacterial infection. I wasn't just mourning my friend, but one of my only confidants. Our relationship was well known, and people reached out to check in on me. For the first time I experienced pain not just within myself, but throughout a community; the pain was sharp, but it was good.

I became obsessed with using art to work through my grief. I painted, did woodwork, and made jewelry to surround myself with memories of M. I ornamented my body with reminders of my trauma, wearing my pain for the world to see. I allowed people to see the pain I had trained my whole life to hide; it was a freedom I had never felt before.

It took until after college for me to come out unapologetically and feel safe calling myself a survivor. I slipped my survivorhood into conversations where I thought it relevant, or simply told the friends I felt should know. Being open about my experiences was and still is the biggest risk I take; but it has also been a way to normalize, to take comfort in shared histories, and to heal. More people than ever know I'm a survivor, and not because I need them to be my saviors, but because the trauma of hiding my experiences was unbearable.

I've finally found a community of trauma survivors, radical Asians, queer folks, and southern activists who are the family I'm my true self around. My new chosen family supplements and complements my biological family in every way. They not only know my truth but also understand my responses. They're a family that calls me out on minimizing my experiences, because they're dealing with similar struggles.

For a long time, I thought my own pain wasn't legitimate because I know survivors who have dealt with so much worse. I wasn't left for dead; I wasn't abused long-term by my primary

> For a long time, I thought my own pain wasn't legitimate because I know survivors who have dealt with so much worse. I wasn't left for dead . . . it wasn't that violent.

caretaker; it wasn't that violent—I even thought my story boring. My assault, like so many, just didn't fit our societal narrative of survivorhood. We live in a world where the only media representation of survivors is that they're perfect (usually white) young women who are violently assaulted by strangers. While recounting their story, they always cry just enough for sympathy but not enough to make you uncomfortable, and it's always at the perfect time. It's either that, or they're absent, and endless droves of talking heads discuss them in the abstract, as if they're not in the room. But what about the survivors who are in between; who aren't included in the publicized narratives? Where is our space to share, cry, joke, and live?

> **I never understand why we don't treat survivorhood like we treat grief. Grief is something traumatic that happens to you. . . . But grief is only a part of you; it does not define you as a person.**

I never understand why we don't treat survivorhood like we treat grief. Grief is something traumatic that happens to you, and that you always carry. But grief is only a part of you; it does not define you as a person. My assault was terrible, and I'm different because of it, but it in no way defines my personhood. It's important that people know I'm a survivor, but I don't want it to be the first thing they describe about me. I want to be called driven, goofy, a science geek, unapologetically political, a caring friend, confidante, and mentor. Those are things that describe who I am; being a survivor, like the death of a loved one, is something that adds complexity to my lived experience.

For so long I squirreled away my pain, feverishly putting back together who I thought I was before my assault. When people said they didn't know any survivors, I never spoke up. I just cried out, in the smallest voice, "But you know me."

Now, I do activism around Asian identities, science literacy, and survivorhood/Title IX, making sure to empower myself to enter spaces and speak my truth. I've found the power in my voice that I avoided for so long because it "othered" me.

Living openly hasn't been easy, and many of my romantic relationships fall apart when I come forward. I've done this so many times that I've perfected when I'm going to tell them and exactly what I'm going to say:

> I have to tell you something important. I'm a survivor of sexual assault and relationship abuse. You can ask as few or as many questions as you want. I won't judge you if you don't ask any questions, but I felt like you needed to know this much at least to understand why I sometimes act the way I do.

No matter what I do, many disappear like my ex. Every single time I tell someone and they vanish, I question whether or not I'm doing the right thing. I question whether or not I am broken, and I fervently fight the temptation to hide. With time, I have learned to catch myself or let myself be caught when I spiral, knowing that the person who deserves to be with me will see me as more than my past traumas. I stand in resolute defiance, refusing to censor my experiences because these men are not strong enough to see me as anything less than perfect.

I will never be fully healed, but I am so much greater than the sum of my traumas. I am endlessly more interesting than a few select experiences, but thanks to my chosen family, I will never again hide my truth. Now, when people claim not to know any survivors, I demand to be counted because the idea that a survivor can't be successful, funny, complete—anything but utterly defined by their assault—is infuriating.

Every conversation where a survivor does not feel empowered to speak adds to their trauma. Every time we treat assault as something incredibly violent that happens to a few unfortunate girls, we retraumatize and silence survivors who never thought their assault was important enough, or worse—who thought their assault was boring.

For all the survivors who are quietly reading this book, pretending it isn't about you, and searching for a community to belong to, there is always an open seat next to me.

I Believe Myself

ON CREATIVITY AND HEALING

A. LEA ROTH AND NASTASSJA SCHMIEDT

When we experience violence, we become reduced to our bodies; it is as though our voices are erased by a perpetrator who chooses to impose their will over our own. Also, through social erasure, victim-blaming, and stigma, trauma becomes unspeakable.

In the process of healing, it is essential to reclaim our voices, narratives, and self-worth. Since many survivors struggle to access a support system—or even an empathetic ear—creativity is one of the most powerful tools of healing accessible to all survivors.

Creativity is a universal process through which we tell ourselves, "My voice and my story matter. I believe myself," and it is a process through which we can invite others to support us in our healing journey. Self-love through creativity can heal the most destructive impacts of violence; self-love is an act of resistance and resilience, countering the isolation, shame, and loss of trust that endure long after an initial trauma.

THOUGHTS I HAVE WHEN I MEDITATE: VOL. 2

IMAGINE THAT YOU ARE ALONE, IN A SMALL CABIN IN THE WOODS. IT IS DUSK, AND EVERYTHING IS QUIET...

OKAY, BUT THERE IS PROBABLY A SERIAL KILLER HIDING IN MY CLOSET.

Ariane Litalien

THOUGHTS I HAVE WHEN I MEDITATE: VOL. 3

Ariane Litalien

My Own Lingerie

ABBI GATEWOOD

And this is random and slightly odd—I've started sewing. I started making my own lingerie. It gives me something to do. I give it to friends. I don't sketch, I just make what comes to mind. They tell me what they want and I picture it and I make it. They give me a color and then I take their measurements and pick out the lace and then I make it.

I've made lingerie for myself. Most of what I make is bras. I feel comfortable because I'm wearing it for myself. Some are intricate and some are regular. I also make bodysuits. The more intricate it is, the more I like it. I don't wear them for anyone; it just makes me feel good.

I was wearing a push-up bra the night I was raped. I have not worn one since and don't know if I will ever again. A push-up bra is very confining. You are stuck and tucked. The bras I make are very light and very

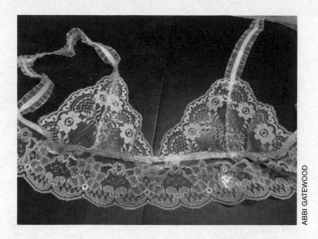

ABBI GATEWOOD

freeing. You're not confined and stuck. The bra is just an accentuation of you. You're not forced into any kind of configuration.

I've learned to not care about what my boobs look like.

If you don't like my face and need to look at my boobs, then I probably won't like you.

"Lux Libertas"

ANDREA PINO

To all survivors, it's okay to not be okay.

I went to the Blue Ridge Mountains of North Carolina for the first time less than a week after dropping out of UNC, hoping that my spirit would feel at peace and return me to myself. My relationship with writing had gone missing for two years (ever since I filed a Title IX complaint against UNC), and writing's absence had been inhibiting many facets of my life. Had I scared off writing with the themes I'd penned, expending my creativity solely on narratives often too painful to read aloud? It's hard to explain just how important writing is to me; I sometimes feel that it will be my own words that lead me to the most danger. My past feels entitled, almost unrelenting in its desire to be written; preserved to remind me that where I am now does not erase where I have been, what I have done, and what has been done to me.

When I feel most vulnerable I remember what my *abuelo* always told me—"Nunca, nunca, nunca pares de luchar"—the motto that helped me grow up.

When I feel most alone, I think of "Lux libertas."

The University of North Carolina's motto is "Light and liberty," and since my first semester at Carolina, I've worn the seal of my university on a necklace. Even today, it reminds me that what prompted my current journey was my love for UNC and my self-imposed duty to seek justice.

My life changed forever when I started at Carolina, and there are days when I think about how my life might have been different if I had gone to Yale, the way I wanted to when I was twelve.

How would my life have been if I hadn't gone to college, if I had stayed home like so many of my high school classmates? Until 2015, I never stopped thinking of what I could have done to have prevented what happened. To prevent my pain, my scars, my fear.

For a long time, I felt that I was wearing a mask, hiding my pain from my family and my friends. I felt that I had to be the strong one, that I had to appear emotionless and resilient at all hours of the day. For too long, I couldn't forgive myself for leaving Carolina without a degree. That was my lowest point.

But it was at my lowest point that I uncovered parts of me I never knew existed. It was then that I felt closest to my family; to my little sister, Angie, my first best friend; and closest to the culture that has always been a part of me. It was then that I met my closest friends (many of them in this book), the people who have given me the love I never knew I needed, and they ignited the strength within me to heal. My *Lux*. It was at my lowest point that I raised my service dog from a shelter puppy to the superhero she is today, and to my guide during my darkest of days. It was then that I realized that what severed my writing from my heart was that I had forgotten to love myself.

I learned that I was worthy of love, and worthy of self-love. I realized that self-love is activism. My *libertas*.

I learned that I was worthy of love, and worthy of self-love. I realized that self-love is activism.

Self-love is sitting under the tallest redwoods in the world, beholding the beauties of the Rocky Mountains (shout-out to Beartooth Pass), running to catch the sun along the peaks of the Badlands, and sleeping surrounded by the cascading waves of Santa Monica beach. Self-love is knowing that I will always have those who loved me during my most difficult times, when I felt farthest away from myself. Self-love is letting myself feel pain and sadness and fear when it is most terrifying to do so; it's the validation to feel both happy and unhappy.

Self-love is radical because our world tells us that sexual assault taints us, that PTSD breaks us, and that we can never be who we were before.

As much as I loved the woman I was, I love every part of the woman I am today.

There are days when she's sad, and days when she's happy.

But every day, she feels loved.

My assault was not my fault, and the mistakes I made along my journey have challenged and shaped me. To those whom I have hurt while trying to find myself, I know that pain may still linger, but I have learned. I'm still learning.

But today, I declare my independence from the guilt that has haunted me.

Today, I am happily unhappy, and I am okay with not being okay.

Women's Studies Built Me

STEPHANIE CANALES

I was born in El Salvador. My parents had a coffee plantation. When I was eight, my parents got divorced and my mom got custody. I was seventeen when we moved to the United States. It was really exciting. Growing up I didn't date much, or go out much, because I always felt responsible for trying to help my mom and watch my younger sisters. My mom was a dentist in El Salvador, and a dentist over here. I loved music and school, but I needed to be a good example for my sisters. I took on a lot of responsibility that was not mine.

In El Salvador, I had been assaulted, starting when I was twelve, by a couple of workers in my mom's office. They each molested me, for a little over a year. After that it was hard for me to trust. So when we got to the United States, I felt like I could live for the first time, away from what had happened to me. I was not aware of the challenges of learning English, or trying to go to college, or trying to get a job over here. I was enamored with the idea of being free and starting over.

We moved to Clovis, California, a small community, very quiet, peaceful. It reminded me of my grandpa's town. Very safe. We could leave our bicycles outside the house.

I had graduated from high school in El Salvador, so I started college in the United States when I was eighteen. I got my associate degree in psychology from Fresno City College when I was twenty.

Around then, I met my first boyfriend; his family and my family were friends. I had never dated before, and I was coming from this painful experience. I didn't feel like I deserved someone to treat me well; I chose an abusive person.

Then I started my bachelor's degree in psychology at California State University, Fresno. I wasn't able to finish. My last class there was women's studies. That class was the pivot point in my life. I was able to find the answers I had been looking for by studying violence against women and the sexual subjugation of women. I had been sexually assaulted, and so had my sister. And when I told my mom, she told me that she had been sexually assaulted, and her sister, as well.

> **My professor said it was important to evolve from "victim to healer, and healer to advocate."**

My professor said it was important to evolve from "victim to healer, and healer to advocate." That for me was huge. After class I went to my car, an ugly half-white, half-black 1994 Toyota Corolla that I had paid $500 for, and I sat in that car and I cried. I was twenty-two.

My professor's name was Elizabeth Swearingen. She looked so strong and powerful. I wanted to be like her. She was not afraid of defending women. She was not afraid of voicing what was wrong about how women are treated in our society, and how the media treats women. She made powerful speeches. I felt inspired by her passion. I thought, "I want to have that, too." She had long blond hair that was purple in the front. She always dressed so fashionably. She was somebody who expressed herself through her dress, through her work, through her life.

After every class in which she talked about violence and sexual violence, I used to cry: "Oh my God, this is exactly where I am." My boyfriend criticized my hair, the way I dressed; he gave me constant criticism. He would make me go change my clothes. I would get a punch in the arm for something he didn't like. He would call me names, say I wasn't going to do anything with my life, tell me I was boring.

I would be sleeping and he would start sex, and if I didn't want to, he would keep going. Or he'd come home drunk and be aggressive and I felt like I didn't have a choice. I was petrified. I would go blank. I was living like a victim.

School was a sanctuary. I confided in my friends.

After that women's studies class, I started therapy.

A couple of years into therapy, I was looking for an internship, so I went to the rape crisis center. They have a forty-hour program that trains students to become interns, and I became an intern, and then I moved from intern to employee.

I wanted to be an advocate: from victim to healer, healer to advocate. At the rape crisis center, I realized that an advocate is the first person a survivor can trust—before the police or their friends or even family. That was very important to me, to be that person someone could trust, because for years I couldn't trust anybody.

I started doing workshops at Fresno State on sexual assault. It was the right timing because, nationally, the White House was getting involved in the issue. Within six months, I was able to help at least five hundred people. We had conversations. People were moved. At the end of those six months, I put together two or three forty-hour trainings, and at least sixty more people became advocates. That was amazing. The rape crisis center started offering internships and scholarships for the women's studies department.

When I finally broke off with my boyfriend, it was not easy. It took seven tries to leave him. I had dated him from the time I was twenty until I was twenty-three, and I was in a cycle of violence. I was going to therapy

> **We both agree it was abusive. I wonder about men's mental health. He tells me he wants to be different and doesn't know how.**

the entire time and trying to graduate. I told him I needed to go to school; the way I framed it was that I wanted to continue with my schooling and was not ready to settle down. I also finally said the relationship was abusive. Now that time has passed and I see him, we both agree it was abusive. I wonder about men's mental health. He tells me he wants to be different and doesn't know how. I tell him to go to therapy.

I've been single since that relationship. I'm dating now but I'm not in a relationship.

Ending that abusive relationship was the beginning of the healing process for me. After that, I became president of People Organized for Women Empowerment and Representation. I started working with Planned Parenthood, because we started giving students information about reproduction and women's health. I had utilized services from Planned Parenthood when I was dating my first boyfriend. Also, when I was working with survivors of rape I would refer them to Planned Parenthood when the survivors didn't want their families to know they had been raped, and of course Planned Parenthood offers confidentiality.

I ended up with two degrees—psychology and women's studies. And my life is so different. The people who surround me are better. My friends are better; my job is better.

I now work at the Leadership Counsel for Justice and Accountability. We advocate for disadvantaged rural communities in the Central Valley of California. People are losing their jobs, drinking bad water, living in crowded conditions.

Rape in the fields is horrible for women. To work in the fields, they often have to do a sexual favor. Women who work in the fields call it "the green motel." They know what they're gonna go through: sexual favors to work there, and being raped in the fields.

The Central Valley of California produces food for much of the country, like corn, almonds, peaches, oranges, and strawberries. And yet people have no idea what these women go through.

I want to go back and get a master's degree in either global affairs or women's studies and then become a family therapist. My goal is to have my own practice or my own nonprofit that helps women, especially those who have been assaulted.

I tell everybody I meet that if they can, they need to take at least one women's studies class: it will help you feel empowered.

Women's studies and therapy built me.

Everybody heals differently. Therapy is not the way everybody heals. Some people heal through art, some people heal through advocacy, some by empowering others. For me, being an advocate meant I was healing. If I could be an advocate, it meant I was strong again and I could help others. "Victim to

> **Everybody heals differently. Therapy is not the way everybody heals.**

healer, and healer to advocate." From the moment my professor said that, it became part of my evolution. I wasn't a victim anymore.

JEREMIAH WHITTINGTON

Fabiana Diaz with teal forks representing nearly six thousand survivors on the University of Michigan campus at the time.

The Teal Forks Timeline

FABIANA DIAZ

3:53 a.m.

It was hard enough trying to fall asleep. Now, I seem to be waking up every hour, tossing and turning, my brain on fire. I know it isn't illegal, and we did mention it to Vice President Royster Harper, and she even gave us the money we used to fork the Diag, the most central location on our campus, where at least ten thousand students walk every day. So there's no way we can get in trouble for this, right?

4:57 a.m.

I might as well get up; my alarm is going to go off in three minutes, anyway. It's still pitch-black outside. Perfect. Forking the Diag. How are we going to do it—only seven of us, with our buckets of teal forks? One thousand two hundred forks in all, each fork representing approximately five sexual assault survivors on campus. Anna did the math—that was Anna's job. Anna, my co-coordinator for this project and my partner in crime.

5:05 a.m.

I shower, thinking about the number—5,806 survivors. The fact that we have almost six thousand survivors on this campus is a scary thought, but not shocking. It makes sense. One in four women is a survivor of sexual assault by the time she graduates. I never thought that I would become a statistic.

5:37 a.m.

Dressed in black, rain boots on, and it's only drizzling outside. As I rush out of my room, scarfing down a banana, I realize I forgot the signposts. The key to this project! If people saw more than a thousand teal forks without any explanation, I would just be getting weird looks.

6:00 a.m.

Everyone is on time. We gather around, hand out buckets, and I yell, "Let's go!" As my knees drop to the cold, wet ground, I begin to fork. The first one is for me. The next one is for my sister. The one after that is for my mom. Next, for my best friend. And then one for my coworker. For my resident. For my roommate. I have someone in particular on my mind each time I drive a fork into the ground. The pain comes in a wave, but the empowerment I feel pushes the pain right out. Holding back tears, I look around. Rain starts to pour down, but everyone keeps on forking. As more and more students arrive to help, I feel I'm swimming in a pool of survivors, and for once I do not feel alone.

7:53 a.m.

Students starting their normal routine—coffee in one hand, phones attached to the other—begin to look up and assess their surroundings. A couple wander over to read the signposts (good thing I went back for them). Then I see this young student who looks a bit lost or maybe sleepy. We make eye contact and she walks toward me. As I slowly get up, she kneels down, grabs a fork, whispering, "For me," and bursts into tears. I embrace and hold her as we sit on the grass, sobbing. Two strangers, united through painful memories and emerging, stronger, from the pain.

8:25 a.m.

We exchange numbers and I mention that the following night there's a free screening of the movie *The Hunting Ground,* with two UNC survivors who began the Title IX work and the producer of the movie in attendance. She thanks me and says she'll be there. I realize that this project is bigger than me, and I feel overwhelmed with emotions. I am furious. I am defeated. I am exhilarated.

9:17 a.m.

"What is all this for?" some student asks. As I walk toward him with my pen and paper in hand, I do not know what to expect. He seems distraught. I tell him what the forks stand for, adding that one in six men will be assaulted in his lifetime.

"That is not true!" he yells back. I am shocked by his reaction and freeze for a second. I feel that if I inquire further I will be prying, but if I don't, he might be offended because I didn't care enough to ask.

I take a deep breath and ask the only question I can think of: "How are you?"

"I just didn't think that was possible. I did not think [my guy friend] could have been telling me the truth," he responds, gulping back tears. I hug him and say, "The survivor's journey is never-ending, and you can choose to be a part of it still. It's never too late."

He thanks me and asks if there are any resources on campus. I tell him about all the student organizations doing amazing work, including SAPAC, the Sexual Assault Prevention Awareness Center. My emotions catch up with me and tears start to trickle down my cheek. Meagan, another coordinator, runs to me with a box of tissues, holds me, and stands in silence with me. I think that sometimes what's hardest for my friends and family is to know how to engage me. I can't speak for all survivors, but from my experience, words cannot always encompass what it means to be a survivor. We are not so much victims of the crimes committed against us as lonely survivors of a sexual war on our bodies and minds.

11:58 a.m.

I decide to sit on a bench and just observe without interacting. The bell tower strikes noon; students pour out of the building. A few hover over the signposts, reading. I see a group of women approach the signs, then drop to their knees and make the sign of the cross. I walk by to hear their prayer.

"The Lord is with thee," they pray in unison. I kneel down and join my prayers with theirs. "In the name of the Father, the Son, the Holy Spirit. Amen."

Then I introduce myself. They share their experiences and say that prayer and faith have helped them overcome what they've been through. That's great for them. As for me, my experience pushed me away from "God" and made me question my twelve years of Catholic school. I questioned it all.

1:10 p.m.

It's time to type up all my notes in detail before I forget any of my interactions or experiences throughout these difficult hours. As I type, everything seems to flow. I realize how much of this process has been healing. For once, I was forced to react and let my emotions be, instead of holding them all back. I let myself feel.

3:07 p.m.
The unexpected happens. As I sit in front of my computer, in the middle of the fishbowl—the computing library—I see him. My assailant. I don't think he sees me right away. My first thought is to get out as quickly as I can. My heart rate is increasing, my blood is boiling. I have fought back tears before, but never this hard. *Don't let him see me cry.* He does see me, though, and this turns into a game of cat and mouse for him. He taunts me, coming right up behind me, without saying a word. I freeze. Looking up, I see him in front of me, with only a 21.5-inch iMac separating us. It isn't enough for him. He needs to get more out of me, as if what he's done already is not enough. He decides that out of all the 250 computers, he needs to sit at the one right next to me. I realize in this moment how much he has altered my life. How every day I make decisions based on that night. My first night on campus. I was naïve, high on my newfound freedom, and felt like I had the whole world at my fingertips, until he forced himself onto me, slammed my face into the dorm room mattress, and left me there, alone and naked. But now, enough is enough. I decide to bear it through. I want to be the cat and he can be the mouse. I feel it becoming uncomfortable for him. Uncomfortable. After everything, that is the least I can make him feel.

11:53 p.m.
For 5,806 survivors, 1,200 teal forks. They healed me.

Then Came Activism

A Chorus

———

I got involved with advocacy work at the university.
There were ways it needed to improve.

My assault was handled very publicly. I used that public-ness as
my way to be open about it and to help others.

I am starting out in business communications and marketing, but
I would love to help men and women get the help they need.

April is Sexual Assault Awareness Month, and we had an event on
campus called "Speak Out." We kept a blog, and anybody could
post an anonymous testimonial. Then every year we would collect
those and members of our group would read them out loud on
campus. It was an organized event, with food, music, and advocates
in case someone got triggered. There was an open mic at the end
so people could share. It was one of my favorite events. The hardest
night, but a healing night.

Activism looks different. It looks different every day. Getting up and
doing anything at all is activism for me.

I wanted to do something, to have a voice. I was on the philanthropy
committee at my sorority. Our philanthropy was domestic violence.
I felt like it was my way of helping people who had been through
situations similar to mine. Working on that committee—that's
when I got my rhythm back.

I'm glad I encouraged my friend to get justice in her life.

Working on myself is the hardest thing I've ever done.
Learning how to accept myself and not hate myself is the
biggest thing. That right now is my activism.

I've come to terms with the fact there's nothing I can do regarding
the assault. I've experienced this gross injustice and I'm not able to
do anything. But it's not okay what they did. Until I do something I
don't think I'm going to get over it.

So after I was assaulted I threw myself into activist work.
That summer, while I was working at the rape crisis center,
one of my good friends opened up to me as a survivor.
She had never told anybody.

My worst fear after being assaulted wasn't that it would happen
again, but that someone I knew was going to have to go through
it. I would think, "If something's gonna happen, let it be to me
because I'm already sort of broken. I don't want them hurt."

We spoke to the police, and we were able to get more sexual
assault awareness training for the campus police. We also got the
school's health center to prescribe Plan B.

It was very important to me, to be that person someone could trust,
because for years I couldn't trust anybody.

I'm now trying to mind my own business and trying to graduate.

When I was a sophomore, I became very involved in an event called
"Consent Day." We would teach students about consent—what it is

and how to obtain it. Of course, the event had free condoms, so that was the incentive for pretty much everyone (especially the guys) to show up. Regarding consent, it is very important to know yourself before starting a conversation with anyone else about what you want. If you like to be kissed, but maybe not touched certain places, that is more than okay! It is *always okay* to stop. You are 100 percent allowed to stop or take a break at any point in any physical interaction with a partner. It may sound simple, but it's true. You only have to do what you want to do—nothing more.

I started working with Planned Parenthood, because we started giving students information about reproduction and women's health. Also, when I was working with survivors of rape I would refer them to Planned Parenthood when the survivors didn't want their families to know they had been raped, and of course Planned Parenthood offers confidentiality.

Advocacy has become my new thing. I want this guy to come to justice, but in nine years, nothing has changed in the whole system. The bathroom is apparently a common place to rape. And these guys convince and coerce the same way. Are they reading a book? How come it's so pervasive? I want it to be over for everyone rather than just find some kind of sanity for myself.

I want to give that guy or that girl who reads this book that same feeling of "Oh my gosh, some girl knows what I'm feeling." I want to be that person in someone's life. I want to give back.

The Professor

SOME NOTES ON MY EXPERIENCE

KATIE ROSE GUEST PRYAL

You decide who touches you.

We have a cat named Richard. When we got her, she was only three weeks old, abandoned by her owners, and we picked out a name we liked. Turned out she was a girl. But we couldn't change her name at that point.

The kids are really good with her and she with them. But sometimes she doesn't want to play. So I say to the boys, "Does it seem like Richard wants to be petted right now? Does Richard get to decide who touches her? Yes, she does, just like you. She's in charge of her body, and you're in charge of yours."

Even now at ages four and six, they don't have to hug people they don't want to hug. I want them to grasp this idea of bodily autonomy.

Remember: *you get to decide who touches you.*

How my career took shape.

I graduated from Duke and got a master's in creative writing from Johns Hopkins. Then I went back to law school at the University of North Carolina, passed the bar, and worked as a lawyer while I also worked through my doctoral program in English.

I finished my Ph.D. in 2007 and started working at UNC as a professor. At first I taught English and also law; then, after a few years, I went to the law school full-time as a law professor. After a few years, I got promoted.

I remember that day clearly. My niece was born, Nelson Mandela died, and I got promoted. Everybody said, "Congratulations!" And I was like, "Oh, my gosh, I'm so unhappy." Sometimes it takes getting exactly what we think we want to show us that we really don't want it at all.

I took an unpaid leave of absence, and that leave made it clear I didn't want to go back. So now I write full-time and do consulting.

I was raped in graduate school. Here's how it happened.

I was dating a person, and we were on the verge of breaking up, but I still really liked him. I was supposed to fly and go see him the next day. But there was this other guy I'd known a long time, a graduate student at UNC. He was really smart, really charming.

I was hanging out with him and others at a bar one night. I remember saying to my friend, "I'm going home with him." My friend said, "Really?" and I said, "Yup, I don't care. I'm so annoyed with the guy I'm supposed to be dating."

I was in a relationship with this person who didn't live anywhere near me. But meanwhile there was this really great guy who could be something more, who was closer to me in age, and who wanted to hang out right now. I didn't think we would have sex; I thought we'd just watch TV and go to sleep. I had done that many times with other guys.

It didn't have to turn into something so ugly.

So I left with X. (That's what I'll call him.) My friend at the bar expressed worry, but I was like, "No, I'm fine!" I wasn't a kid, I was close to thirty. I knew I was drunk, but I thought things would be fine. Why wouldn't they be? We all knew each other. We'd known each other for years.

I remember X not talking to me at all in the car. I remember thinking that was weird. This funny sweet guy from the bar disappeared as soon as we got in the car.

Once we got to his apartment, I couldn't walk. I couldn't open my door or undo my seat belt. He had to help me out. We entered his place through a sliding glass door that had a lip to it, and I tripped over it and fell on the carpet. When I fell, I burst out laughing. He said, "Shut up. My brother is sleeping."

His words were really harsh.

After he spoke to me, I was like, okay, fine, this guy's an asshole. I proceeded to stretch out on the carpet and go to sleep. My attitude was, "Fuck you, go upstairs to bed without me. I'll just sleep here."

But he picked me up and got me upstairs to his bedroom. He had a giant bed. I said, "Excellent," and plopped onto the bed fully clothed, with shoes. I was instantly asleep.

He woke me by grabbing my feet and pulling off my shoes. He was standing at the foot of the bed, naked. Then he grabbed my pants and yanked. I remember hanging on to my underwear with both hands. I hung on to my underwear and said "No" the whole time he was touching me.

He took my shirt off. Then he pulled my bra off without unclipping it, and I remember how violent that felt—my unclipped bra got caught on my hair, my earrings, my face. He just ripped the bra over my head. And I was this floppy thing. I could barely sit up. He was holding me up

> I was drunk, but I thought things would be fine. Why wouldn't they be? We all knew each other. We'd known each other for years.

with one hand and tearing my shirt and my unclipped bra over my head with the other.

I don't own that shirt anymore. I gave it away.

He was bigger than me, and I was still holding on to my underwear with both hands, hanging on for dear life. He flipped me over. Put an elbow in my back, tore my underwear to the side, and raped me from the back with my underwear still on. I do remember he used a condom.

I passed out.

The next day I remember I woke up to the daylight and sounds of birds. Everything hurt. I was so sick—there are no words for how sick I felt.

> I was so sick—there are no words for how sick I felt.

I can't remember asking X for a ride but I must have done so. Somehow I got home, got my bag, went to the airport, and got on a plane.

I vomited the entire plane ride, until I was dry heaving. The flight attendant was so nice to me. And I was trying to be funny, too, making jokes about being airsick. But I'd never really thrown up from drinking or from flying, so I wondered if I had food poisoning.

Sitting there, on that plane, I was thinking inane thoughts. "Wow, what did I eat? Was it the crab cakes?"

How about, "I was brutalized for the last six hours?"

When did the reality that I was raped hit me?

Right away. No doubt in my mind. I was lying there, holding my underwear, yelling, "No!"

But I didn't report him.

I was raped off campus. I didn't know who to report it to. I could cancel my flight, get a rape kit, report to a doctor? No way.

Also, I have a psychiatric disability: bipolar disorder. I was diagnosed when I was twenty-one. In my mind, the prosecutor would say, "We can't believe anything she says."

Another reason: I was raped before, when I was thirteen.

After I was raped the second time, I thought, "Am I doomed to be a victim forever?" The next day, at the airport, I called a friend and said, "I can't believe I'm a person who was raped twice. What does that say about me?"

Then my brain shut off. I put it away. I had other things to do—I was busy, I had to finish my doctorate in three years! And luckily I never saw my rapist again.

Years later, I decided to report.

I didn't report it to the police, only to the university. I wanted to have it counted. And I finally had enough cultural capital where I felt like I wouldn't feel demeaned.

I thought I had nothing to lose, but I was wrong.

Reporting was awful.

Here's how it went:

In July 2014, I decided I was going to report.

So I called, and it took four or five people to get me to the right office at UNC, an office where someone could take my report.

The whole time I was thinking, "If I weren't me, if I weren't a law professor at this university, if I were a scared eighteen-year-old, when would I give up?" There were so many hurdles I had to cross. The website was so bad I couldn't find anything. There was no "If you have been raped, call this number," except to call 911. And I didn't want to call 911.

Was the website hurdle too high? I think it was too high for 50 percent of the population. Then UNC would lose another 25 percent with the phone tag I had to play. I finally reached the guy, and he told me to come back next Tuesday. That waiting period? Having to wait so many days, UNC would lose all but 5 percent of rape survivors who want to report.

So as I got ready to go to the Title IX office, I put on a nice dress, nice shoes. I wanted to look, literally, as powerful and forbidding as possible. I'm a law professor. I have a Ph.D. I introduced myself to the reception-ist on the phone as "Dr. Pryal." My reporting experience, I believed, was going to be very different from that of the undergraduates who feel so powerless in the face of these administrators.

I wondered, "Why is it that I am meeting with a white guy? Was there not a woman available to fill this role? They couldn't find a single woman to do this job?"

I was going to talk about one of the most deeply personal events of my life with a white male who, given his biology, could not have had my experience. He was not a woman who had been raped by a man, and never could be. As I was ush-ered into an office with windows instead of walls, and with other people milling around outside, I felt totally exposed.

> I wondered, "Why is it that I am meeting with a white guy? Was there no woman available to fill this role?"

Before going to UNC that day, I had written a detailed statement because I didn't want to describe the play-by-play of my rape aloud. I handed this man the paper. After he read it, he said, "Where was your assailant's apartment?" I said, "I don't know." I was super poised. I knew that if you get too emotional, they might think you're nuts, especially if (like me) you have a major mental illness.

Then he told me that my reporting would likely not have any effect on anything because my rape had happened so long ago. And because the location was unclear, his department wouldn't be able to tell if the university had responsibility for it or not. I knew he was talking about Clery stuff. He didn't mean to be harsh. But I still felt like I'd been gut-punched.

My whole point in going through the reporting process was to get it on the books that a rape happened, perpetrated by a UNC student. But nope, it turns out that my coming forward was likely all for nothing. Hearing his words was really demoralizing. I'd dredged up the horrible memories for nothing. I'd shared them with this stranger for nothing. I felt weak, and I felt totally naked.

Depression set in. My suicide attempt was a few months later.

Was my depression triggered by the experience of reporting my rape?

I can't speak to that. I do know that I wrote about the experience of reporting my rape shortly after I reported, and that the experiences of reporting and then writing took a lot out of me. The piece was "Being Counted: Reporting My Rape at a School Under Title IX Investigation," published on *The Toast*. After writing that piece, I was a wreck for a week.

Later, I wrote another piece for *The Toast* about attempting suicide, "A Mother's Suicide Attempt and the Guilty Burden of Statistics." As with the first piece, writing this second piece was very draining.

So why write?

I think it's important to talk about breaking taboos. The taboos around both those topics—rape and suicide—need to be broken. I'm an activist and writer, and I wanted to help other people by sharing my story. That's why.

How can the Title IX offices at colleges and universities improve?

They could pull a page from rape crisis centers that take a holistic approach to caring for survivors. Forty percent of people who have experienced sexual assault will develop serious psychiatric disabilities as a result of their assault, and those people often have no resources.

But the campus Title IX office has two goals: to protect the university and to make sure the university complies with Title IX. Therefore, that office's ultimate goal is not to help rape survivors if helping rape survivors doesn't align with those two goals—and often the two do not align.

Title IX offices often send survivors on their way even when survivors need more services than that office can provide. There's no follow-up, no connection between the Title IX office and Title II, which is the disability office.

Title IX offices need to be proactive. If you made it all the way to the Title IX office, they should make sure to add a simple question: "Do you mind if we have someone from the disability support office give you a call?" That student could get a call in two weeks. If it turns out that she hasn't left her room in two weeks, someone will know there's a problem.

A trained person could go to her room and provide guidance. Don't wait until she's flunked out of her classes. Give her a two-week phone call, three-month phone call, six-month phone call. We don't think about how trauma is waiting in the wings. Which speaks to suicide.

> **Give her a two-week phone call, three-month phone call, six-month phone call.**

After I kissed my children good-bye, dressed in dark clothes, and walked into traffic to die, I kept my suicide attempt a secret, from my husband, from everybody, from my amazing psychiatrist. I had to ask myself, "Why are you keeping a secret from people who take care of you and love you?"

I sat down and figured out why, and then told everybody: I had been afraid. I'd been afraid my doctor would commit me involuntarily. I didn't want cops to show up at my house with shackles. And that happens. So I said to my doctor, "I don't trust you to not commit me," and she said, "All right, here's a plan." And we made a plan for the future, for when I'm depressed, so I won't be afraid to tell her things.

I was afraid my husband wouldn't love me anymore. And that sounds so stupid to say out loud now. I'd thought, "If I'm dead, he can find someone who is less trouble than I am, who is a better mom and a better wife." That's a depressed brain's thoughts.

Now we talk about my depressed and suicidal feelings. He can get more proactive without me being annoyed. We struck a deal: I don't get to be pissed off when he asks about my moods, and he promises to ask more often.

I've told him, "As soon as I get these feelings in the slightest sense, I want to tell you right away."

You have to pull the fire alarm right away. If you wait until later, it gets worse. Worse and worse.

As soon as you have that first ugly thought, pull the alarm, tell somebody. But you have to have a team and you have to have a plan. People you trust. A support system.

I've thought about keeping my suicide attempt a secret from my sons. Would that protect them? Now I think not. I tried to die because there was no one I could tell. And there was no one I could tell because suicide was taboo.

And I feel that removing the taboo-ness will help solve the problem.

If one of my kids is in high school or college and hears that a girl was raped, I hope his reaction is, "Who's helping her? Who took her to the hospital?" I want him to run toward her, with a gentle, helping spirit, instead of backing away with disgust. They can learn that through me. It's my job as their mom to teach them.

Someday, their father and I are going to have that conversation with them. And when I tell them about my rape, I hope the message they learn is about having empathy, and that kindness is a rare and precious commodity.

Some days I go to bed a "survivor"
and wake up a "victim"; some days I go to
bed a "victim" and wake up a "survivor."

—Kamilah Willingham

Music affects us in ways prose cannot. Some of us associate certain songs with times in our lives, whether a romantic relationship, a high school graduation, or a breakup. The same is true for many survivors of sexual assault and abuse. Music helped get us through times when we felt isolated or needed to feel empowered. For example, one song that was on repeat for hours before we filed the complaint about the mishandling of our cases was "Titanium" by David Guetta, sung by Sia. As survivors started connecting to one another, we started to share the songs and playlists that helped get us through our processing and healing. Here is one example. You can also find it on Apple Music as "Songs for Survival" by Nastassja Schmiedt.

Songs for Survival

A PLAYLIST

A. LEA ROTH AND NASTASSJA SCHMIEDT

1. "Put Your Records On"—Corinne Bailey Rae
2. "Green Garden"—Laura Mvula
3. "I Need"—Maverick Sabre
4. "Til It Happens to You"—Lady Gaga
5. "If I Ever Feel Better"—Phoenix
6. "Hold On"—Good Charlotte
7. "Move Along"—All-American Rejects

8. "Let It Be" (long version)—Carol Woods, Timothy T. Mitchum

9. "Private Party"—India. Arie

10. "That's Alright"—Laura Mvula

11. "On My Way"—Axwell ∧ Ingrosso

12. "Battle Cry"—Angel Haze feat. Sia

13. "Q.U.E.E.N."—Janelle Monáe feat. Erykah Badu

14. "Hate On Me"—Jill Scott

15. "i"—Kendrick Lamar

16. "Powerful"—Empire Cast feat. Jussie Smollett and Alicia Keys

17. "I Choose"—India. Arie

18. "Fight Song"—Rachel Platten

19. "Heroes (We Could Be)"—Alesso feat. Tove Lo

20. "Sun Is Shining"—Axwell ∧ Ingrosso

I Am a Phoenix

BRENDA TRACY

I was born in Alaska in 1973. My parents divorced when I was one and a half, and my dad stayed in Alaska. I mainly grew up in the Salem, Oregon, area. My mom remarried when I was two. I went to Alaska every summer until I was twelve—rode the plane by myself, starting in the first grade. I carried a backpack with crayons and stuff. My dad remarried and had two boys.

My stepdad and my mom fought a lot. My mom yelled a lot. I was an only child, so I spent a lot of time in my room. I had a TV, cool wallpaper, and lots of toys. I was physically taken care of but emotionally neglected.

When I was nine, my stepdad got sober. He told me, "I'm sorry. I have a sickness, and I'm going to get help." My mom and stepdad started going to AA, and to church and to Al-Anon. And they started being involved parents.

I had been a latchkey kid, but our next-door neighbor, a high school girl named Amy, became my babysitter.

Amy had a boyfriend who would sneak over after my parents left. One night something woke me, and I saw Amy's boyfriend standing next to my bed. He tore the blankets off and lay on top of me. I had on a long flannel nightdress that buttoned to my neck and had ruffles. He tried to rip the nightgown off me and it wouldn't come off because it was buttoned. I remember extreme burning pain and not being able to breathe because he was lying on top of me and I was pinned inside my nightgown. To this day if I get stuck in something I'm wearing, I panic. I don't know where Amy was. I don't remember him saying anything during the rape. I was very afraid of him. He lived down the street. There were times when I walked home from the bus, he'd be standing in the window watching me walk by. His expression was like, "You better not say anything or I will kill you."

Somewhere along the line, I decided the rape didn't happen. We moved out of that neighborhood when I was about eleven. I thought, "I don't see him anymore, so I can be a normal kid. I don't have to be afraid anymore." But I was still afraid.

When I was twelve, two things happened that brought it all back. The first was that I was riding my bike down the street and a car slowed as it came toward me and I looked and it was him. We locked eyes for a second, and I knew it was him and I panicked. I looked behind me and I saw brake lights. I rode home as fast as I could. When I got home I broke a Coke bottle and started furiously scratching my wrists and my inner forearms. The cuts ranged from superficial to a little deeper than that; bleeding, though not enough to require medical attention. But I felt like my body was exploding. I didn't know what to do.

> We locked eyes for a second, and I knew it was him and I panicked.

Shortly after that, I saw a movie on TV called *Something About Amelia*, with Ted Danson. In the movie, Amelia was being molested by her father. Amelia had the same type of nightgown that I'd had when I was nine, and it triggered me. My friend across the street came over and I was crying and upset and I told her I'd been raped. So she brought her mom over, and then her mom told my mom. The next day my mom called the Salem police and made a report. I remember thinking this was a big, big deal; my life was gonna change.

A few days later my mom said, "Brenda, I'm sorry, nothing can be done. The statute of limitations is up."

After that, I became an angry, rebellious child. I started running away. I went back to that place I had learned to be in: alone, by myself, and It Didn't Happen. School was where people loved me—the teachers loved me. I did well in my classes. I tried to excel where I was accepted and loved. I kept my chin down. I played basketball and volleyball.

But there was something very sexualized about me from a young age. A family member who I saw once in a while was very inappropriate with me from when I was two until the age of five. I had a very warped sense of what love was.

In my senior year of high school, I met Antwan. I felt like this was it. I was in love. We had sex right away. It was the first time I'd ever had consensual sex. I immediately got pregnant. I wanted my baby; I wanted to feel that connection of love.

I got really sick during my first trimester. Started skipping school. Didn't tell anyone. But eventually the school called my mom and said, "We're dropping Brenda from the roster."

My mom said, "Are you pregnant?" I said yes, and she and my stepdad started crying. I told them I wanted to keep the baby, and they said, "Okay, we will help you." I couldn't believe it. I thought they would be angry and hate me.

I was supposed to graduate in June 1992.

One of my teachers was angry with me for getting pregnant and wouldn't let me make up the work I missed during my first trimester. I was half a credit short of graduating. They allowed me to walk, but I didn't really graduate.

I had my son Darius in November.

Antwan stayed around. He drank and did drugs and would get violent when he drank. He wasn't violent when he was sober but, when he drank would kind of torture me. He'd keep me awake all night, kick me or pinch me or pull my hair. He used to bite me, terrorize me. But I felt like I had to marry him. We got married when I was nineteen. The night before, I cried and cried.

One night he was passed out, and he was gurgling. Vomit was coming out of his mouth. I remember thinking, "I could just let him die." I was really contemplating that, and then I heard, "Mommy, what's wrong with Daddy?" Darius was standing over Antwan. So I ran over and turned Antwan onto his side.

I had another son with Antwan, Devante. I didn't want Darius to be alone. I had grown up alone. I thought, "Maybe if he has a brother he'll be okay."

The final straw was when Antwan threw a remote at me, and Darius, who was three or four, said, "Daddy, don't hurt my mommy!" Antwan looked at Darius for a second, then said, "Fuck it, I'm out of here." Darius looked at me and said, "You bitch, I hate you!" He was saying what he'd heard his dad say.

I was done with Antwan. I packed and moved in with my parents. I was twenty-two. I got a restraining order.

I went into a depression. I had two children, a failed marriage, no high school diploma, no job, and I was on welfare. Then I met a friend, Karmen, and we wanted to hang out and have fun, so we started going to clubs. I needed to be in control, so I didn't do drugs or drink, but I was promiscuous; my attitude was "I'm going to use you. I'm going to use you before you use me."

In October 1997 I met this

> I went into a depression. I had two children, a failed marriage, no high school diploma, no job, and I was on welfare.

football player, Anthony. He went to Oregon State. And we had an immediate connection. I stopped sleeping around. Anthony graduated. Then in June 1998, when I was twenty-four, I went with my friend Karmen to visit her boyfriend's apartment. The boyfriend was one of Anthony's teammates. There were five guys in all there. Karmen went into the back bedroom with her boyfriend. The other four guys drugged me and I was gang-raped, for hours.

The next morning I woke up on the floor, a blanket from the couch halfway thrown over me. I had a used condom stuck to my stomach, chips all over me, dried vomit in my hair, and gum stuck in there, too. I felt like a piece of garbage.

One of the men walked up and said, "Are you going to suck me off now?" I said no, and then Karmen and I left, and I fell apart.

Karmen called my mom, and my mom came to my side.

We went to the women's crisis center. The nurse there suggested I go to the hospital. I was in a lot of pain. We went to the Salem hospital. Mom was driving, holding her hands at ten and two, so stressed, and I remember looking at her and thinking there was no safety for me on this earth and that I hurt people. In that moment I decided the only answer was death.

I reasoned that my sons couldn't love me or respect me or be proud of me and that I brought my parents only pain, and that all I had ever known was abuse and pain. So I resolved that it was okay to die, that it would be better for everyone without me. I felt really calm. This was the answer to all that pain and suffering. I made this decision on the car ride to the hospital.

As a last wish for my mom, I agreed to do the rape kit. Jenny was my nurse. She didn't look at me like I was gross. She was very warm, and kind, and she just looked at me like she loved me. I didn't understand how someone could look at me like I was beautiful. And in that moment I remember asking God, "What is the point of me being here?" And He said, "I want you to be a nurse and take care of your sons." Getting that answer was so deep and so profound.

During the rape kit exam I started asking Jenny, "So how did you become a nurse?" We ping-ponged back and forth during the entire exam. She'd pluck a pubic hair and I'd ask, "So where did you go to school?" She'd swab me and I'd ask, "How much does nursing school cost?"

Jenny didn't know I was suicidal, but by the time we were done with the exam, that had changed. By the time I got back into the car, I had decided I wanted to live. I turned to my mom and said, "Mom, you know what?" She was exhausted. We'd been there for hours. I said, "I'm gonna be a nurse."

Since I had decided to live, I wanted to press charges, so I needed to make a statement. We left the hospital and drove to the police and I made a statement. The next day, I pointed out the men and identified the apartment. The police arrested all four of them. They were booked.

The hospital report said, "This appears to be nonconsensual."

People started taking sides. Karmen showed up at my house and essentially said, "I will testify against you if you go to court." We never talked again. Anthony decided he wanted nothing to do with the trial. He said his friend didn't deserve to go to prison for twenty years.

I received two death threats over the phone. An older gentleman said my kids and I would be hurt. All four of the men arrested were athletes. One was recruited to UC Berkeley, two were from Oregon State, and the other guy played for a community college. They were all football players. The DA said it was a "he said, she said," and that there would be four separate trials. Based on that, and the backlash, and the fact I was traumatized and just wanted to go to nursing school, two weeks later I dropped the charges.

> I received two death threats over the phone. An older gentleman said my kids and I would be hurt.

Still, I wanted some kind of justice. So I went to Oregon State and talked to a sexual assault counselor there. I didn't want these men to do this again. I was told that the university took my concerns "very seriously." I left there that day feeling like they were going to do what they were supposed to do. Meanwhile, in the athletics department, the football coach gave the two Oregon men a one-game suspension. (And the university required that they perform twenty-five hours of community service, but I didn't know this until years later.)

I was angry but tried to rationalize it. I went to nursing school and pretended everything was fine. I got my RN degree, then my bachelor's, then my master's in business and health care. I put a bunch of letters behind my name to prove my self-worth.

Getting my nursing degree—that was a joyous day. Getting that degree had been such a struggle, but having it was like winning the lottery. I went from being on welfare to making a lot of money all at once.

I felt like Jenny had given me the gift of life and compassion, and I wanted to pay it forward to my patients. I always remember that you don't know what a person's going through, and sometimes they just need someone to be compassionate. That's what I love so much about nursing: you get the opportunity to serve every day.

I got my first nursing job in 2003, not long after graduating. And nursing was my calling. But I was two different people. There was Professional Brenda, who was this success story, but behind the scenes I was suffering. I hated myself. After the rape, I stayed in a relationship with Anthony, off and on, for ten years. After what had happened to me, I figured no one else would want me.

I had nightmares and wanted to die and was angry because I couldn't. I resented my children because I couldn't die. I had a borderline eating disorder. I would binge and then starve myself. Take fat burners to wake up and sleeping pills to sleep. I had PTSD. To this day I can't have anybody behind me and I can't be in the dark.

Antwan, the father of my sons, has now turned his life around in many ways, but back then he drank and ended up in prison. Darius acted out. My mom had cancer. I went through bankruptcy. Then depression. There was always some kind of trial. I was working full-time and going to school. How did I get through it? I adopted that "Just Do It" slogan from Nike. Every day it was, "Get up: Just Do It. Take a breath: Just Do It."

Then, in 2010, I went to a business conference. On the weekend, they had a church service. I went, and I got saved.

One of the first things I heard was that I didn't have to be perfect for God to love me. I remember thinking, "Wow, God will love me the way I am." I started believing that with God, anything is possible. I started leaning on Him. But I was still not thinking my issues came from being raped.

Then that family member who had molested me when I was little died. I felt this sense of peace; then I felt guilty. Two weeks later I was watching the evangelist Joyce Meyer on TV, and she said, "If you bury anything alive, it will come screaming back at you from the grave."

I said, "Okay, God, what have I hidden and buried?" And God said, "You need to forgive that family member who molested you." At that moment, I saw a vision of me in a yellow dress on a porch. I was two, and he was tongue-kissing me. I got nauseous and vomited, and the floodgates opened. My life came crumbling down. I had a breakdown.

I got to the parking lot at work, but I couldn't get out of the car. My son had started going to a counselor. I called her and said, "Can I come see you?" She met with me and immediately said, "Go to the doctor and get medication and come see me every day or I am going to put you in a hospital." I wanted to die. I didn't want to be inside my own body. I wanted to peel off my old skin, but you can't—you can't get away from yourself.

That family member who molested me died in February and I started counseling at the end of March. I was forty. By August I started talking about the gang rape in counseling. I was ready to do whatever I needed to do to heal and get better.

I told my counselor that I had always hated myself for giving up on prosecuting the men for the gang rape. In the same breath I said, "But I went to the school and other women were saved because of me." And my counselor said, "Are you sure the school did something?" I said, "I assumed they did." And she said, "Hmmm."

She said, "Let's call them." So I called the Student Conduct Office and said who I was, that I was raped and that two of the rapists were Oregon State students, and that I wanted to know what the student code of conduct disciplinary action was. I said, "I have a police report if you need it." They said something about records and that they'd call me back.

A week later, I called again. That same day, a woman called me. She said she was from Oregon State. She said, "I haven't read all the emails, can you explain?" And I thought, "What emails?"

She said, "Why do you want this information? Are you planning to litigate?" And I said, "No, I'm in therapy and trying to heal." She mentioned FERPA, a student privacy law, and said she might have to ask my attackers to sign off on the records. She said something about her email not working and could I send the police report to her coworker's email. I felt like something was really sketchy and called my counselor and she said, "No, don't send in the report."

My counselor said, "Maybe we need to consult a lawyer." I looked up the name of the woman who had called me. She was a Title IX person at Oregon State. She was not from the Office of Student Conduct, and it was her boss that she wanted me to send the police report to. That was super sketchy to me. So I called three lawyers and all of them told me they couldn't help me, that I should just give the Title IX woman the police report and try to work with the school.

I felt victimized all over again.

I was frustrated and angry, so I decided to talk to Coach Mike Riley. He was the coach when the rape happened, then he left for the NFL, and then came back to Oregon State. I decided to write him a letter. I wanted him to understand how profoundly he had hurt me. So I Googled him. And all I found were articles about how great he was. This was a guy who had suspended players for one game for a gang rape. Then I found a 2011 article about one of his players being convicted of domestic violence; Riley gave the player a one-game suspension.

Very impulsively, I wrote to the reporter of that article. I wrote an angry email, telling him all that had happened to me and how nothing had happened to those men. I said, "Thanks for letting me vent," and signed it "Brenda." He emailed me back one minute later.

He was John Canzano, the head sportswriter for the *Oregonian*.

A week later, I met him in the lobby at his workplace, handed him my police report, and dumped my story on him. He said, "If you want to meet with Mike Riley, I will set that up for you, but if you want to tell your story, I will do that."

At the time I didn't think I had a story. I was surprised he was acting like I had something to say. He said, "You know you have a story, right?" I said, "Okay, but we have to put my name and my face on it. I don't want to be anonymous." He started investigating and calling people. This was September 2014, and the story came out in November.

During those three months, I was nervous and I was scared. I thought the article was just going to be a sports column. Then John called and said, "Normally my stories are twenty inches long. Yours is one hundred and seven inches." The *Oregonian* didn't want to cut it down. They ran it on the front page in a series of four articles, and it also appeared on their website, which is how I first saw it.

John texted me a few minutes after it went up and said, "The article is up. You're a hero." When I went online to read it, I immediately started to cry. I had to take deep breaths and stop a few times to get through it, but I called John, literally sobbing on the phone, thanking him. I remem-

> John texted me . . . and said, "The article is up. You're a hero."

ber specifically feeling like it was the very first time I didn't feel ashamed about what had happened to me. And even more important, I felt like my two lives were finally merging.

I became one person that day, in that moment that the world read about me. I had lived in a prison of shame and silence for so long. I had lived in the public as one person—Brenda the independent, put-together single mom and RN, and then behind the scenes there was the Brenda who was ashamed, depressed, and suicidal. But once my secret was out, it was liberating. I walked out of prison that day.

My plan was to *not* read the comments, because I knew I risked being attacked by the public. But John told me it was safe to read them, so I did, and there was an amazing outpouring of love. Reading those comments was a healing experience. It helped restore my faith in humanity, literally. I don't say that lightly. My life experiences have caused me to question humanity. Reading that first article was a deeply pivotal moment that set the course for my life's purpose and my destiny. I will always be grateful to John for what he did for me. He is my hero.

The Title IX woman from Oregon State had never called me back, but about a month after I talked to her, while John was reporting the story, she left me a voice mail and said, "Oh, Brenda, I realized I never called you back. Oregon State would love to help you." But it was too late. I didn't call her back.

> I became one person that day. . . . I had lived in a prison of shame and silence for so long. . . . But once my secret was out, it was liberating. I walked out of prison that day.

All along, I had had the police report but I had never read it. Two months after being raped, I had started nursing school, and because I was depressed and failing my classes, I was put on academic probation, so I got the police report and sent it to the school and said, "Can you cut me some slack? I was just raped." And they did. After that I stuck the report in a manila envelope and never read it.

But when my story came out in the *Oregonian,* I finally read the report. Turns out, all the men had confessed to wrongdoing and had implicated each other. My account corroborated their accounts, from the condom to the white tank tops to the flashlight—the whole scene.

John had uncovered meetings between Oregon State and the DA and the police. The DA had misled me when the DA's office told me I had no case. Three years after my rape, the police destroyed my evidence. They had audiotapes of the men implicating each other and the DA had told the police to keep them, and they had destroyed them.

The athletic department officials had felt that my rape scandal would bury them. The school was in the hole financially. In 2001, my attackers went to the Fiesta Bowl.

So I politicized my pain. I've helped pass three bills, including one to double the statute of limitations for rape in Oregon. Coach Riley issued an apology. The president of Oregon State, Ed Ray, came forward and apologized on behalf of the university.

I've been hired as a consultant at Oregon State. One of the first things I did was to go there for Take Back the Night. That was in April 2015. Somewhere between five hundred and eight hundred people showed up. (The year before, forty people had shown up.) I spoke, and a basketball coach, Rachi Wortham, spoke after me. They've really embraced me and asked me to be a part of what they're doing. I talk to all the athletic programs. Recently, I told my story to every male and female athlete at Oregon State. There are 520 of them.

I'm still nursing. I'm a coordinator for a mobile dialysis team. I do treatments and oversee the team.

And more than ever, I'm focusing on education. But the right kind. We need to stop trying to educate women about how to prevent their own rape and engage the men. Women can't stop rape. If we could we would have already done it. There are good men out there, but they're not speaking up and doing their part. And we're not paying enough attention to the men who are speaking out.

PHOTOGRAPHY BY AJAY

Brenda Tracy and her sons, Darius Adams, twenty-two, left, and Devante Adams, twenty-one, on the right. "We were at a gala in May of 2015 for the nonprofit foundation Sparks of Hope. They help children who have been sexually abused. I was given the advocacy award."—Brenda Tracy

Riley coaches in Nebraska now, so I'll go there to talk to his team. I'm hoping to get Nike engaged in some campaigns. How do you get to men? Through sports. How do you get to men through sports? Nike.

I'm still a single mom, with two college-age boys. My boys were really nervous when the story came out. But they supported me. When there was such an outpouring of support, so many people saying, "Your mom's courageous," they felt the love from the community. They had carried some of my shame. When I became free, they became free, too. They're very proud of me, and I've seen a lot of healing.

Now I think, "It *happened* to me; I didn't *do* anything." I'm not going to carry around the shame of the men who hurt me. I did that for a long,

long time. I'm giving them back that case of bricks: "You take this shame. It's not mine anymore. You can carry it around."

In May 2014, at the capitol in Salem, Oregon, I was testifying in support of a bill, a resource bill for college students. If you're sexually assaulted on campus, the school has to tell you what your rights are. I was testifying, saying that if I had known what my rights were, my life could have been very different. I spoke of how I struggled for sixteen years and wanted to kill myself. And I realized at that moment that I don't think about dying anymore; I think about living and helping others. I thought, "Wow, I haven't thought about killing myself in six months." Somehow, the love within me was finally out-tipping the hate. Love for myself was finally tipping the scales.

PART V

DECLARATIONS OF INDEPENDENCE

I believe that telling our stories, first to ourselves and then to one another and the world, is a revolutionary act. It is an act that can be met with hostility, exclusion, and violence. It can also lead to love, understanding, transcendence, and community. There's nothing more powerful than truly being and loving yourself.

—Janet Mock, *Redefining Realness: My Path to Womanhood, Identity, Love & So Much More*

What we've been through doesn't define us, and we are fighting back.

Some of us hold protests, some of us go to the press, and some must work within the safety of silence.

We are trying to dismantle systems that operate as if our circumstances of sexual assault are statistically inevitable.

Some of us have moved past the daily reminders of our trauma; for others, simply getting out of bed in the morning is an act of defiance, resisting the visible and invisible aggressions that put us in the position of writing these declarations.

We will not allow the current oppression of women, people of color, and LGBTQ-identified individuals to continue. Our acts of resistance, simultaneously boldly public and intentionally private and everywhere in between, have value.

We declare our independence from the oppression that silences us.

We are using our words and sharing our lived experiences as tools to chip away at the status quo.

We need both legislative action and cultural change to end sexual violence. But we cannot legislate cultural change. Through everyday activism, we collectively change the way people talk about survivors of sexual violence. Through consciousness raising, we change the vocabulary of our legislators, our college presidents, our school board members, our families, and our friends.

We know change takes time. And we stand on the shoulders of those who came before us, those who offered and invented the language for us to share our stories.

Our activism is our storytelling. And our activism is not over.

What follows is Chloe Allred's artistic statement for a self-portrait, Rape, *pictured on page 79 of this book.*

Statement from the Artist on Doing a Self-portrait About Rape

When I woke up, I didn't know where I was. Somebody's hands were on my body, groping my breasts and stomach, running between my legs and inside me. I didn't know how long they had been doing this or what else they had done to me. I shifted my body, stirring. The hands froze, they shrank away. Details surfaced in my mind: I was at my friend's house. I had stayed the night after a party because I didn't think it would be safe to walk home late at night. A guy who I thought was a creep had slept behind me that night. He invaded and violated my body while I slept. I confronted him that morning and he pretended not to know what I was talking about.

At first, I tried to forget what had happened. But I couldn't. A deep repulsion churned in my stomach. Just months before, my aunt had been raped and murdered in a park that I'd frequented as a kid. The grief from her death weighed heavily on me. The man who killed her had committed many atrocities on other women. He had slipped through the cracks of the legal system, ending with my aunt.

The violation of my body left me feeling fragmented, numb. I wanted to address what had happened to me. I wanted to hold him accountable.

After two days I called the police and filed a report. The detective I met with told me that what happened to me was a form of rape. He was sorry but thought that little would happen legally because of the lack of evidence.

I told my friends about it. Some of them ignored what I had to say. This felt like a new violation. To not acknowledge my rape was to deny that my grief was valid. My true friends stuck by me, listened, and made sure to be a consistent presence in my life. I was raped. I will not feel guilty about that. I refuse to shut up or feel ashamed about something that I didn't do. The rapist did something horrible and should feel ashamed. I will not take that on for him.

Chloe Allred, *Winter, Plucked* (oil on canvas)

Tattoos

ANNIE CLARK

Much to my parents' chagrin, I got a tattoo; my first was in the summer of 2009, when I was doing an internship in Washington, D.C. I got a small female symbol, the one that comes from Greek mythology—it's said to be Venus's comb and mirror. I didn't tell anyone what my tattoo meant to me until much later, and often I had it covered up with a brace-let or a watch. I had contemplated getting "survivor" or something else in text, but while I wanted something purposeful, I didn't want some-thing obviously connected to sexual violence. With this tattoo, I could always say it symbolized my dedication to women's issues and equal rights instead of disclosing what it meant to me. My tiny tattoo was a reminder that I had survived something and that, though I wasn't over it, I was getting through it.

I got my second tattoo in January 2013, the day five of us filed two federal complaints with the U.S. Department of Education against the University of North Carolina at Chapel Hill. This time, my ink wasn't about marking my survival; it was the recognition of learning my rights

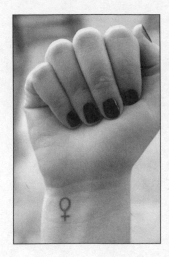 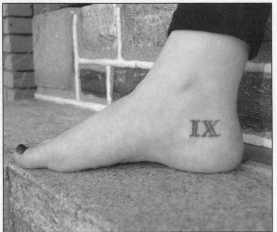

ANDREA PINO (BOTH PHOTOGRAPHS)

and fighting back. I wanted to hold the university I loved accountable for violating Title IX. Although my assault had occurred off campus, the treatment I received when I disclosed that crime for the first time to a campus employee meant that something had to change for UNC students. The quarter-sized "IX" on the inside of my right ankle represents taking a bold first step.

Lilly Jay adapted this piece from a speech she gave on September 19, 2014, introducing Vice President Joe Biden at the White House launch of the It's On Us initiative to raise awareness of campus sexual assault. It's On Us specifically encourages that bystanders intervene to prevent sexual assault.

Reclaiming College

LILLY JAY

Getting into college is difficult. Getting your college back, reclaiming it as your own after a sexual assault, is nearly impossible. I was raped a few weeks into my freshman year. I became a student by day and prey by night. For a year, I pantomimed learning, and I watched educational opportunities slip away.

The day I found out that the student who had assaulted me had raped someone else, I filed a disciplinary complaint against him. I joined survivors across the country in announcing our truth. My newfound activism seemed like a promising antidote to the loneliness of surviving assault. But the truth is, it didn't help me reclaim college.

Whether you're thinking about it because you're scared of the boy down the hall or because you're planning a meeting with the college president, recalling rape always hurts.

That's the terrible irony of sexual assault activism: using your experience to protect others from rape is so empowering, but it also tethers you to your pain. In order to be heard, I had to talk about the night in which violence silenced me.

When nonsurvivors step up and say, "I don't need to be hurt to care about assault," they give survivors permission to move our hearts from the edge of our sleeves back to where they belong. Hearing my friends, family, and professors say, "You don't need to stay hurt to convince us to care" freed me. That's when I got back my college experience.

Every moment or statement of support makes it easier for survivors to finally mourn for our younger selves and find reasons to love our communities again. Allies do more than prevent future assaults; they help carry the heavy truth that colleges are not safe, but they can and should be. Only nonsurvivors can ensure that when we look back, we can say that compassion, not trauma, changed the world.

School After

A Chorus

———

I dropped one of my classes because I had started having so many nightmares and panic attacks.

I didn't go to tutoring. I didn't leave my dorm. If I walked down the hall, people would look at me and stare. I could tell they knew.

I'd had Bs and I started getting Fs.

I dropped out.

For the most part I was always able to sleep, but I wouldn't go to bed until almost morning. Then I would sleep during the day.

I got behind on my thesis, got really depressed.

I kept running into my rapist on campus, so I left early.

I came back to school and kept trying to be normal and live a normal life, but I couldn't. I couldn't go to parties anymore.

I fell out of love with the school.

I went into group therapy at school. Most of us had been assaulted by other students. We were men, women, trans people.

So for now I'm taking summer classes. I'm going to
Bryn Mawr College, outside of Philadelphia, an all-women's
school. I'm excited about that.

This is my university just as much as it is his. I'm gonna go back.

I threw myself into my work and that numbed me out. I did a bunch
of Adderall and I did a bunch of work. I graduated.

My women's studies class was the pivot point in my life.
I was able to find the answers I had been looking for.

School was a sanctuary.

It's only because I love my university and feel like it's my home that
I can stay and try to make a difference.

I will graduate with him. I know a lot of people transfer. But I felt
that my leaving would be because of him, and that any new
environment would be tainted because of that outlook.

There are no awards at graduation that say, "This person got out
of bed and went to class every day, and followed up with therapy,
and took their medication."

I just feel very betrayed by my university, and so angry. Not just for
myself but for the other girls who go through this.

I'm going to graduate. I want that degree. I want to say,
"Screw them and all their attempts to make me feel low."

I graduated.

I ended up with two degrees—and my life is so different.

I don't know that I will finish the Ph.D. program, and it
doesn't matter as much. They tried to give me allowances but
the work requires you to be 100 percent focused,
and I've stopped feeling that. And I don't know if my brain is
100 percent there.

After two years, I talked to one of the detectives. She said she was
there the day I graduated, that she had to hold herself back from
running up to me and hugging me. She told me, "I was so proud of
you for sticking to your guns and graduating."

Dear Harvard: This Fight Is Not Over

ARIANE LITALIEN

Dear Harvard,

I am writing this piece as I sit in my own dining room, hundreds of miles away from the guy who pressured me into sexual activity in his bedroom one night in 2013. I do not know how to express the bitter-sweet taste of this moment in words. The joy of still being alive, and the anger I still have toward you for failing survivors of sexual violence almost two years after my piece, "Dear Harvard: You Win," appeared in the *Crimson* and went viral. The sense of peace that I've come to reach about one night in February 2013, and the overwhelming feeling of bereavement that I have to overcome every day because of the way you handled my assault. The support I have gotten from so many friends and strangers, and the reality that, after everything that was said, done, written, and rewritten, so many survivors at your school still do not feel heard.

I am writing this piece on a Friday afternoon, after finishing my eleventh week as a first-year medical student at McGill University. To most strangers, I probably look like any other female student in her twenties, busing around my textbooks on the subway, cramming in a coffee shop before an exam, going to dinner parties with old friends. I manage to study on most days, I only wake up once a night, and I regularly work up enough of an appetite to squeeze three meals in a day. I am able to laugh sincerely, to take care of myself, and to appreciate little moments that make life beautiful. These are huge victories.

But in spite of all this, my anxiety and the ghost of depression still haunt me. I've tried doing yoga, practicing mindfulness, adopting a cat, painting, picking up photography again. I've tried writing about the good things, writing about the bad things, not writing at all. But none of these has been able to erase the certainty that something terrible is about to happen to me, that I will imminently be betrayed by someone I trust, that I will fall again into a pattern of self-harm and suicidal ideation until I finally gather enough courage to act on my thoughts. I still can't drink coffee or alcohol without risking a panic attack. I have had to take sick days at work and at school to deal with severe bouts of anxiety. I am on four types of medication, and probably will be for the rest of my life. For me, this fight isn't over.

After seeing so many administrators repeatedly turn their backs on me following my assault, my piece in the *Crimson* became, in a way, the only means I had left to ensure my voice would be heard by someone, somewhere. The day my op-ed was published, after several months of work with *Crimson* lawyers to get legal clearance, I stayed up until five a.m. to watch my words go live on the *Crimson* website. It was a cold and cloudy Monday in early spring, over a year after my assault, and I had an organic chemistry midterm later that week. But as my fellow classmates worked their way through aldehydes and ketones in the library, my eyes were glued to my Twitter feed, a few feet away from their textbooks. I remember the constant tingling at the bottom of my stomach and the restlessness of my eyes as I scrolled through dozens and dozens of supportive tweets, from strangers in France and from Mia Farrow;

from classmates who did not know I was the author and from U.S. Senator Kirsten Gillibrand. After all those days spent in bed and those nights crying myself to sleep, after all those conversations with Harvard administrators that ended with the same refusals to acknowledge my pain, and after almost being hospitalized for suicidal behavior, people were finally saying that I had been right all this time, and that those administrators were wrong. People were saying that I was *right*. It was, and still remains, the best day of my life.

There were, of course, Reddit users, other online commenters, and conservative writers to say that that night in February was just "sex that I regret," to claim that I never said no, never screamed, and never ran away, and even to bring forth some twisted conspiracy theory about how I framed my assailant. The fear of such comments is what kept me from coming forward with

> **People were saying I was *right*. It was, and still remains, the best day of my life.**

my story—at Harvard initially, and in the *Crimson* for many additional months after. To physically survive a sexual assault means being constantly flooded with raw pain, anger, self-hatred, shame, sadness, and distress, and these feelings are often the only things you know to be real before you begin to process what happened to you. In this context, to be told that your feelings are not justified, that your assault was just a misunderstanding, and that you are overreacting has the very real potential to completely destroy you.

And so I didn't publish "Dear Harvard: You Win" for a long time because, in addition to being scared that my institution would retaliate against me, I was scared that readers would tell me that I had not been sexually assaulted, just as Harvard had done before. I did not think I could take any other attempts to suppress my voice. Eventually, I realized that the judgments, the comments, the dismissals—none of them mattered. I was not going to give up one of the few things I had left: the power to judge for myself what had happened to me. To this day, the certainty that my distress was real and that my assailant went beyond the boundaries of my consent is what shields me from any misguided comments on my assault.

And eventually, in spite of my believing otherwise, things got better. I moved to a new house at Harvard, got to know the academic and career advisers there, attended a few formal events, and met my new resident dean, who proved to be the polar opposite of the administrators I had encountered before. He was kind and understanding and did not shy away from echoing my thoughts whenever Harvard seemed to be failing me. One of my professors, learning about my fight with her institution, and seeing that I was about to fail her class, gave me a clean slate midsemester. I successfully filed for a restraining order against my assailant, and became one of the complainants in a Title IX complaint against Harvard College. I moved to New York City, got a job, and never heard from Harvard officials again. After submitting a long letter that explained the extenuating circumstances behind poor grades in my last three premed courses, I got into medical school.

Some people may take my medical school admission as the ultimate victory against you, Harvard, but I will never see it that way. You took away pieces of me that I will never get back: my tendency to trust and see the good in people; my optimism; and, more important, my ability to function normally in society. Yet you've also given me resilience, the strength to speak up for what I believe in, and the pragmatic understanding that is necessary to change the system—all of which will make me a great advocate for survivors, and a great doctor. As a medical student, I want to raise awareness about the ways health care providers can avoid retraumatization when they encounter survivors of sexual violence. And I know that, as a doctor, I can do for survivors what Harvard didn't do for me: listen to them, and, even more important, believe them.

And yet, Harvard, I am also writing this piece a year after your Title IX coordinator refused to incorporate the concept of affirmative consent into the school's new sexual assault policy. I am writing this piece knowing all too well that a student found guilty of sexual assault by your disciplinary board was recently allowed back on campus to finish his degree. I am writing this piece two days after nineteen professors at your law school—an institution found in violation of Title IX by the U.S. Department of Education's Office for Civil Rights—attempted to silence a former student and survivor through intimidation in an

> I know that, as a doctor, I can do for survivors what Harvard didn't do for me: listen to them, and, even more important, believe them.

open letter.* I am writing this piece after too many of my own friends have come forward about their sexual assaults on your campus, but whose voices will never be heard because the task force you created to address sexual violence still does not allow them to participate in—or even sit in on—its meetings. And for them, Harvard—for us—I want you to know that this fight isn't over. But someday, I know, we will win.

—Fall 2015

---

*On November 11, 2015, nineteen Harvard Law professors sent out a press release denouncing the documentary *The Hunting Ground*, because they felt that it portrayed Kamilah Willingham's case against another Harvard Law student in a manner that was "unfair and misleading."

An Important Event

A STATEMENT GIVEN ON FEBRUARY 26, 2014,
AT THE UNIVERSITY OF CALIFORNIA–BERKELEY

SOFIE KARASEK

Good morning, and thank you for your attendance at this important event. My name is Sofie Karasek and I am a third-year student here at the University of California–Berkeley. We are here today to announce the filing of two federal complaints against Berkeley for failing to prevent, investigate, or discipline assailants in cases of sexual violence and harassment.

This past May, eight students and I filed a federal Clery Act complaint against U.C.–Berkeley. Over nine months have passed, and we still have not been told whether or not the federal government is planning to investigate our complaint. After multiple failed attempts to reach the Department of Education about our case, we are now filing yet another Clery Act complaint against Berkeley, in addition to a Title IX complaint with the Office for Civil Rights. Our complaint has grown from nine to thirty-one cases. It is unacceptable that as we wait for the federal government to respond to our complaint, more students are being sexually assaulted, and continue to have their cases dismissed, mishandled, and ignored if they choose to report them. Several of our complainants had problems with the administrative process even after the first federal complaint, and even after the State of California began auditing our school.

While the intentions of the Department of Education and U.C.–Berkeley may be different, the impact of their deliberate indifference to sexual violence is the same. Neither the Department of Education nor U.C.–Berkeley has made the efforts necessary to address the pervasive culture of sexual violence on our campus. This is not only disappointing; it is also dangerous for the students who attend college here, and is representative of a larger problem: the federal government is not adequately enforcing its own laws.

Now I'd like to ask the staff of the Clery Compliance Division and the Office for Civil Rights to consider a similar question to the one that I recently posed to the U.C. Board of Regents: How do you sleep at night, knowing that students are being assaulted because of your inaction? How would you feel if one of your children or someone you know went through this utterly useless, demeaning process?

Nearly two years ago, I went to report my assault through the campus process. The assault happened on an off-campus trip in February 2012; he was a leader in the student organization, and I was a freshman who had never been involved in the group before. After it happened to me, I quickly learned that I wasn't the first person he had assaulted. Another leader in the organization

How do you sleep at night, knowing that students are being assaulted because of your inaction?

approached me about it, and she met with representatives from the Gender Equity Resource Center to seek guidance for how to address his presence in the organization.

To my surprise, someone at the the Gender Equity Resource Center, which is often a positive and inclusive space for many students, advised her against removing him from the organization. The representative said that our organization should "keep him close in case he does it again" so that he would "have a community of friends to support him in processing it." Why should his healing process take precedence over the possibility that he could assault me again, or assault another person?

Shortly afterward, he was pressured into resigning from his leadership position in the organization. I had hoped that this would be a significant enough deterrent so that he would not assault anyone again. But not even a month went by before he assaulted another person. At that point, I connected with three other survivors who were all assaulted by him, and we turned to the university to officially report our assailant together. I never received any confirmation of anyone having read my statement, and was not contacted to take part in an investigation.

After waiting seven months for a reply that never came, and after learning through a friend that the assailant was going to graduate early, I inquired into my case. After multiple attempts to contact the administration, I finally received two short emails telling me that my case had

"been resolved through an early resolution process" and that he had been found in violation of the student code of conduct, without specifying whether any disciplinary action had been taken against him. Two days later, he graduated.

It wasn't until September 2013, a year and a half after my assault, that I learned of the sanctions. According to the Center for Student Conduct, he was put on "disciplinary probation" and had "engaged in counseling measures." They also said that "any further misconduct during that probationary period could have resulted in further disciplinary action." How many survivors does it take for a serial perpetrator to be punished?

I have now waited for nine months to hear back from the Department of Education about our federal complaint, which is longer than it took me to hear back from Berkeley.

I Write On

ANNIE CLARK

Her name is Tori. I'm not sure if it's spelled with an "i" or a "y." I don't ask. My friend from elementary school was named Victoria. She had curly black hair and she spelled her nickname "Tori," so I'm going to go with that. Tori is the name of my server at the Coupe, a restaurant in the Columbia Heights neighborhood in Washington, D.C.

The Coupe is where I have decided I will put pen to paper and write a part of my story for the first time.

The restaurant is divided into three sections. The left side is serving Sunday brunch, with traditional table service. The section in the middle is self-serve; it has a coffee counter with couches and rustic chairs where millennials sit and peck away at their keyboards. The middle is a conversational mix of D.C. politics and venture start-ups, and the interior decoration reflects that fusion. On the right side is a bar, which also offers food and coffee. Hipsters hide behind their electronics as they drink local drafts and lagers and wait for their friends.

I choose the bar side. I first sit at a small table with one wooden chair. It feels stiff. This wooden table is the wrong place to write something so personal. I move. I walk to the back, to an armchair. I cross my legs and sink into the chair, as if I'm expecting some sort of emotional comfort from a piece of furniture. Judging by the lack of lumbar support, this chair has been here, or somewhere, for some time. The chair, upholstered in a golden flower pattern, is stained with dirt and thoughts.

Tori comes back to ask me what I want. I haven't even glanced at the menu. "Thank you, please give me a minute"—I'm really indecisive on basic things. "I'll be here awhile," I confess.

Originally, I thought I would do most of my writing about sexual assault from my bedroom, a place I affectionately call my nest. But my nest has become an intentional safe space of sorts: I leave emotional matter at the nest entrance. I have strung tiny cable cord LED lights ($17 from Amazon) around the ceiling and I have had every friend who has visited me sign a brick on the wall where the door is located. I have painted the wall opposite my bed a slate gray and have stickered "JUST BREATHE" in the center in white. My nest is a place where I can read fiction, listen to loud music, study academic journals, watch bad TV, and not have to think about my job or about my rape. My nest is safe.

And so I find myself at the Coupe, sitting cross-legged in a back corner of a bar in a golden-flowered chair, silently scribbling my story. My only witnesses include Tori, the wallpaper graffiti art, and a painting of acrylic and mixed media (including empty chai canisters and electrical wire shells) hanging crookedly behind me.

Tori meanders back to my chair, and I order the Dragon Tea. She's probably annoyed that I'm sitting on the bar side drinking two-dollar tea. I hope she can guess that I'll tip her well. What she probably can't guess is that I ordered the tea simply because it was called Dragon Tea. Dragon. That feels strong. I don't feel so strong.

BEFORE: GROWING UP

To be fair, I really like tea, and I offer this nonessential information to Tori when I order. She manages an I-have-to-smile-to-the-customer face and asks if she can bring me anything else. I say "No thank you, ma'am." She turns her head back at me, with some confusion. Even in a big city, if I don't say please and thank you, I feel off kilter. I'm southern born and bred.

Growing up, I loved sweet tea. I loved scooping cups of sugar from an old blue ceramic cylinder into a pitcher of tea at my grammy's house. How could so much granulated sugar dissolve into the warm tea? That disappearing act fascinated me.

Growing up, I was a middle-class, precocious kid. I made fun of my mother's southern accent, the one I have since partially adopted and begrudgingly embraced.

Growing up, I had braces, and I experienced the humiliation of digging a retainer out of the school cafeteria garbage can. I fought with my little sister, who attended the same elementary school as I did, and who knew I loved her more than anything in the world.

Growing up, I was the first female student in my high school class to earn a letter in a varsity sport. But I wanted to run on more than the field and the track. I wanted to run for office. My grandfather had been a Democratic congressman from North Carolina. He remains one of my role models, even after his death.

Growing up, I wanted to play on the U.S. Women's Soccer Team. I believed Jif peanut butter was a superfood, and would have a spoonful before every one of my games. I won the state championship with my team in 2004 and had knee surgery shortly thereafter.

Growing up, I was terrified of receiving a "B." I measured much of my worth by my grades. I was awful at geometry but kicked ass in pretty much everything else academically.

Growing up, I experienced my parents' divorce, just like 50 percent of my friends. I have one sister, two stepsisters, and one stepbrother.

Growing up, I went to—and got used to giving extemporaneous eulogies at—the funerals of more than twenty of my friends and family members, including one who fell asleep at the wheel, one who died of an overdose, and one who had been my first boyfriend.

Growing up, I loved watching crime drama shows, particularly *C.S.I.* and *Without a Trace* on Thursday nights. Afterward, I would sing in the shower to my Christina Aguilera CD. I knew I sang poorly, but I sang anyway.

Growing up, I equated bravery with people who fought and reported crimes.

Growing up, I thought I would be one of those brave people.

Growing up, I never expected to be sexually assaulted.

I am still growing up.

———

I have to run to the restroom. I'll take my notebook and my purse and ask Tori to watch the remaining half of my Dragon Tea. In the bathroom, I'll go into a stall and I'll come out of it. Then, I'll wash my hands as I look at myself in the mirror, just like I did the night of my assault.

HOW IT HAPPENED

He pushed me up against a wall and he penetrated me; that's the word the law uses. I really hate that word. *Penetrate.* It's active on the part of the assailant. Though *penetrate* is the technical word for a criminal act in some states, it renders the victim an object.

In the moment of that verb, you are nothing more than an object, an object to be penetrated: an object to be acted upon.

Reporting to the police never crossed my mind. I didn't even want the friends who were out with me that night to know, much less my parents or siblings. I had always been a strong, independent young woman, and I thought that I could push the assault to a back corner of my mind.

I could hide and be strong and no one would know. My assault could be an invisible scar.

Just like I can sit in the corner of a restaurant and write, and no one has to know what I am writing.

I sip my Dragon Tea. I don't add the honey that comes in packets on the side. I don't like anything too sweet anymore.

I told myself that I was too strong for "breakdowns." I told myself that things like this didn't happen to girls like me. I had GRIT. I was made of GRITS. And Girls Raised In The South just learn to get over things.

HEALING

> Just looking in the mirror is a reminder.
> —Text message from an individual very close to me,
> who was assaulted during the writing of this book

After this penetration happened, I found myself in a bathroom. I used cheap toilet paper to clean myself up and forced myself to try to clean up my mind. It hurt.

Little did I know that my mind wouldn't be disinfected; in fact, my brain would be altered. That night would be carved in memory and retold in flashbacks.

I guess I always knew deep down there was something I would have to address eventually, even though I could not immediately put words to what had happened. I don't know how long I was in the bathroom that night. I remember putting both my hands on the sink, hunching over, and looking at myself in the mirror and knowing that was my reflection, but the person I was seeing didn't feel like me.

Just looking in the mirror is a reminder.

I think I was in shock.

When you're in shock, sometimes there are no emotions. There are only actions. For the rest of the night, and for a few days to come, I was simply robotic. I didn't have my own voice. I wrote down song lyrics over and over again. I wrote down the lyrics to "SuperSoul," an original song by Dilana, a South African rock star who had competed on one of those audition-to-be-in-the-band TV shows a few years earlier. In "Super-Soul" the narrator is harmed yet also somehow "bulletproof"; in the end, her scars heal and she has a "super soul."

~

They're turning down the lights in the restaurant. Even though it's late afternoon, the sun goes down early now. Bar mood-lighting follows. I think Tori will be leaving soon because she asks if I will close out my check. Having worked in the restaurant business for years, I empathize. I say, "Of course."

It's interesting to write about healing in the darkness of the bar. There is no light, no pathway, no prescriptive narrative of healing, and the sound bites the media perpetuate are glossy and unrealistic.

To be able to tell one's story is a privilege, but it's also a vulnerability, a risk, and a sacrifice. Pieces of you are misconstrued and forgotten; your identity is chiseled to fit the mold of what sells, not what is real.

Tori brings back my credit card and says thanks.

There's nothing special about our interaction, and why would there be? To her, I am a white, blond, blue-eyed, five-foot-seven-inch, athletic woman working on the weekend. I'm privileged; that's what our society sees as normal. I'm average to her. I'm probably a near likeness of 25 percent of her customers. Tori doesn't know or care that I'm writing about my rape. Tori doesn't know or care that I'm bisexual.

I never intended to tell people at all about either of those things, much less lots of people at once.

I gulp the last of my Dragon Tea. I try to decipher the meaning of the recycled art piece on the adjacent wall. I pine for an excuse not to be so vulnerable to my notebook. Part of the reason I didn't want everyone knowing what had happened to me in 2007, beyond the hurts from the slings and arrows of a victim-blaming culture, is that at the time, I was also coming out as a member of the LGBT community, and I had no clue how people who had known me my whole life would react to that. Each of these pieces of information was heavy in itself, and I thought that delivering them together would be throwing medicine balls at people who wouldn't be able to catch them.

1. Would people think the only reason I was interested in dating women was because I was assaulted by a man?
2. If I told people I was assaulted at the same time as I told them I was bisexual, would that be too much to process and would it therefore lesson the impact of each bit of information?
3. If I told conservative family members or friends both things at the same time, would they just judge me on the basis of my sexuality, and forget the rape part?
4. If I told my more liberal family and friends, would they not care about my sexuality and ask me a lot of questions about my assault?
5. If, years later, I talked about my sexuality in a documentary, would people take sexual assault less seriously?
6. If, years later, I let media sources constantly cut out my sexuality, or I was silent about it, was I being unfair to the LGBTQ community and to myself?

This list of complex social- and integrity-cost calculations doesn't end. I have questions 7, 8, 9, 10, 11, and on and on. My mind reels with these questions.

I grappled with what to say and with how to phrase these two things and to whom for years. By the time I graduated from college, almost everyone in my circle of friends and my family knew that I wasn't heterosexual, but only a handful knew about my sexual assault.

So when I look into a mirror, I see things that the media doesn't capture, facets of my identity that are never conveyed through a magazine photo shoot for a story about my activism. I'm getting through my assault, but I'm not over it. I'm angry at the erasure of parts of my identity, and more angry at the complete erasure of so many others' experiences.

I might be on camera talking strongly about policy, but I still struggle sometimes in the greenroom, always doing a last-minute check to make sure my mascara hasn't run. And because of that mascara and my long hair, most at home won't know I'm bisexual. But I hope that people reading this will know that whatever their identity or struggle is, they are believed and not alone.

Tori has left, and my tea is gone. And I press my pen to my notebook a bit harder. I want to feel the words I'm writing more viscerally. I will write on.

I Have Been Told That My Skin Is Exceptionally Smooth

REGINA GONZALEZ-ARROYO

I was born in Mexico and we moved to California when I was three.

Growing up as an undocumented Mexican immigrant was hard. I didn't speak English until I was seven, and even when I got to junior high and became a citizen, kids still mocked me and called me wetback. I was eager to leave Orange County, which is very white and very conservative.

In middle school I had an artsy friend who talked about someday going to CalArts, so that's when I started researching it. That college seemed like a utopia. I desperately wanted to be a part of an open and diverse community. I had never been to a school that was inclusive. I applied to major in film.

The college is like a large high school. There's only a cafeteria and a lounge, so not a lot of places to eat or hang out. You know everyone and know their major. It's kind of claustrophobic at times.

I started school in the fall of 2013. I felt really privileged to be there, so my first semester I was trying to convince myself that I belonged. I was a bubble of positivity. I was just trying to embrace the environment, which sounds really immature now that I look back.

The assault happened my second semester. He was in the same program as I was, and also a freshman. We hooked up a few times over a month and a half. Then we had a falling-out because he was manipulative—he would want to see me only when he wanted sex. I didn't see that as abusive until a friend said she didn't want me around him. So I told him, "I don't want to see you anymore, have you touch me anymore."

At the beginning of second semester I was invited to a film department party. I didn't know he was going to be there. I got there and realized I was one of the only girls at the party. I started feeling really uncomfortable. About an hour into the party, other girls arrived, including one of my best friends. I hung around her until people started leaving. I was very intoxicated. I couldn't stand. I sat on a staircase talking to my friends, then at some point the guy I had dated came and sat really close to me, almost on top of me.

I go upstairs to use the bathroom and the guy I used to date appears up there. He drags me into the bathroom, closes the door, and turns off the lights. That's when the assault begins.

After the assault, I tell one of the guys at the party, "I wanna go home." At some point the rapist comes out and hovers around us as they're walking me home. I start saying, "I don't want him here. I hate him!" One of the guys is recording it. They're trying to walk me home and I don't remember where I live. One guy looks up my email and finds an order for Amazon, finds my address, and gets me home.

The next day I woke up with my dress on. It was dirty and torn. I was bruised and sore. I had messages from friends: "Where are you?" I showered and went on a friend's film set as I'd previously planned. On set someone said the word *rape* and I started crying.

I broke down for the next week. I didn't want to go to school, didn't want to talk to anyone. Didn't know whether to get a rape kit. Friends kept telling me to go to the hospital or at least to the school to get help.

I was scared of what would happen. I didn't want my family to know. I wanted my parents to trust me. I wanted to make them proud. I was the first in my family to go to college. I was supposed to be an example. My parents are so conservative and I didn't want them to blame me.

So I wrote about what happened on my blog. Now I know that one of my good friends was following me on Tumblr and forwarded the post to my perpetrator. That night, one of my perpetrator's friends called me and told me, "You need to talk to him and work this out." I was scared. I never wanted to see him again much less "work things out." My friends took my phone away from me. They were worried I would end up answering out of anxiety.

The guy and his friends were trying to hunt me down. I moved to another friend's apartment for a few days. That's when I realized this wasn't going away and I couldn't ignore it.

My friends convinced me to report to the school but I still waited until three or four weeks after the assault. I confided to another student, a teacher's assistant. She told me to report to the film school's director and I ended up telling the associate vice president of the school and the human resources officer. They told me they would take immediate action and that it might take thirty days.

They removed him from my classes and all student events, but he would still show up. The rules weren't enforced. I was always afraid of running into him. His friends cornered one of my friends and screamed at her. They posted on Facebook that they would shit on me for what I did; they approached me and cursed me.

The school's investigation took two months. The school administrators interviewed a professor's teaching assistant and asked her to compare my art to his. They asked me what I was wearing that night, how short it was. If I had feelings for my rapist. If I had climaxed during the assault. And if I had issues regarding climaxing. They asked me how oral rape was possible and I had to describe how he was choking me and forcing me. They didn't get it.

Months later, I realized that they wanted to keep him in school. He was paying full tuition and he had a lawyer. I was on scholarship. He comes from a very wealthy, powerful family. He's white. He couldn't take no for an answer. He had ownership over me.

I like my school. I love my professors and my friends. But it's not a healthy environment. I wish I could take a semester off, but because of my student loans, I'm imprisoned.

The school came out with its decision in May and the sanctions were super light. He was only suspended for an academic year. That's been one of the hardest things: the institutional retaliation and betrayal. You've dreamed of being there and they turn their backs on you. I went home that summer upset and hurt. I researched Title IX and got in touch with End Rape on Campus and Laura Dunn.

I told my parents when I got home. Not immediately but about a month into the summer. It was almost an accident. One of my sister's friends told a rape joke and I started sobbing in front of my mom. My dad was just getting home from work and was pulling into the driveway. I ran out and met him. I told him I needed to talk to him but not at home. We drove to the nearest Starbucks and talked.

I was trying to look composed. I explained Title IX and said, "Hey, this law exists, and my school violated it, and I'm going to file a complaint, Dad, and I need you guys to support me." He kept trying to get me to go to the police and I kept trying to explain why it wasn't an option. He looked the saddest I've seen him.

We got home and I was a crying mess again. My dad called my mom and my sister, and my mom started crying and we hadn't even told her yet. Their questions were painful. I didn't want to tell them and they wanted to know every detail.

I took them to a screening of *The Hunting Ground* at school. That was the first time they realized this is a huge issue and I'm not the only one. I send them articles for parents of victims but it's still not a conversation they like to have.

My assailant was allowed back in school as of the fall of 2015. But, so far, he hasn't reenrolled. His friends said he was going to reapply but to a different program. On September 30, 2014, the U.S. Department of Education opened an investigation into CalArts for Title IX violations.

I'm looking for a therapist. I am learning, and I'm around a close-knit group of nurturing people. In a few years I'll be close to where I want to be. I am trying to raise awareness through film and art. Film is my artistic voice and my activism. In December 2014, not long after my assault, I made my first movie about sexual violence. I was supposed to make a documentary about a location for a class. So I went back to an actual location where he'd been aggressive. The film is called *I Have Been Told That My Skin Is Exceptionally Smooth*.

I want to show the escalation of violence and the horror of rape. I've hardly ever seen an effective rape scene—a realistic one that makes you sick. So I force the audience to endure my film. A lot of people feel sick and gross after watching it, and that's the point. One professor told me it was the best because it successfully re-created the experience.

I want people to think about it and understand why I made the film. It's not enjoyable. It's not something that can just stop. I'm taking advantage of the audience because I'm not letting them know what they're getting into. I wanted to feel that power, because I've had to struggle to regain it. If I get any reaction, the film is successful.

A screenshot of Regina from her film, *I Have Been Told That My Skin Is Exceptionally Smooth*

This reflective film essay about one of my traumatic encounters has a running time of five minutes.

Accompanied by darkness and on-screen text, it consists of twenty-four images, a reference to the standard number of frames projected in a second.

It's not an easy film to watch because I have deconstructed narrative, documentary, and film-essay formalities. The audience is in unfamiliar territory, forced to participate. It becomes powerless, like the narrator.

While inviting the audience to enter such a vulnerable setting, I also create a space where I can reenact, perceive, and reflect on my experience under conditions to which only I have consented.

From 2012 to 2015, Emily Yoffe, then a contributor to the online magazine Slate, *wrote a number of widely read pieces on sexual assault, including several "Dear Prudence" advice columns (in 2012), which encouraged women to avoid assault by adjusting their own behaviors, and the articles "College Women: Stop Getting Drunk" (October 2013), "College Women: Don't Depend on 'Bystanders' to Rescue You from Assault. Rescue Yourselves" (February 2014), "The College Rape Overcorrection" (December 2014), and two pieces critical of the documentary* The Hunting Ground. *In the first of those, a review (February 2015), she deemed the film a "failure" for "privileging the claims of accusers," and in a second piece (June 2015), she asserted that one of the personal stories in the film—Kamilah Willingham's and a friend's assaults at the hands of a Harvard Law School classmate—was not an assault but rather a "spontaneous, drunken encounter." The student whom Kamilah accused of sexual assault was later convicted of misdemeanor (nonsexual) assault of her friend, but he was not indicted for assaulting Kamilah.*

Dear Emily Yoffe

KAMILAH WILLINGHAM

Dear Emily Yoffe,

While a student at Harvard Law School, I was assaulted during the January term of 2011. And a month later, I started the class "Race and Justice: *The Wire*," taught by a prominent Harvard Law professor, Charles Ogletree. This class used the HBO crime series *The Wire* to explore some of the realities and legal issues in many black communities, especially the consequences of America's "war on drugs." I found the course both refreshing and disappointing. It was refreshing, as a black law student at Harvard, to have a space where we could have honest and important conversations about race. It was disappointing because, like many conversations about race and justice in America, the course treated blackness as if it is defined by the experiences of black *men*.

In these types of conversations, black women are treated as a footnote—a side story, at most—in the broader story of the struggles and injustices faced by black Americans. In these conversations, we can acknowledge how black men are victimized by systemic oppression and entrenched racism, citing police violence and mass incarceration as examples. But what about black women, who are subject to these same oppressive forces *in addition to* the abuse of patriarchy *and* must endure and fight white supremacy as well as forcefully dominant masculinities? Is there room in that conversation for black women who are subject to abuse, too often at the hands of black men?

As I noted in a paper I wrote for that class, "In the study of equality and rights, it is as if we—as academics and professionals in a wide spectrum of fields, but especially legal—cannot think of people in more than one dimension. When the topic is rights or inequality, it is as if we can only think of two groups: oppressors and the oppressed; villains and victims."

In your June 2015 piece for *Slate,* "How *The Hunting Ground* Blurs the Truth," you fell into this same kind of one-dimensional thinking, Emily Yoffe. You wrote in the introduction to your piece that an assault against me, a black woman, and against a female friend of mine, who is white, by a black man was the "story of an ambiguous sexual encounter among young adults that almost destroyed the life of the accused, a young black man with no previous record of criminal behavior." And again, to make sure this "subtle" point was not lost on your audience, you awkwardly reiterate, before walking through the timeline of the night my friend and I were assaulted: "Both Willingham and Winston are black," going out of your way to point out my assailant's blackness, as if it supported the "story" you believed you were uncovering (me being a "bad victim," and thus the documentary *The Hunting Ground* being inaccurate). In setting up your story this way, you irresponsibly and outrageously played on one-dimensional cultural fears of further victimizing black men.

This diversion tactic—inverting notions of victimization—is pretty clichéd among those who, for whatever reason, set out to deny the occurrence, prevalence, and effects of rape. In writing your piece, you set yourself up to be an objective finder of facts, but what is "objective" in the prioritization of men and the acceptance of the inherent unreliability of women? You seem to be asking, "Who is the true victim here? Are the victims these women who seem so demanding, with their incomprehensible pain and anger? Or is this victim this promising young man, who had such a bright future ahead of him?"

Of course "innocent until proven guilty" is a valuable principle, but do you really think there are only as many rapists as there are defendants who have been proven guilty in a court of law? The type of writer you are—the supposedly objective proponent of "reason," but, in fact, a principled denier of rape—seems to embrace an inverse of this innocent-until-proven-guilty principle. That is, to you anyone who says they were sexually assaulted is lying and/or crazy unless they can produce, for your satisfaction, incontrovertible proof (a handy videotape they made or photographs they took *while they were passed out*?) that they were violated. To you, anyone who says she or he was assaulted is confused and oversensitive, if not malevolent. Again, the true victim is the poor, innocent man being persecuted as a result of the crazy woman who woke up to find someone trying to put his finger inside her and who thinks that is assault.

You used my assailant's race to prop up your demented "true victim" narrative. You wrote your piece during a year when mass media was focused on the victimization of black men by a racist and overzealous criminal justice system, a year when Ferguson, Missouri, had become a domestic cops-versus-black-people combat zone; you wrote a month and a half after Freddie Gray was murdered while being transported by the Baltimore police department, ten months after Eric Garner was choked to death by New York City police on suspicion of selling illegal cigarettes. Yes, there had been yet another bad year for black men. Truly. So, because it was a black man who was being accused of raping me and my friend, did you figure that the idea that *he* might be falsely accused would be especially powerful to your audience?

One of the things that shocked me the most about the campus proceeding that looked into the assault against my friend and me was that at first our assailant didn't seem to dispute many of the facts. He simply seemed to have trouble differentiating between unconsciousness and consent.

He essentially told the faculty, "Yeah, I did this, what's wrong with it?" and they ultimately said, "Yeah, don't punish him for being a boy!"

Our schools, our courtrooms, and our society (that's you, Emily Yoffe) can't accept this "Boys will be boys" excuse anymore. Not when "Boys will be boys" includes undressing and fondling an unconscious woman. Is it okay for that to be considered "normal"?

Yes, black men are victimized in our culture, but I hate that you played into the victimization of black men in this case, because this perpetrator is not part of that narrative. Yes, he's black, but this isn't someone who is being targeted or overpoliced because he's black. He's not the victim here.

A lot of the framing of the struggles of black people in America leaves out black women. We're even more marginalized by the criminal justice system and authority than black men are.

What was your intention with that piece in *Slate*? What it looks like is an opportunistic move by a white woman who doesn't seem to care about the treatment of black Americans in the criminal justice system if they are black women. The kind of accusations you make about me are the same kind of accusations that were lobbed at Bill Cosby's black victims when they came forward—that we're betraying something more important than our own selves by publicly calling out a black man. The potential for that kind of accusation was something I grappled with before I came forward to identify my assailant.

But the horror of his actions outweighed that reluctance.

Only a few days before your piece came out, you started calling my former employer. They promised not to give you my contact information—even though you contacted them repeatedly—because I did not want to speak to you. Why would I feel safe talking to the "journalist" who writes about campus sexual assaults with articles like "College Women: Stop Getting Drunk"—how could I trust that you would treat me objectively or fairly? It was one of the most dreadful feelings, knowing that someone who treats victims with such disdain would be singling out my case.

In the days before your article came out, I couldn't make it out of my room. I woke up with a pit in my stomach and my heart racing. "Keep breathing," I thought, and when I was about to leave the room I had a full-on panic attack. I was sobbing, hyperventilating. It was scary.

I called my aunt who lives in Germany and she gave me massive pep talks: "You made a decision to speak out, and you knew it was not going to be easy. It's not personal; you're being attacked for what you represent. Put up walls around yourself. You have to be strong, and think about it as a job you've taken on. You can stop if you want to, but know that this isn't about you. What woman in our family has not been attacked at some point? We all fight back in whatever way we can; this is how *you've chosen* to fight."

Whether or not I chose to continue fighting, I knew there was nothing I could do to stop the renewed feelings of assault that your story would trigger—I could only brace myself. I became so anxious, I couldn't eat or sleep. My weight started dropping immediately, and I'm already underweight. I felt like I was disintegrating.

But back to your awful piece: the morning it came out, I got a text from a friend with a link to it. Not knowing what to do, I called my boyfriend, who had already left for work on his bike. He said he was turning around. My heart was racing. I sat on my living room couch and began reading your piece on my phone. I barely got through the first page—through the part where you mockingly describe me explaining in *The Hunting Ground* how "the events continue to haunt" me, through the part where you, grossly, describe me and my assailant as "both tall and good-looking" and write about us romantically connecting.

I was shocked. I was not prepared to read a sensational reimagining of the beginning of my nightmares, an imagining in which my assailant is the true victim and his most convenient retelling of events is taken as unscrutinized truth. He and I were not romantically involved. If you actually examined the voluminous court record, you'd have seen that even my assailant confirmed, on record, that there was absolutely no romantic connection between us, that we were, as I understood it, just "friends." Do you know how disgusting it is to read someone writing about your assault as if it happened in a romantic context? Can you imagine how devastatingly powerless and at the same time outraged that would make you feel?

You say that an "ambiguous sexual encounter" ruined a promising young black man's life. What about my life, Emily? I was once a promising young law student—a young black woman with a bright future ahead of me. My life and my career were derailed as a result of that awful encounter—as a result of his actions. I spent four years bracing, in crisis, for a trial that was continually delayed. Four years of nightmares, flashbacks, and panic attacks. Sometimes I still don't feel safe falling asleep in my own bed, not until the sun comes up and I'm sure I don't have to relive those awful hours when I was "ambiguously sexually encountered" while unconscious.

After the trial I thought, as plaintiffs and defendants in trials probably often think when the legal contest is over, "Okay, I'm done being in battle mode and I can relax. Nobody's going to come after me. Nobody's going to attack my integrity or my sanity." And I also thought what crime victims may also often think after a trial,

> I was once a promising young law student—a young black woman with a bright future ahead of me. My life and my career were derailed . . . as a result of his actions.

"No one can make me relive what happened again."

But thanks to you, I was back on trial, back under attack; this time, in the court of public opinion.

One of the things you mentioned is that once I kicked him out of my bedroom, I allowed him to stay in the other room. It's something they asked about at Harvard too: "Why would you do that if you'd just been assaulted?"

Well, if you ask that question, you have no idea what sexual assault looks like, and no idea of how trauma works. Why didn't I beat him over the head and call the police? Because in the real world that rarely happens.

Yet every assault victim is asked, "Why didn't you fight? Kick?"

How do you respond to trauma? Fight, flight, or freeze. In this case I was barely conscious, and not prepared to fight, especially because I was looking at someone I had considered one of my best friends.

My flight, in what I now understand is common in such situations, was mental. I thought, "This can't be happening." You disassociate in the moment.

After he left my room, I sat for an hour, wondering, "How can I possibly wrap my head around this in a way that doesn't make somebody who was my friend into a monster?" I was the first person who tried desperately to defend him. And then I realized I could not.

If you decide to keep reporting on this issue, I suggest you study research on the effects of trauma.

You certainly added to mine.

As I tried to brace myself to keep reading your piece, my chest became so tense, it hurt. I had to stop reading, but I couldn't put down my phone. I suddenly felt claustrophobic; I had to get outside. I took my dog for a walk, storming down the street, still grasping my phone in one hand, afraid to look at it but unable to let it go. I didn't feel safe outside, either. I live in a quiet neighborhood and the streets were empty, but I felt as if, from behind their windows, my neighbors were scrutinizing me and imagining the night I was assaulted while unconscious, imagining what happened from your warped point of view. I walked faster and my dog trotted behind me, and I noticed that I was breathing in short, quick breaths.

While I tried to slow down and force myself to breathe normally, I pulled up my phone and got ready to text my boyfriend that I was having a panic attack in the street. And then it fell over me—that familiar, merciful feeling of numbness. Instead of texting my boyfriend, I began reading your piece again as I turned around and started making my way home.

When I got home, my boyfriend was there. He sat with me as we both read the rest of your piece. He asked how I was, and all I could do was just sit there in silence. I felt the way I did that morning when I realized that my friend and I had been assaulted. I felt the way I did when I had to relive that awful night in front of the police; in front of my assailant and a room full of law school administrators; before a grand jury. I felt the way I did during the criminal trial when, on my second day on the stand, my assailant's attorney shouted the details of my assault at me, as if outraged that I was still telling the same story after four years. I didn't want to deal with it, I didn't want to have to be strong, I didn't want to do anything. I wanted to fade into the furniture and not believe that any of it was happening. I didn't want this to be my life.

And I was so angry with you for bringing me back to this place where I have to put on my armor. Once again, I had to harden myself, tell myself that even though it feels like a personal attack, it's not. Still, I don't want to have to be strong all the time.

I know that this attack on my credibility is not personal. It does feel like some private, essential part of me is being attacked—my truthfulness, my character. But I know that your attack, like all other attacks of this kind, is not personal, uniquely aimed, or even nuanced in any way. It's not personal, but it's still painful. It seems to me that people just hate women who try to stand up for themselves.

On the one hand, if you're a survivor who speaks up, you put yourself in this battle and you want justice and redemption; and on the other hand, the reaction you face is not necessarily individualized; it's a barrage of every sexist stereotype about who you're supposed to be, and of dangerous notions of what men are entitled to and how their sexuality functions, regardless of context.

With my armor on once again, I remembered the pep talks my aunt had given me when I was bracing myself for your article to be published: "It's not personal; you're being attacked for what you represent. What woman in our family has not been attacked?"

Endurance is part of many black women's identities, because we get it from all directions.

We are attacked within our families and our communities. In a lot of ways we're at the bottom of the social hierarchy. We're dismissed by feminists like Madonna and the actress Patricia Arquette, who said, "It's time for all the women in America, and all the men that love women and all the gay people and all the people of color that we've all fought for to fight for us now!" Well, that's a punch in the stomach. It's not just white women who are feminists. Black women—and gay women—have *always* been part of that fight, even when you refuse to acknowledge our existence. Likewise, the struggle for racial equality is not just about straight black men.

But we're told by both groups: Not you, not right now.

Not you right now, because equality for black people is equality for black men.

Not you right now, because equality for women is equality for white women.

So we constantly have to assert ourselves. We can be incredibly psychically resilient, when we have to be. A lot of women, especially women of color, feel we can't afford to focus on our own victimization because we have to be strong and appear strong in order to survive. It's never "our turn" to say that we are being hurt, that what's happening to us is criminal and we demand an end to it. People like you have been trying to erase the voices of people like me since the beginning of history. You're on the wrong side of it, Emily.

I don't understand why you write the stories that you do. I don't understand why a journalist would make it her niche to single out and attempt to discredit victims of any crime, let alone sexual assault. It makes me sad. Maybe you've internalized many of the oppressive ideas about gender and sexuality that hurt us all—men and women.

I'm sure your stories get lots of clicks, you get the readers and are probably hailed as a tough-minded ("objective") leader at work, and a hero among those who mistake their insecurities for "objectivity."

But do you truly believe in what you're doing?

Or do you do this simply because you don't want to live in a world in which the reality and frequency of sexual assault is what countless survivors, activists, bystanders, and researchers say it is? I don't want to believe that I live in that world either, but denying it doesn't make it go away. Denying it hurts people, and enables perpetrators.

The message you're sending to the world is this: "If you've been violated, keep it to yourself. Don't demand justice—don't demand anything, because I won't believe you. No one will believe you." What better way to empower perpetrators, who rely on the silence of their victims?

I don't hate you. I am angry with you, though. I think you're capable of doing better. I think you're capable of not actively doing harm in the world.

Kamilah Willingham
June 14, 2015

UNITED STATES DEPARTMENT OF EDUCATION
OFFICE FOR CIVIL RIGHTS

400 MARYLAND AVENUE, SW
WASHINGTON, DC 20202-1475

March 1, 2013

Annie E. Clark

Eugene, OR 97403

Re: OCR Complaint No. ███████
          Notification Letter

Dear Ms. Clark:

I write with the evaluation of your complaint filed with the District of Columbia Office for Civil Rights (OCR), within the U.S. Department of Education (the Department), on January 17, 2013, against the University of North Carolina (the University). Based on the information you provided in your complaint and in extensive supplemental documentation, we are opening your allegation for investigation. You allege that the University failed to ███████████████████████████

███

OCR is responsible for enforcing, among other civil rights statutes, Title IX of the Education Amendments of 1972 (Title IX) and its implementing regulation, which prohibit discrimination on the basis of sex in any education program or activity receiving Federal financial assistance (FFA) from the Department. These laws also prohibit a recipient or other person from retaliating against an individual for the purpose of interfering with any right or privilege secured by them or because that person has made a complaint, testified, assisted, or participated in an investigation, proceeding or hearing under the laws enforced by OCR. Because the University receives FFA from the Department, it is subject to the provisions of the above laws.

We are opening the allegation for investigation ██████████████████████

*The Department of Education's mission is to promote student achievement and preparation for global competitiveness
by fostering educational excellence and ensuring equal access.*

www.ed.gov

How to Become an Activist

ANNIE CLARK AND ANDREA PINO

We are often asked, "How do you become an activist?" The answer is different for everyone. Violence is entrenched in our culture; it manifests in transphobia, racism, ableism, homophobia, and misogyny. It can be subtle and it can be vivid, and because of that, there are roles for every kind of person to play. While protesting and speaking out publicly might be ideal for some activists, for others, teaching their children or friends about consent is how they choose to exercise their activism. And still for others, getting out of bed and eating a bowl of cereal is activism, because self-care is radical and necessary. Audre Lorde once wrote, "Caring for myself is not self-indulgence, it is self-preservation, and that is an act of political warfare." Though we all engage with activism differently, there are things allies can do on a daily basis to help chip away at the stigma of our violent culture and alleviate the shame and silencing our society bestows upon survivors.

Participate in the conversation. Ending our culture of violence should not be the sole responsibility of those who survive it. Call out "rape jokes" and comments that perpetuate violence. Get involved with your school's antiviolence organization, and if there isn't one, start one. If you are not a survivor, work to center the voices of survivors. Prioritize the needs of survivors of color, queer survivors, and transgender survivors; if they aren't part of the conversation at your school, challenge that and fight to change it.

Advocate for better federal, state, and local policy regarding consent and healthy relationship education. Boys and girls are exposed to the painful silence around violence at a very young age; we should not wait until they reach college age to start talking about consent.

Learn about Title IX, and make sure your friends, children, and partners know that all students have the right to a safe and equal educational experience.

Give someone this book. It is difficult to encapsulate the power in every narrative in this book, and the lessons shared in the beautiful words printed on these pages. Writing the introductions for this book was difficult, as every story can stand alone, and carries a complexity that is difficult to summarize. For centuries, the stories of survivors have been kept in the shadows and kept from print, but we must free them and share them.

Believe survivors. As we've said throughout this book, and as our fellow survivors have reiterated, the most important thing is to Believe Survivors. Believing survivors is a type of radical everyday activism, since we live in a society that suggests that you do completely the opposite.

Believing survivors is a type of radical everyday activism, since we live in a society that suggests that you do completely the opposite.

RIGHTS AND RESOURCES

HELP 101

What to Do Immediately After Experiencing Violence

If you are ever a victim of crime, it is never your fault. You may be experiencing a wide array of emotions, all of which are valid. Something happened that was unwanted, and it's hard to know how to react in the aftermath. You and your safety are important.

- If you are in immediate danger, call 911 if possible.*

- If you do not feel safe, think about going to a place where you do feel safe, if possible, and finding a family member or friend for support.

- If you are intoxicated, or under the influence, most universities and local hospitals have amnesty clauses that will protect you and/or your friends if you wish to seek medical help after an assault.

- If you are unsure where to go, you can call the 24/7 National Sexual Assault Telephone Hotline at 800-656-HOPE (4673). They can also offer guidance and support as you navigate your next steps.

- Many people don't want to seek medical attention alone. If you would like an advocate, most rape crisis centers have designated advocates who are trained to accompany and support survivors after their assault. If you choose to have a sexual assault examination performed, you should not have to pay for your own rape kit.**

* We recognize that survivors may not feel comfortable calling the police, especially survivors of color and queer survivors. In many states, rape statutes are very narrow, and we recognize that not all survivors have this resource available to them, nor are all police adequately trained.
** According to the U.S. Department of Justice, there were an estimated 400,000 untested rape kits in the United States as of 2014, and it is not unheard of that survivors in rural areas, and queer and transgender survivors, are often dissuaded from getting, or not offered access to, a sexual assault examination. We recognize that much more needs to be done to assure that rape kits are available to all survivors and are tested promptly.

RESOURCES

Our Top Picks

Further resources, including those that can help you in a time of crisis, are listed below:

American College Health Association: www.acha.org

Promotes campus health care for students and advances the interests of college health with advocacy, education, and research.

Clery Center for Security on Campus: www.clerycenter.org

Works with college and university communities to create safer campuses.

End Rape on Campus: www.EndRapeOnCampus.org

End Rape on Campus (EROC) works to end campus sexual violence through direct support for survivors and their communities; prevention through education; and policy reform at the campus, local, state, and federal levels.

FORGE: www.forge-forward.org

FORGE is a nonprofit that provides comprehensive resources primarily to those on the female-to-male (FTM) gender spectrum and Significant Others, Friends, Family, and Allies (SOFFAs).

The Hunting Ground Film Campaign: www.SeeActStop.org

A coalition of survivors, students, alumni, parents, educators, and supporters who refuse to tolerate campus sexual assault.

It's On Us: www.itsonus.org

It's On Us is a campaign initiated by President Barack Obama to end campus sexual assault. The initiative encourages bystander intervention.

Joyful Heart Foundation: http://www.joyfulheartfoundation.org/learn/sexual -assault-and-rape/resources/hotlines-and-more-information

Runs programs for survivors of traumatic events, addressing the physical, emotional, mental, and spiritual effects of the events. They advocate for survivors of domestic violence and abuse and educate the public on these issues, bringing them into conversation, changing the way society thinks about, talks about, and responds to sexual assault, domestic violence, and child abuse.

Know Your IX: www.knowyourix.org

Know Your IX is a national survivor-run, student-driven campaign to end campus sexual violence.

Men Can Stop Rape: http://www.mencanstoprape.org

Men Can Stop Rape seeks to mobilize men to use their strength for creating cultures free from violence, especially men's violence against women.

National Sexual Violence Resource Center: www.nsvrc.org

NSVRC acts as a communication hub connecting people with the information, resources, tools, and expertise needed to effectively address and prevent sexual violence in all communities.

National Women's Law Center: http://www.nwlc.org/
Champions laws and policies that work for women and families.

No More: www.NoMore.org
No More is a unifying symbol and campaign to raise public awareness and engage bystanders around ending domestic violence and sexual assault.

Not Alone: www.notalone.gov
NotAlone.gov includes information for students, schools, and anyone interested in finding resources on how to respond to and prevent sexual assault.

Only with Consent: http://onlywithconsent.org/
Only with Consent is committed to teaching consent in a compelling and interesting way that engages students and promotes discussion and open dialogue.

PAVE: http://pavingtheway.net
Promoting Awareness, Victim Empowerment (PAVE) is a multi-chapter national nonprofit that uses education and action to shatter the silence of sexual violence through targeted social, educational, and legislative tactics.

Rape Abuse Incest National Network: www.RAINN.org
RAINN (Rape, Abuse & Incest National Network) is the nation's largest anti–sexual violence organization.

Safe Horizon: http://www.safehorizon.org/page/rape-and-sexual-assault-13.html
Runs a 24/7 confidential hotline for victims of violence, providing crisis counseling, safety planning, assistance with finding shelter, referrals to Safe Horizon programs or other organizations, advocacy with the police, and other services.

Students Active for Ending Rape (SAFER): www.safercampus.org

Started by Columbia University students in 2000, SAFER is the only organization that fights sexual violence and rape culture by empowering student-led campaigns to reform college sexual assault policies.

SurvJustice: www.SurvJustice.org

SurvJustice is a national not-for-profit organization that improves the prospect of justice for survivors of sexual violence by providing legal assistance, training institutions, and supporting change-makers.

Trans Lifeline: www.translifeline.org

Trans Lifeline is a 501(c)3 nonprofit dedicated to the well-being of transgender people. They run the only crisis hotline staffed by transgender people for transgender people.

If you need immediate help, please call their crisis hotline:

U.S.: (877) 565-8860   Canada: (877) 330-6366

The Trevor Project: www.thetrevorproject.org

The Trevor Project is the leading national organization providing crisis intervention and suicide prevention services to lesbian, gay, bisexual, transgender, and questioning (LGBTQ) young people ages thirteen to twenty-four.

If you need help, please call their 24/7 crisis hotline: 866-488-7386

Victim Rights Law Center: www.victimrights.org

The VRLC's mission is to provide legal representation to victims of rape and sexual assault to help rebuild their lives, and to promote a national movement committed to seeking justice for every rape and sexual assault victim.

"WHY DIDN'T YOU GO TO THE POLICE?"

Annie Clark

Those of us who become frustrated with our school's response to an assault are often asked, "But why didn't you report it to the police?"

In the United States, students who have been assaulted have the option of reporting their assault to the police or to their school or to both or to neither. There are risks and benefits to each of those options.

An institution of higher education can support an assault survivor in ways that a police department cannot. Schools can expel perpetrators or require them to take time off using different criteria and within a much shorter time than it takes to prosecute a criminal case. Also, the federal law Title IX is in place to ensure that schools provide equal access to educational programs and activities regardless of a student's sex. Thus, schools can offer educational accommodations to a survivor who might be experiencing gender-related trauma in the aftermath of a sexual assault so that the survivor can continue their studies. A school can switch a survivor's chemistry section so that she is not in the same class as the person who attacked her, can move a survivor's dormitory room so that she does not live in the same building as the attacker, can allow extra test-taking time if the survivor has developed a PTSD-related disorder that necessitates extra time, and so on and so forth.

Reporting the assault to the police and pursuing a case through the criminal justice system are other options. Some survivors do go immediately to a hospital, have a rape kit done, report the crime to the police, and have a good enough experience with a trauma-informed officer; and some even have a positive prosecutorial outcome. But other survivors do not want to do any of those things. Many simply want to move on; they do not want to put someone they know in jail, and/or do not want their parents to find out what happened, and/or do not want to endure an often long, arduous, and unfruitful criminal prosecution process.

Trauma impacts each person differently, and sharing an experience of sexual assault with the police or undergoing a physical examination can be harmful to survivors if they are not ready. Some studies (such as *The Psychological Impact of Rape Victims' Experiences with the Legal, Medical, and Mental Health Systems* by Rebecca Campbell of Michigan State University) have shown that survivors who go through a criminal prosecution tend to experience worse mental health outcomes than those who do not.

Furthermore, some colleges and universities, hoping to keep their crime statistics low, have, in the past at least, heartily discouraged students from reporting an assault to the police. Other times, friends or family members have actively dissuaded a survivor from reporting. And some survivors, particularly survivors of color, undocumented survivors, and LGBT survivors, feel unsafe going to the police or to a hospital.

Thus, while many of us find safety, healing, and satisfaction in the pursuit of health and justice in our schools and communities, others experience a secondary trauma because of the way school or public officials respond to them. If the goal is to heal, the possibility of reinjuring oneself by undergoing the trauma of a hostile dean or an inept police report is a risk many survivors do not wish to take.

TITLE IX

(Public Law No. 92-318, 86 Stat. 235 [June 23, 1972])

No person in the United States shall, on the basis of sex, be excluded from participation in, be denied the benefits of, or be subjected to discrimination under any education program or activity receiving Federal financial assistance.

CAMPUS SEXUAL ASSAULT VICTIMS'
BILL OF RIGHTS

- Survivors shall be notified of their options to notify law enforcement.

- Accuser and accused must have the same opportunity to have others present.

- Both parties shall be informed of the outcome of any disciplinary proceeding.

- Survivors shall be notified of counseling services.

- Survivors shall be notified of options for changing academic and living situations.

The Campus Sexual Assault Victims' Bill of Rights is part of the Clery Act, signed into law in July 1992.

A NOTE ON REPRESENTATION

Andrea Pino

Sexual violence exists in every arena of our society—even the places we consider the safest. Assault can and does happen to anyone: to people of all classes, religions, races, genders, ethnicities, abilities, identities, and sexual orientations. There is no single "assault narrative" and it is dangerous to assume there is one. When the media only report on middle- and upper-class white women, they erase the experiences of so many and reinforce damaging narratives about what sexual assault looks like. These constricting narratives exclude women of color, whose likelihood of surviving (and not surviving) violence are very high; they exclude the experiences of boys and men whose experiences are silenced by a culture that promotes toxic masculinity; they exclude the daily realities of transgender women, who are the least likely to survive violence.

In the United States, approximately 40 percent of black women report coercive sexual contact by age eighteen.[1] The National Violence Against Women Survey (NVAWS) found that 6.8 percent of Asian/Pacific Islander women in the United States reported rape in their lifetime.[2] Asian/Pacific

Islanders are also less likely to report rates of rape and other forms of sexual violence than are women and men of other backgrounds.[3] According to a U.S. study of intimate partner violence, Latina women report rape by an intimate partner 2.2 percent more often than white women.[4] For survivors who are undocumented immigrants, the risk of being deported seems to outweigh the potential benefits of reporting their assailant to the police. (Under the U.S. Violence Against Women Act of 1994, undocumented survivors can apply for "U visas" if they agree to cooperate with a police investigation. Unfortunately, by law only ten thousand such visas are issued each year, and applications far exceed that number.)

Sexual assault and interpersonal violence among Native Americans is 3.5 times higher than for all other races, and the U.S. Department of Justice found that one of three Native American women will be raped or sexually assaulted in her lifetime.[5] We recognize that our book does not include the experiences of native survivors, and we acknowledge we must do more to support native voices in survivor spaces.

Despite the lack of media coverage, sexual and interpersonal violence happens at incredibly high rates among the LGBTQ community. One in eight lesbian women and nearly 50 percent of bisexual women and men experience sexual violence in their lifetime.[6] Nearly four in ten gay men experience sexual violence in their lifetime.[7] Transgender individuals— who are met with more incidents of all forms of violence than anyone else—are the most likely to be affected by sexual violence, with an alarming 64 percent of transgender people[8] reporting having experienced sexual assault in their lifetimes.

Furthermore, while dominant narratives seem to suggest that most sexual assaults happen between strangers, statistically we know that these are actually a minority of the cases. While stranger rapes do happen (we— Annie and Andrea—are two examples), 80–90 percent of college-aged sexual assault survivors know their assailant.

We want to acknowledge all of these statistics because we recognize that some survivors cannot come forward, whether their reason is fear for safety, fear of being ostracized by their community and family, or fear of not being believed. Some of us can't tell our full stories yet, fearing what will become of our lives in the aftermath of our openness. Some of us don't want to ever share our stories, clinging them tightly to our chests, and that's okay too. When putting together this project we sought stories of survivors whose experiences were not reflected in the current conversation about sexual violence on campus, and realized that many survivors of color and queer survivors will never be able to come forward, but we must always seek to support them.

1. National Black Women's Health Project.
2. U.S. Department of Justice (USDOJ), Office of Justice Programs (OJP), "Extent, Nature, and Consequences of Intimate Partner Violence: Findings from the National Violence Against Women Survey," 2006.
3. Center for Disease Control and Prevention, "Highlights in Minority Health," 2004.
4. USDOJ, OJP, "Extent, Nature, and Consequences of Intimate Partner Violence: Findings from the National Violence Against Women Survey," 2000.
5. Lawrence A. Greenfeld and Steven K. Smith, "American Indians and Crime," Bureau of Justice Statistics, USDOJ, OJP, NCJ173386, 1999.
6. The National Intimate Partner and Sexual Violence Survey 2010 findings by sexual exploitation.
7. Ibid.
8. National Transgender Discrimination Survey.

GLOSSARY

An **advocate,** in general terms, is someone who has comprehensive knowledge of certain laws and policies, and protects the rights of or acts as a representative for others in a legal or official context. With regard to campus sexual violence, an advocate is usually appointed by a university, the police, or an organization dealing with trauma, to help survivors of sexual assault in their dealings with the police and other adjudicating bodies.

Clery Act, or the Jeanne Clery Disclosure of Campus Security Policy and Campus Crime Statistics Act, was signed into law in 1990. It requires all colleges that receive federal funding to disclose, to students and to the public, information about crimes on and around their campuses, as well as their efforts to improve safety. This act also ensures that students who have been subject to violence or the threat of violence are provided physical and psychological protection from perpetrators.

The Clothesline Project was started in 1990 by a coalition of women's groups on Cape Cod, Massachusetts. A visual artist, Rachel Carey Harper, suggested the concept of shirts hanging on a clothesline to raise awareness of violence against women. Anyone who had experienced violence could tell her story through words or art, designed on a shirt, and hang it on the clothesline. The campaign has grown exponentially since then, with about five hundred projects currently in the United States, many of them in colleges and universities. www.clotheslineproject.org

Consent, in the context of sex, is an affirmative, conscious, and voluntary agreement to engage in a sexual activity. It is given when each person knows to what they are agreeing, decides freely and voluntarily to participate, and expresses this intent to participate. Consent cannot be given when a person is intoxicated, unconscious, mentally or physically unable to give consent, under the threat of violence, or under the age of consent.

Dissociation, in psychology, is an experience of detachment from surroundings or events; an experience that ranges in severity from mild to severe, it can be fleeting or a longer-term disorder.

Emma Sulkowicz is a graduate of Columbia University in the city of New York, where she studied visual arts. In the 2014–15 academic year, her senior thesis was an endurance performance art piece that involved her carrying a mattress similar to the ones used in the school's dormitories whenever she was on Columbia University property. The piece was titled *Mattress Performance (Carry That Weight)*. She said that she would carry the mattress as long as her alleged rapist was allowed on campus. The project received attention in the national media, and students across the United States joined her in carrying mattresses on their respective campuses in a show of solidarity and to draw attention to the problem of sexual assault. Sulkowicz carried the mattress around her campus until her graduation day, even taking it with her to the commencement ceremony.

FERPA, or the Family Educational Rights and Privacy Act, was signed into law in 1974. It requires all schools that receive federal funding to give parents and eligible students the right to protect the privacy of students' education records.

A **genderqueer** person identifies outside of the gender binary (male/female, man/woman). They might conceive of gender as fluid, choosing when to perform the gender of their assigned sex, and they might identify as both genders, or as neither.

Health Services is a college or university department that employs primary care physicians and other health care professionals to treat students' illnesses and ensure their well-being.

A **hearing** is a meeting at which evidence is presented before a judge or judicial body. Colleges and universities often have hearings for sexual assault cases; the survivor and the accused have the opportunity to give statements to a group of people affiliated with the university who will decide the case.

The Hunting Ground is a 2015 documentary, directed by Kirby Dick and produced by Amy Ziering, about the problem of sexual assault and its cover-up at U.S. colleges and universities.

IPV, or intimate partner violence, is the physical, sexual, or psychological abuse by someone with whom the victim is or has been in an intimate relationship.

It's On Us is a campaign initiated in 2014 by President Barack Obama to address campus sexual assault, with the belief that it is the responsibility of the U.S. government and its citizens to actively recognize sexual assault, identify situations where it may occur, intervene in situations where consent has not been given, and create an environment in which sexual assault is unacceptable.

Latin@ is a gender-neutral shorthand for Latino/Latina, a person who has origins in Latin America.

LGBT (alternatively LGBTQ or LGBTQIA) is an umbrella term used to describe people who identify as lesbian, gay, bisexual, transgender, queer, intersex, or asexual.

The **Office for Civil Rights** (OCR) is the branch of the U.S. Department of Education that ensures equal access to education through enforcement of civil rights in American schools. OCR handle Title IX complaints (*see* Title IX *and* Title IX complaint).

A **panic attack** is defined in the *Diagnostic and Statistic Manual of Mental Disorders*, Fifth Edition (DSM V), as "a discrete period of intense fear or discomfort," during which a person experiences four or more of symptoms including 1) palpitations, pounding heart, or accelerated heart rate, 2) sweating, 3) trembling or shaking, 4) sensations of shortness of breath or smothering, 5) feeling of choking, 6) chest pain or discomfort, 7) nausea or abdominal distress, 8) feeling dizzy, unsteady, light-headed, or faint, 9) derealization (feelings of unreality) or depersonalization (being detached from oneself), 10) fear of losing control or going crazy, 11) fear of dying, 12) paresthesias (numbness or tingling sensations), and 13) chills or heat sensations. In a panic attack, the symptoms develop abruptly and reach a peak within minutes.

Post-traumatic stress disorder (PTSD) is a term for people's experiences of intense stress after a trauma. PTSD can involve flashbacks, nightmares, and severe anxiety, and it often affects survivors of sexual violence and soldiers returning from war.

Psychiatric Services is a department in some colleges and universities that employs mental health professionals to provide counseling and other mental health services for students.

QTPOC means "queer and/or trans people of color." The term originated online and is used by people of color who identify as queer and/or trans, to express their solidarity with one another.

Rape culture is the term for the social phenomenon by which attitudes about gender and sexuality result in sexual violence occurring frequently and seeming normal.

A **rape kit,** also called a sexual assault forensic evidence (collection) kit, is used to collect and preserve evidence of a sexual assault. The forensic examination is conducted by medical professionals, within 120 hours of a sexual assault. It provides physical evidence that a rape happened, and can be helpful in sexual assault trials. People who have undergone this exam often describe it as an invasive procedure.

The Red Zone refers to the first six weeks of freshman year in college, the period between Labor Day and Thanksgiving, when students are at highest risk for sexual assault.

A **Resident Assistant** (RA) is a student with peer-to-peer leadership training who supervises and counsels other students living in campus housing. RAs are often affiliated with the Office of Student Life (*see* Student Life).

"The *Rolling Stone* story" refers to the article "A Rape on Campus," first published in *Rolling Stone* magazine on November 19, 2014, about the supposed gang rape of a student in a fraternity house near the University of Virginia. After several challenges to the veracity of this story, including a *Washington Post* report and several different updates to the article online, *Rolling Stone* retracted it, deleting it from its website on April 5, 2015, and replacing it with a report by the Columbia School of Journalism detailing where *Rolling Stone* failed to properly fact-check its story. Because that story proved to be untrue, rape deniers lean on it to support their point of view, and activists point to it as a moment after which, for a time at least, a journalistic failure made it even more difficult for survivors of sexual assault to come forward and be believed.

Student Life, or Office of Student Life, is the department of university administration that manages student housing and organizes activities.

"They" is not only a third-person plural pronoun but can also be a third-person singular pronoun used in referring to an individual who does not identify with the pronouns "he" or "she." In 2015, the American Dialect Society chose singular "they" as its word of the year.

Title II of the Americans with Disabilities Act of 1990 (Public Law 101-336, July 26, 1990; 104 Stat. 337) ensures that "no qualified individual with a disability shall, by reason of such disability, be excluded from participation in or be denied the benefits of services, programs, or activities of a public entity, or be subjected to discrimination by any such entity."

Title IX refers to Public Law No. 92-318, 86 Stat. 235, which states: "No person in the United States shall, on the basis of sex, be excluded from participation in, be denied the benefits of, or be subjected to discrimination under any education program or activity receiving federal financial assistance." Title IX was most frequently used to prevent discrimination against women in college sports, but is now also used to hold colleges and universities more accountable for the way they handle sexual assault cases. As of December 31, 2015, 186 schools are being or have been investigated for violating the rights of student assault survivors under Title IX.

A **Title IX complaint** is a document filed with the U.S. Department of Education's Office for Civil Rights when a student believes that they have been subject to an act of discrimination on the basis of sex or gender.

"Title IX people" refers to the administrators on college campuses who are charged with handling Title IX complaints.

A **transgender** person identifies as a gender different from their assigned sex. This includes an individual who might identify as a man or a woman, as well as someone who identifies as both or neither. A **cisgender** person identifies as the gender of their assigned sex.

Trigger, in the context of sexual assault and other trauma, is a word, phrase, sight, sound, smell, or place that might evoke anxiety or flashbacks in survivors.

Jameis Winston is a quarterback for the Tampa Bay Buccaneers. In 2013, when still a student athlete at Florida State University, he allegedly raped another student, freshman Erica Kinsman. The case has received much attention, thanks to Winston's athletic profile as the 2013 Heisman Trophy winner and the number one NFL draft pick for 2015, and because of Kinsman's appearance in the 2015 documentary *The Hunting Ground*.

OUR FULLER DEDICATION

We dedicate this book to those who did not survive, and to those whose stories the media have kept from us, the stories that societal intolerance, racism, homophobia, and transphobia have kept from us.

To Faith Danielle Hedgepeth, who was found murdered in her bedroom her junior year, and who should have received her University of North Carolina degree in the mail around the time of this book's initial publication. Her story was kept out of the news at the time, but her life and death still impact every Tar Heel, reminding us that the life of a promising student can be ended by sexual violence. To all survivors of color whose stories are silenced and forgotten, and to the Hedgepeth family and the Haliwa-Saponi Indian tribe, we dedicate this book.

To Tynesha Stewart, who was murdered by her ex-boyfriend her freshman year at Texas A&M, and whose story still makes us shake, and to Tynesha's family, and to survivors of interpersonal violence whose stories are seen as "imperfect" or whose stories of dating abuse are taken less seriously because they knew their assailants well. To all survivors of domestic violence, interpersonal violence, and dating violence who were disbelieved by individuals and institutions who claimed to have their best interests at heart, we dedicate this book.

To Lizzy Seeberg, who took her life after her beloved institution failed to protect her, and whose assault was not taken seriously because of the status of the man she accused. To all survivors who struggle with anxiety, depression, post-traumatic stress disorder, and other invisible disabilities, who are made to feel inferior after sexual assault, we dedicate this book.

To Deah Shaddy Barakat, Yusor Mohammad Abu-Salha, and Razan Mohammad Abu-Salha, students whose lives were taken during the writing of this book. To students who feel marginalized not just on campus, but in our greater society, to individuals who are discriminated against because of their faith and who they are; to the families of those who have lost loved ones due to violence and who still feel loss and fear, we dedicate this book.

We as a society are failing our students because we care more about headlines, politics, and "school pride" than we care about the people who make up our student body.

We are failing our students because we care more about the number of touchdowns in a season than we care about the number of assaults in a semester—even if the latter is a higher number.

We are failing our students because we are complacent about the machine that continues to finance campus violence and the cover-up of that violence.

We are failing our students because what is right is not always comfortable to our donors or our alumni. We place power, prestige, and institutional ranking above student safety. We cling to a culture of legal compliance instead of to our mission statements that speak of commitment to all students and for all students.

We didn't know Faith Hedgepeth, Tynesha Stewart, or Lizzy Seeberg personally, but they could have been our friends. They are too similar to the people we met in our classes, who lived in our dorms, and who stood next to us at graduation—except that they didn't get to wear their robes or toss their cap in the air. They did not get to take graduation pictures with their roommates or hug their parents after commencement.

Violence impacts every community, and while this book is being published and sold, we recognize that there will be more survivors of violence.

To all survivors reading this book, we dedicate it to you.

You are not alone.

It's not your fault.

We believe you.

ACKNOWLEDGMENTS

FROM ANNIE CLARK AND ANDREA PINO:

Thank you to every contributor in this book—our coauthors—Aditi, Chloe Allred, Anonymous A, Andrew Brown, Stephanie Canales, Julia D., Fabiana Diaz, Johanna Evans, Sari Rachel Forshner, Elly Fryberger, Abbi Gatewood, Regina Gonzalez-Arroyo, Anonymous H, Princess Harmony, Aysha Ives, Lilly Jay, Anonymous K, Kevin Kantor, Sofie Karasek, Lauren, Ariane Litalien, Katie Rose Guest Pryal, Zoë Rayor, A. Lea Roth, Anonymous S, Nastassja Schmiedt, Elise Siemering, Brenda Tracy, Anonymous V, Liz Weiderhold, Alice Wilder, Kamilah Willingham, Anonymous XY, and A. Zhou. Thank you for trusting us with your lives, hearts, hopes, and stories. You continue to awe us with your courage and strength.

Thank you to Laurie Bernstein, our wonderful and tenacious agent, who encouraged us to write this book and believed that survivors' stories merit publishing. Thank you to Amy Herdy for working with many of the contributors and helping us pen their stories. And thank you to Barbara Jones, our editor and Yoda, who has been patient, meticulous, and nurturing not only to us but to every contributor in this book. And to Helen Rogan. And to Gillian Blake, who believed in us, and to the rest of Henry Holt's army of publishing pros, especially: Leslie Brandon, Kelly Too, Lucy Kim, Molly Bloom, Kanyin Ajayi, Stella Tan, Kenn Russell, Jason Liebman, Maggie Richards, Patricia Eisemann, and everyone else at Holt and Macmillan. You know who you are.

And to every person reading this book, thank you for reading our stories, and to the survivors who have connected with our stories whether silently in dorm rooms or aloud, by sharing your experiences publicly, we believe you. You are not alone.

FROM ANNIE CLARK:

Thank you so much to my amazing coauthor and partner in preventing crime, Andrea Pino.

Thank you to Laura, Deb, Lynn, T, K, and so many other LGBTQ folks, particularly in the South, who gave me the permission to be me.

Thank you to Megan Wise, who listened.

Thank you to all of my fellow Carolina students, alumni, faculty, and staff who make me so proud to be a Tar Heel.

Thank you to the team at *The Hunting Ground*, my End Rape on Campus family, and the Sweet Suite.

I'm grateful to Soraya Chemaly for your fierce commitment to culture change and to Katie Rose Guest Pryal for your consistent writing (and life) advice. Thank you to Senator Kirstin Gillibrand and staff for fighting for our rights and to Anita for your mentorship.

Thank you to my uncle, Carter Monroe, for inspiring me to write, and my aunt Jean for her traveling tips.

Thank you to my family, to Martha and Jerry Stevens, John Clark, Rachel, Jennifer, Jessica, and Matthew for their love, support, and belief in me.

Finally, I'm forever grateful to Trina McDonald, Leslie, A, C, D, J, M, and S, and so many other survivors of violence who picked me up, let me know I was not alone, and that surviving and thriving were possible.

FROM ANDREA PINO:

I have many people to thank but first, foremost, my partner in all of this, Annie, my constant supporter and rock.

Thank you to Senator Kirsten Gillibrand who has always pushed Annie and me to fight for what we believe in.

Thank you to my family, especially my father, Mario J. Pino, my mother, Evelyn Pino, and my sister, Angeline Pino, who have always believed in my storytelling and the power of my words; and to my *abuelito* Antonio Silva, and my *abuelita* Evarista Silva—*ustedes seran mi guia por el resto de mi vida*. Thank you to Swati Rayasam, for your friendship, for challenging me to write my truth, and to learn from my mistakes. To Daisy Hernandez—*gracias, amiga*.

Thank you to Dr. Barbara Friedman, Dr. Anne Johnston, Dr. Frank Baumgartner, and Dr. Alice Dawson, for always believing in my research and my academic and professional commitment to fighting against sexual violence, and for your tireless personal support of me and my work, and to Cari Simon, for pushing me forward. It is thanks to you all that I never gave up on my journey toward my bachelor of arts at UNC.

Every time I sat down to write acknowledgments, it seemed impossible because there are too many people to whom I am indebted. I stand on the shoulders of activists and survivors before me, and had it not been for all of you, we wouldn't have the vocabulary to write this book. Thank you.

ABOUT THE AUTHORS

ANNIE E. CLARK is one of the founders of the survivor advocacy organization End Rape on Campus (EROC) and a lead complainant in the Title IX and Clery complaints against the University of North Carolina at Chapel Hill, where she graduated Phi Beta Kappa with a BA in political science. She has a certificate in business and is a former administrator at the University of Oregon. She is a contributing writer to the *Huffington Post*, MSNBC, and the Chronicle Vitae. Working with Senator Kirsten Gillibrand, she helped write the Bipartisan Campus Accountability and Safety Act. In 2013, she was listed alongside President Barack Obama as one of the most influential forces in higher education, and she is featured in the campus sexual assault documentary *The Hunting Ground*.

ANDREA L. PINO is one of the founders of the survivor advocacy organization End Rape on Campus (EROC) and is EROC's director of policy and support. She attended the University of North Carolina at Chapel Hill, where she majored in political science. Her activism has been featured in *The New York Times, Vogue,* CNN, and *Good Morning America*, among many other media outlets. Working with Senator Kirsten Gillibrand, she helped write the Bipartisan Campus Accountability and Safety Act. In 2013, she became the first student featured in *The Chronicle of Higher Education*'s Influence List and was listed as one of the *Huffington Post*'s most influential forces in higher education. Her work and personal journey are prominently featured in the award-winning documentary *The Hunting Ground*.